Adobe® InDesign™ for the Mac®

Check the Web for Updates

To check for updates or corrections relevant to this book and/or CD-ROM visit our updates page on the Web at http://www.prima-tech.com/updates.

Send Us Your Comments

To comment on this book or any other PRIMA TECH title, visit our reader response page on the Web at http://www.prima-tech.com/comments.

How to Order

For information on quantity discounts, contact the publisher: Prima Publishing, P.O. Box 1260BK, Rocklin, CA 95677-1260; (916) 787-7000. On your letterhead, include information concerning the intended use of the books and the number of books you want to purchase.

Adobe InDesign for the Mac

Carla Rose

A DIVISION OF PRIMA PUBLISHING

© 2000 by Prima Publishing. All rights reserved. No part of this book may be reproduced or transmitted in any form or by any means, electronic or mechanical, including photocopying, recording, or by any information storage or retrieval system without written permission from Prima Publishing, except for the inclusion of brief quotations in a review.

A Division of Prima Publishing

Prima Publishing and colophon are registered trademarks of Prima Communications, Inc. PRIMA TECH is a trademark of Prima Communications, Inc., Roseville, California 95661.

Adobe, the Adobe logo, Acrobat, Adobe PhotoDeluxe, GoLive, Illustrator, InDesign, PageMaker, Photoshop, PostScript, PressReady, and Type Reunion are either registered trademarks or trademarks of Adobe Systems Incorporated in the United States and/or other countries. Apple, Mac, Macintosh, ColorSync, TrueType, AppleWorks, and ClarisWorks are registered trademarks of Apple Computer, Inc., in the U.S. and other countries. Microsoft, Microsoft Windows, Microsoft Word, and Microsoft Internet Explorer are either registered trademarks or trademarks of Microsoft Corporation in the United States and/or other countries. Pantone and Pantone Hexachrome are trademarks or registered trademarks of Pantone, Inc. Trumatch is a registered trademark of Trumatch, Inc. Dreamweaver and Fontographer are registered trademarks of Macromedia, Inc. Extensis and the Extensis logo are trademarks of Extensis Products Group. Creativepro.com and the Creativepro.com logo are trademarks of Creativepro.com, Inc. Netscape Navigator and Netscape Communicator are registered trademarks of Netscape Communications Corporation in the U.S. and other countries. Corel, CorelDRAW, and WordPerfect are registered trademarks of Corel Corporation or Corel Corporation Limited in Canada, the United States, and/or other countries. All other brand and product names are trademarks, registered trademarks, or service marks of their respective holders.

Important: Prima Publishing cannot provide software support. Please contact the appropriate software manufacturer's technical support line or Web site for assistance. This book is an independent publication of Prima Publishing and is not affiliated with or sponsored by any manufacturer mentioned herein.

Prima Publishing and the author have attempted throughout this book to distinguish proprietary trademarks from descriptive terms by following the capitalization style used by the manufacturer.

Information contained in this book has been obtained by Prima Publishing from sources believed to be reliable. However, because of the possibility of human or mechanical error by our sources, Prima Publishing, or others, the Publisher does not guarantee the accuracy, adequacy, or completeness of any information and is not responsible for any errors or omissions or the results obtained from use of such information. Readers should be particularly aware of the fact that the Internet is an ever-changing entity. Some facts may have changed since this book went to press.

ISBN: 0-7615-3029-0
Library of Congress Catalog Card Number: 00-107338
Printed in the United States of America
00 01 02 03 04 DD 10 9 8 7 6 5 4 3 2 1

Publisher
Stacy L. Hiquet

Marketing Manager
Judi Taylor-Wade

Managing Editor
Sandy Doell

Acquisitions Editor
Jawahara Saidullah

Project Editor
Cathleen D. Snyder

Technical Reviewer
David Fields

Copy Editor
Linda Seifert

Interior Layout
Marian Hartsough Associates

Cover Design
Prima Design Team

Indexer
Sharon Shock

Proofreader
Lisa Shaw

To Natty and Grace

Acknowledgments

No project this large could be completed without help from a lot of people. I'd like to thank the people at Prima Publishing for their hard work in turning my manuscript into the pages you see here. Specifically, I would like to thank Jawahara Saidullah for giving me the opportunity to write this book, and Cathleen Snyder for keeping me on track as I worked on it. Thanks go to Linda Seifert for a thorough copy edit, and to David Fields for his equally thorough technical review. Applause to Marian Hartsough for designing an attractive and readable layout. Thanks to my friends on Delphi's ABC forum, who helped keep me sane as I worked long hours, and let me use their newsletter in my examples. Finally, many thanks and much love to my wonderful husband, who took care of everything else while I wrote.

About the Author

Carla Rose has written over two dozen books on various aspects of Macintosh computing and graphic design. She is a graduate of the School of the Museum of Fine Arts, Boston, and holds a degree from Tufts University. She is a contributing editor of *digitalFoto* magazine. She lives near Boston with her husband, sound guru Jay Rose, and two neurotic cats, and welcomes mail sent to carla@graphicalcat.com.

Contents at a Glance

Introduction xxii

Part I	**Getting Started** **1**
1	What Is InDesign? 3
2	Understanding the Pasteboard and Menus 15
3	Using the Tools and Palettes 37
4	Opening and Saving Pages 57

Part II	**Understanding Frames and Lines** **71**
5	Creating Text and Graphics Frames 73
6	Working with Frames and Lines 91

Part III	**Document Basics** **107**
7	Using Master Pages 109
8	Working with Layers 125

Part IV	**Text Techniques** **139**
9	Preparing Text for Import into InDesign 141
10	Working with Imported Text 151
11	Flowing Text through Your Document 167
12	Applying Character and Paragraph Formatting 181
13	Using Styles and Style Sheets 197

CONTENTS AT A GLANCE

Part V **Typography 209**
- 14 Working with Special Formatting 211
- 15 Using Type as a Design Element 227

Part VI **Pictures on the Page 239**
- 16 Importing Graphics 241
- 17 Making Changes to Your Images 251
- 18 Working with Special Effects 267
- 19 Creating Original Graphics 283

Part VII **Working with Color 295**
- 20 Using Color Models and Color Modes 297
- 21 Applying Color 311

Part VIII **Putting It in Print 325**
- 22 Outputting to Your Own Printer 327
- 23 Working with Service Bureaus 343
- 24 Going from Print to the Web 355

Appendix: Keyboard Shortcuts for the Toolbox 365

Glossary 367

Index 377

Contents

Introduction xxii

PART I GETTING STARTED 1

Chapter 1 What Is InDesign? 3

How We Did It before Computers 4
How Computers Changed the Process 5
Understanding the InDesign Idiom 5
    Overview: The Pasteboard 6
        Pages and Master Pages 7
    Overview: Frames 7
        Text Frames versus Graphics Frames 8
    Overview: Styles 9
    Overview: Plug-Ins 10
Installing InDesign 10
    System Requirements 10
Getting Started 12

Chapter 2 Understanding the Pasteboard and Menus 15

Working with the Pasteboard 16
Exploring the Menus 18
    The File Menu 18

| The New and Open Commands 18
            The Save Commands 19
            The Place Command 19
            The Document Setup Command 20
        The Edit Menu. 21
            The Undo Command 21
            The Paste In Place Command 22
            The Step and Repeat Command 22
            The Find/Change Command 23
        The Layout Menu. 23
            The Margins and Columns Command 24
            The Ruler Guides Command 24
            The Create Guides Command 24
            The Layout Adjustment Command. 25
            The Navigational Commands 25
            The Insert Page Number Command 25
        The Type Menu 26
            The Story Command 26
            The Insert Character Command 26
            The Fill with Placeholder Text Command. 27
        The Object Menu. 27
        The View Menu 29
        The Window Menu 30
        The Help Menu 30
    Using Shortcuts. 32
        Using the F-Keys 32
        Exploring the Command Key Combinations 33
    Setting Preferences 33
        Adjusting Document Preferences. 34
        Adjusting Online Settings 35
        Adjusting Color Settings 36

Chapter 3 Using the Tools and Palettes 37

Working with the Toolbox. 38
    Changing the Toolbox Layout from Two Columns to One . . . 39
    Using the Selection Tools 39
    Using the Path Tools 40
    Using the Type Tools. 41
    Using the Line Tools 42
    Using the Shape Tools. 42
    Using the Transform Tools 43
    Using the Eyedropper Tool 46
    Using the Gradient Tool 47
    Using the View Tools 47
    Using the Stroke and Fill Tools 47
Using Palettes Instead of Menus 48
    Docking Palettes 49
    Using the Palette Menus 49
    Working with Palette Options. 49
    Exploring the Pages, Layers, and Navigator Palettes. 50
    Exploring the Transform and Align Palettes 51
    Exploring the Stroke, Gradient, Attributes,
        and Color Palettes. 51
    Exploring the Swatches Palette 53

Chapter 4 Opening and Saving Pages 57

Starting a New Document. 58
Opening Existing Pages. 59
Making Changes to Your Document 60
    Resizing Margins 60
    Changing the Default Margin Settings 61
    Adding Pages 61
        Adding Pages to the Middle of a Document 62
        Adding Pages to a Spread 63

Removing Pages 63
Saving Pages 64
Setting Up Guidelines and Grids. 64
    Changing the Zero Point 65
    Using a Grid. 66
Creating Templates and Stationery 67

PART II UNDERSTANDING FRAMES AND LINES 71

Chapter 5 Creating Text and Graphics Frames. 73
Creating Frames 74
    Working with Text Frames 74
        Setting Text Frame Properties 76
        Aligning Text Frames to a Grid. 79
        Moving and Resizing Frames 81
Creating Graphics Frames. 84
Deleting Unwanted Frames 86
Drawing Shapes 86
    Drawing Filled Shapes 87
    Working with Corner Effects 88

Chapter 6 Working with Frames and Lines 91
Adding Fills and Gradients to Frames. 92
    Adding Fills 92
        Working with Color Fills 93
        Applying Spot Colors 94
    Using the Swatch Libraries 95
    Adding Gradients 96
Drawing with the Pen Tools 100
    Drawing Compound Paths 102
Using the Scissors Tool 103
Stroking Lines. 104

Drawing Lines with the Line Tool............................ 104
    Changing the Weight of a Line........................ 105
    Starting and Ending Lines............................. 105
    Moving and Resizing Lines............................ 106
    Changing Colors..................................... 106

PART III DOCUMENT BASICS 107

Chapter 7 Using Master Pages 109

Creating Master Pages...................................... 110
    Deciding What to Include on a Master Page............. 112
    Applying Grids and Guides............................ 112
    Numbering Pages and Sections........................ 114
        Placing a Page Number Marker.................... 115
        Dividing a Publication into Sections................ 116
Creating Multiple Master Pages.............................. 118
    Overriding a Master Page............................. 119
    Removing Overrides................................. 119
Multi-Page Documents..................................... 120
    Specifying Page Count............................... 121
    Removing Extra Pages................................ 122
    Arranging Pages..................................... 122

Chapter 8 Working with Layers 125

What's a Layer?... 126
Exploring the Layers Palette................................ 128
    Creating a Layer.................................... 130
    Naming Layers..................................... 130
Working with Layers....................................... 131
    Selecting Objects on Layers.......................... 132
    Placing Objects on Layers............................ 132

Moving Objects and Layers........................... 133
Merging Layers..................................... 133
Deleting Layers.................................... 135
Reducing Palette Icon Size 136
Saving Layer Objects to an Object Library 136
　　Exploring the Library Palette 137
　　Adding an Item to the Object Library.............. 138

PART IV TEXT TECHNIQUES 139

Chapter 9 Preparing Text for Import into InDesign 141

Translating Word Processor Formats 143
　　Using Import Filters 143
　　Using Add/Strip 146
　　Choosing a Format for Text Creation 147
Importing Text 147
　　Using Tagged Text................................. 148
　　Deciding Where to Format Text 150

Chapter 10 Working with Imported Text 151

Editing Text 152
　　Showing Hidden Characters 152
　　Getting around the Page 154
Finding and Changing Text............................. 155
　　Using the Find/Change Command 155
　　　　Searching by Metacharacter.................... 156
　　　　Finding and Changing Formatted Text 160
Checking Your Spelling................................ 161
　　Adding Words to the Dictionary 162
Working with Tabs 164
　　Adding Tab Leaders 165

Chapter 11 Flowing Text through Your Document....... 167

Placing Text in Frames 168
  Typing Text in a Frame 168
  Placing Text from the Clipboard 169
  Using Drag-and-Drop Text Placement 170
  Placing Text Using the Place Command 171
    Flowing Text Manually 172
    Flowing Text Semi-Automatically 173
    Flowing Text Automatically (Autoflow)............. 173
Threading Text Frames 174
  Threading Text through Frames...................... 175
  Adding a Frame in an Existing Thread 175
  Unthreading a Frame............................... 176
  Working with Leftover Text 176
Managing Links 176

Chapter 12 Applying Character and Paragraph Formatting................... 181

Understanding Character and Paragraph Formatting 182
Formatting Characters Using the Character Palette 182
  Changing Fonts and Styles 183
  Choosing a Size and Style........................... 185
  Using Other Style Options 186
Setting Leading and Tracking 188
  Applying Leading 188
  Applying Kerning and Tracking....................... 188
    Working with Kerning 189
    Working with Tracking 191
  Changing Horizontal and Vertical Scaling............... 192
  Using Baseline Shift 192
  Skewing Type 192

Formatting Paragraphs Using the Paragraph Palette. 193
    Setting Alignment. 193
    Setting Indents 194
    Setting Paragraph Spacing. 195
    Aligning to the Baseline Grid 195
Using Drop Caps 195

Chapter 13 Using Styles and Style Sheets 197

Creating Styles 198
    Defining a Style 199
    Applying Styles. 203
    Editing Styles 204
    Removing Unused Styles. 204
Working with Character Styles 205
    Creating Character Styles 206
Removing Styles 206
Using a Style Sheet 207
    Working with HTML Style Sheets 207

PART V TYPOGRAPHY 209

Chapter 14 Working with Special Formatting 211

Using Hanging Indents. 212
Creating Bulleted and Numbered Lists 213
    Adding Bullets 214
    Working with Numbered Lists 216
Using Dingbats and Symbols. 217
Applying Run-In Heads 219
Using Foreign Characters 219
Formatting Tables 221
    Placing Rules into Tables. 223

Chapter 15 Using Type as a Design Element 227

Using Different Kinds of Type. 228
    Serif Type 228
    Sans Serif Type 228
    Character Fonts 229
Rotating Text 232
Importing Headlines from Illustrator or Photoshop 234
Transforming Text into a Path 235
Using White Space 236
    Leading the Reader's Eyes 237
Creating Coherent Documents 237

PART VI PICTURES ON THE PAGE 239

Chapter 16 Importing Graphics 241

Preparing Graphics to Import 242
    Understanding Bitmaps and Vector Graphics 242
    Choosing a File Format 243
        Working with TIFFs 245
        Working with EPS Files 245
        Working with PDFs 246
        Working with PICT Files 247
Placing Graphics Files 247
Working with Inline Graphics 249

Chapter 17 Making Changes to Your Images 251

Cropping a Picture 252
    Centering an Image within a Frame 254
    Reshaping Frames 256
Resizing an Image 257
Applying Rotation and Skew 258
    Skewing an Image 261
Adding Borders and Backgrounds 262

Chapter 18 Working with Special Effects 267

Text Wrapping 268
   Wrapping Text around a Frame 268
   Wrapping Text around a Bounding Box 270
   Setting Text to Jump a Graphic 272
   Setting Text to Jump to the Next Column 272
   Using No Text Wrap 273
   Applying Inverted Wraps 273
   Solving Text Wrap Problems 274
Working with Clipping Paths 276
   Saving a Path as a Clipping Path 277
   Creating Automatic Clipping Paths 278

Chapter 19 Creating Original Graphics 283

Drawing Closed Shapes 284
Drawing Open Shapes 285
Filling a Shape 285
Drawing Freeform Shapes with the Pen Tools 285
   Using Anchor Points 288
   Using the Scissors Tool 289
   Working with Compound Paths 290
Applying Stroke and Fill 293

PART VII WORKING WITH COLOR 295

Chapter 20 Using Color Models and Color Modes 297

Working with Color Models 298
   The RGB Model 299
   The CMYK Model 300
   The LAB Color Model 301
Working with Color Modes 302
Using Color Management Systems 303
   Understanding Color Profiles 305

Getting Consistent Color 306
   Obtaining CMS Profiles 307
   Considering the Working Environment 308
Color Management for Prepress 308

Chapter 21   Applying Color 311

Understanding Spot Colors 312
Defining Colors 313
   Defining Spot Colors 315
   Working with Tints. 317
Using Color Blocks with Text 321
   Reversing Text. 322
   Filling Text with a Graphic 323

PART VIII   PUTTING IT IN PRINT 325

Chapter 22   Outputting to Your Own Printer 327

Getting Ready to Print a Proof 328
   Printing to an Inkjet Printer 330
   Setting up Pages 331
Running a Preflight Check 333
   Understanding the Preflight Summary. 333
      Working with Preflight Fonts 333
      Working with Preflight Links 335
      Working with Preflight Colors and Inks 336
      Working with Preflight Print Settings 336
Almost Ready to Print. 337

Chapter 23   Working with Service Bureaus 343

Preparing Files for the Service Bureau 344
   Color Trapping 345
   Making a Document Package 346

	Outputting to PDF Format	349
	Sharing Documents over a Server	352
	Working with Cross-Platform Issues	353

Chapter 24 Going from Print to the Web ... 355

	Understanding the Differences between Web and Print	356
	Preparing Files for the Web	358
	Planning a Site	358
	Constructing Documents for Web Publishing	359
	Exporting a Page as HTML	362

Appendix: Keyboard Shortcuts for the Toolbox ... 365

Glossary ... 367

Index ... 377

Introduction

Publishing comes from a Latin word meaning "people." When you publish something, you're putting it into some form that can be read by other people. The early cave dwellers mixed clay and animal fat to make crude crayons with which they drew pictures of the animals they had hunted or were planning to hunt. They published their successes or their intentions. It's hard to say which. . . .

The first desktop publishers were the ancient Sumerians, who scratched words in cuneiform script on clay tablets with a reed stylus. Many of these tablets survived, giving scholars a firsthand look at Sumerian newsletters and flyers. The Egyptians, meanwhile, carved their messages in sandstone. It was publishing, of a sort. The Hebrew scribes patiently copied the Pentateuch onto vellum scrolls. Monks learned to copy their bibles and prayer books, but in the Dark Ages, only the clergy and a few noblemen could read.

In the 1440s, Johannes Gutenberg made publishing history (and made it possible to publish history, theology, and steamy novels) with the invention of moveable type. Gutenberg, originally a goldsmith, had the idea of using techniques of metalworking, such as casting, punch-cutting, and stamping, for the mass production of books. European books of the time were hand written by monks and scribes in a Gothic script with lots of flourishes and ligatures (interconnected letter pairs). To imitate this "look," Gutenberg fashioned a font of over 300 characters, much more comprehensive than the fonts we use today. To make it possible, he invented the variable-width mold, and perfected the blend of lead, antimony, and tin still used by the few remaining type foundries that set metal type.

Gutenberg's type and printing press took publishing out of the hands of solitary scribes and made it a group effort. You needed people to write the books, to set the type, to operate the presses, to bind the books, and to distribute them. It has been that way until relatively recently. But now, thanks to computers, laser printers, and the technology that's given us PostScript fonts and desktop publishing programs like InDesign, we've come full circle. Once again, one person can create and publish a document. The power of the press is yours.

Conventions Used in This Book

Throughout this book, you'll find icons in the margins, drawing your attention to helpful features. Look for:

> **NOTE**
>
> **Notes** are in-depth explanations of specific InDesign functions and other features.

> **TIP**
>
> **Tips** are helpful suggestions to make your pages beautiful as well as useful.

Buzzwords are quick definitions of technical terms that might not be familiar to you.

How This Book Is Organized

There are twenty-four chapters in this book, divided into eight sections. The sections, or *parts*, are as follows:

- **Part I: Getting Started**. This section introduces you to the program, and to the tools and pasteboard on which you'll assemble your publications. You'll also learn how to start a new page and how to save your work.

- **Part II: Understanding Frames and Lines**. Here you'll learn about frames, InDesign's "containers" for text and graphics. You'll also learn how to place frames and lines on your pages.
- **Part III: Document Basics**. This section covers master pages, which can save you time if you work with multi-page documents, or those that retain the same format but often contain new material. You will also learn about layers, which are another timesaver.
- **Part IV: Text Techniques**. Words are the "meat" of your document. In this section, you'll learn all about working with text. You'll learn how to import text from a word processor, how to enter text directly into InDesign, and how to format the text you've entered. You'll also learn about checking spelling and hyphenation.
- **Part V: Typography**. In this section, you'll treat type as an object on the page, rather than as text. You'll learn about special formatting, using foreign characters and dingbats, and how to set bulleted lists and tables. You'll also learn to use type as a design element. You'll learn about text rotation and setting headlines, and how to make your documents coherent.
- **Part VI: Pictures on the Page**. This section deals with graphics, from how to import them into InDesign to how to crop, rotate, and resize them once they're in place. You'll learn about wrapping text around a graphic, and how to draw simple shapes and objects with the pen tools.
- **Part VII: Working with Color**. This section explains color modes and models, and how to apply them so you get accurate color in print or on the screen. You'll also learn the difference between spot and process colors, and how to work with color on your InDesign pages.
- **Part VIII: Putting It in Print**. In this final section, you'll learn about printing your InDesign publications. First, you'll learn about printing your pages on a home or office laser printer, then you'll learn how to prepare your documents for commercial printing and service bureaus. Finally, you'll learn how to convert your publications into Web pages.

Use this book as a guide to working with InDesign. You'll find clear instructions on how to do everything from bringing text onto a page to setting drop caps, pull quotes, and fancy corners. Have fun!

Adobe InDesign

PART I
Getting Started

1

Adobe
InDesign

What Is InDesign?

Back in the early days of Macintosh, two things happened that forever changed the way documents of all kinds—from lost dog flyers and yard sale posters to magazines and books—were published. The first was the introduction of the Apple LaserWriter. The LaserWriter was an affordable printer that made use of the then brand-new type description system called Adobe PostScript. PostScript defined type as vectors, lines, and curves rather than as dots on the page. Previous printing systems had placed dots of ink representing the pixels on the screen. In larger fonts, the pixels were simply printed larger. Your message appeared to have been built from bricks, similar to what you see in Figure 1.1. The computer, as far as graphics went, was still a toy until the LaserWriter and PostScript made it a useful tool.

The second thing that happened was the release of Aldus PageMaker, the first practical desktop publishing program. Taking advantage of the new printing technology, PageMaker provided a way to assemble type and pictures on a page. It was revolutionary.

How We Did It before Computers

My very first job was as a paste-up artist, a sort of human PageMaker. I worked for a small weekly newspaper, laying out and pasting up all the advertising for the paper. My workspace featured a drafting table, a stack of heavyweight paper with light blue grids printed on it, a typesetting machine called a Headliner, a cabinet full of Instant (rub-on) lettering, and a gadget called a hot waxer that coated papers with a thin layer of wax. There were also scissors, Exacto knives, some drawing tools, and a scrapbook full of pictures that could be used to perk up the ads.

Figure 1.1
Type, before and after Adobe PostScript

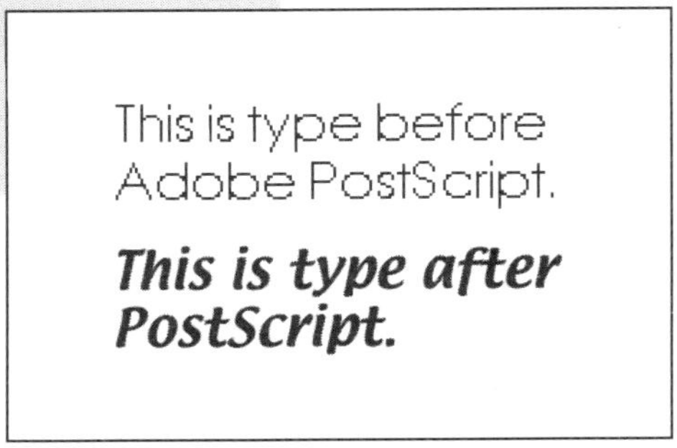

This is type before Adobe PostScript.

This is type after PostScript.

When an ad came in—for instance, the weekly grocery store page—I'd check to see what copy, if any, was small enough to be set on the Varityper. I'd hand that off to the typist, who would give me back a galley (a long sheet of glossy paper with my type set in blocks). Meanwhile, I'd choose a big plastic platter with the appropriate font (Futura, Helvetica, or Times) and set the big type. It came out of the Headliner on a strip of photo paper the same size as 35mm film. Then, I'd wax the galley and the headline strips, pick up a piece of grid paper, and start laying out my ad. Using wax instead of rubber cement made it easy to move things around on the page. I'd cut out the headlines, press them down lightly, and then see if I had space enough for a picture. If bananas were on sale, for example, I'd find a photo of bananas in the file. But it was almost never the right size, so off I'd run to the photo department to get a reduced or enlarged photostat, a copy of the original art. Finally, I'd get everything put together, rub it all down so the pieces would stay put, and send it down to be included with the other pages being sent out for printing. At the printer, each page would be photographed onto same size film and then "burned" onto a flexible metal plate for printing. It was a lot of time and effort for something that cost a quarter and ended up on the floor of a birdcage.

How Computers Changed the Process

Not long ago, I went back to visit the paper where I'd worked. Instead of an entire building full of typists and artists and photographers, there were a half-dozen desks. Each one had a Macintosh, and as I looked around, I saw a reporter editing a story in Word, a photographer downloading a digital camera's flashcard onto a Zip disk, and an artist retouching another photo. The woman who put the pages together had gone to lunch, but I peeked at her computer and saw the front and back pages of the first section, almost complete but waiting for the words and photos that were being worked on. Most of the other pages had already been uploaded to the printing company, and were ready to be run off and folded. It was a very different process.

Understanding the InDesign Idiom

The people who designed InDesign, and PageMaker before it, must have been artists. Even though you're working on a computer, when you work with

InDesign, you feel as if you're sitting at the drawing board, assembling your headlines, pictures, and text. The only real difference is that now it's much easier, and you needn't go running off to another machine to set a piece of type or resize a photo. The tools are right at your fingertips.

Overview: The Pasteboard

When you open InDesign, you'll see a toolbox and some palettes. You won't automatically see a new page, because the creators of InDesign realized that much of the time you'll be working on files you've created previously. When you create a new page you'll also see the pasteboard, shown in Figure 1.2.

The pasteboard is the white area. There's a light blue grid covering the entire pasteboard, and the outline of your page is drawn on it in black, with a nifty little drop shadow. The margins are drawn in pink, and there is a pair of column guides at the sides of the page, indicating that the page is currently one column wide. Because the column guides are in blue, and sit on top of the pink margins, they look purple. The pasteboard is just like those sheets of grid paper on which I used to mark the edges of the pages and add lines for margins.

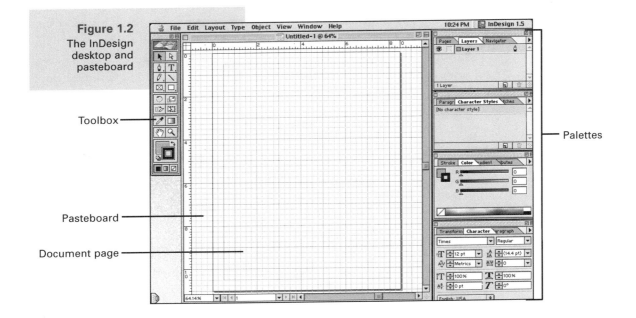

Figure 1.2
The InDesign desktop and pasteboard

Looking at the desktop, you can also see the toolbox on the left. Those windows down the right side of the screen are called palettes, and they give you information about the document and the tools you're using.

Pages and Master Pages

There are two kinds of pages you'll be concerned with: master pages and document pages. Document pages are the pages from which you print. Master pages are essentially templates you build to make your document pages look alike. If you're using InDesign for a single page flyer, you probably won't bother to make up a master page, unless you know that you'll have to do several similar flyers. But if you are creating a multi-page newsletter, a booklet, or some other item that has the same elements on all pages (for example, page numbers, column sizes, and logos), putting these elements on a master page can save you lots of time—you'll only have to place them once, not once on each page.

Overview: Frames

Master pages aren't the only timesavers you'll use in InDesign. Frames are another very useful feature. Frames act as placeholders when you're planning a page layout.

Back in the good old days, if I had to design an ad from scratch, lay out a newsletter, or start a new project, I'd begin by taking a blank piece of paper and sketching the dimensions of the page or ad I was working on. Then I'd scribble in headlines, text blocks, and maybe even a picture. These scraps of paper were called "dummies," and every artist made as many as a dozen different ones before ordering type or planning an illustration. Figure 1.3 shows what a newsletter dummy might have looked like.

Today, paste up artists still use a sort of dummy. Because this is the age of computer graphics, it doesn't make sense to grab a pencil and a piece of paper every time you need to plan a page. That's when you need frames. Figure 1.4 shows the same newsletter dummy, planned with frames in InDesign.

You can set your headlines, throw in a couple of frames for photos, and add the fake print called "greeking" to see how your pages will look when they're finished. Using frames, it's easy to slide things around, or to change the size of the type or the width of a column.

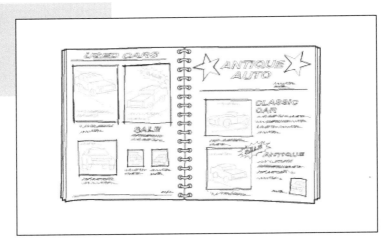

Figure 1.3
Dummies were very rough, and done very quickly.

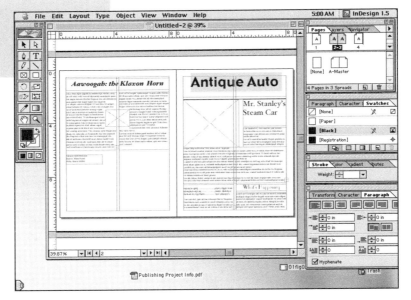

Figure 1.4
Frames make planning a page much easier.

Text Frames versus Graphics Frames

There are several different kinds of frames. Text frames hold text, and graphics frames hold pictures. Logical? Yes, but that's only the beginning. InDesign has rectangular, elliptical, and polygon frame shapes for both text and graphics. You want text set in a circle? Simple. You want your photos in oval frames? No problem. Just use the frame tool to draw the frame shape and size, and then pour in your text or place your graphic. (Don't worry. You'll learn exactly how to do this soon.) Figure 1.5 shows some uses of different frame shapes.

Overview: Styles

Frames and master pages aren't the only timesavers built into InDesign—you've also got styles. If you're familiar with any of the current word processing software, you already know about styles. Styles are automatic formatting attributes that can be applied to a selected range of text.

There are two kinds of styles. Character styles describe the attributes of a particular kind of type, such as "flush text" or "headline." Paragraph styles include both character and paragraph formatting attributes and are applied to a selected paragraph or set of paragraphs.

Styles can save you time when you apply and revise text formatting. They also help provide a consistent look for your pages. If you change the formatting of a style (for example, if you change the font from Times 12 to Palatino 11), all text to which you have applied that style will be updated with the new font and size.

Figure 1.5
Odd-shaped frames add some excitement to a page, but they're not for everyday use.

Overview: Plug-Ins

Plug-ins are, in effect, mini-programs that run within the framework of another program. They're stored in a Plug-ins folder in the main InDesign folder. If you sneak a peek in the Plug-ins folder, you'll see folders that contain plug-ins for InDesign's tools and palettes. Unlike most software, InDesign is built on an architecture of plug-ins. That's why it's so much faster and more flexible than other desktop publishing programs. It doesn't have to keep everything in memory; instead it can turn on a plug-in when it's needed. That makes your Macintosh run faster, and saves you time.

There aren't as many third-party plug-ins (created by companies other than Adobe) for InDesign as there are for some other programs. Photoshop, for example, has well over two dozen third-party plug-ins available. But, if you need to set many complex tables, add scalable borders to your pages, or create an index and table of contents, there are InDesign plug-ins to help you. You can find some interesting and useful free and demo plug-ins in the Goodies folder on your InDesign installation disk. As more plug-ins are written, you will find information about them at http://www.adobe.com/products/plugins/indesign/main.html.

Installing InDesign

Before you install Adobe InDesign, make sure your system is up to the task. Have you defragmented your hard drive(s) recently? If not, you need a disk defragmenting utility such as Norton Speed Disk, a part of the Norton Utilities for Macintosh. While defragmenting is not mandatory, installing new software on an already fragmented disk slows down all computer operations considerably.

System Requirements

Does your computer meet these requirements?

- ◆ PowerPC 604 or faster processor (PowerPC G3 or G4 recommended)
- ◆ Apple System Software version 8.5, 8.6, or 9.0
- ◆ 48 MB of installed RAM with virtual memory on; 96 MB with virtual memory off (128 MB recommended)

- 120 MB or more of available hard-disk space for installation
- 832×624 monitor resolution (high-resolution 24-bit screen display recommended)
- Adobe PostScript Level 2 or higher required
- Internet connection recommended

If your computer does not meet these requirements, you may find yourself dashing off to the computer store for additional RAM, a system upgrade, or even an external hard drive.

> **TIP**
>
> Not sure what level of PostScript your printer uses? Find out by going to the Chooser and selecting the appropriate PostScript printer. Click the Setup button under the printer list. Then select Printer Info, and read all about the inner secrets of your printer.

Installing an Adobe application is remarkably simple. Insert the CD-ROM in the drive and open the Read Me file. This file contains important information about the files on the CD, and tells you what you might need to install in addition to InDesign. To save yourself time, make sure no other applications are open.

Ready to rock and roll? Double-click Install InDesign. You'll see the "splash screen." Click the button to continue, and enter your country of residence. The next screen is all the legal stuff; accept it. If you have more than one hard drive or if your hard drive is partitioned, you will need to tell the Installer exactly where to install the software. Figure 1.6 shows the Adobe InDesign Installer dialog box. Click Select Folder if you need to switch to a different folder or disk for installation.

Next, you'll be asked for your name, company name (if any), and most importantly, the serial number of the software. The serial number is a string of letters and numbers on a sticky label inside the disc package. Be sure you enter it correctly, using uppercase letters as needed. You might also see a box asking your permission to shut down any other open applications while InDesign installs. Now, sit back and relax while the Installer decompresses files and copies them onto your hard drive. This is also a good time to write the serial number on the flyleaf of your manual, just in case you lose the sticker. You will need the number for upgrades and technical support.

After the InDesign is installed, you'll see a registration screen. Fill out the requested information and send it electronically, if you have access to an Internet connection. It's just one less thing to think about, and if you need tech support in the future, you'll be in the database of legitimate InDesign users. If you don't have an Internet connection, print the form and mail or fax it as directed.

Getting Started

The first thing to remember is that you can't break anything. Try out a few of the features and get a general feel for the program. Open InDesign and type Command+N to start a new page. Use the default settings and click OK. Then, take a good look at the palettes on the right side of the screen. Each tab on the palette changes what you see in the window; only one of the palette tabs can be active at a time. If you don't see the palettes, click Window and choose Pages, Swatches, and Stroke; doing so will open those three palettes. Then, go to the Type menu and click Character to open the Type palettes. At the upper right of each palette is a black triangle; click it to see the options for the active palette. Then, click a different palette and look at its options.

Go to the toolbox and click the diagonal line to select it. It's a Line tool, which draws straight lines. In the document window, click and drag to draw a line. You'll notice an x in the middle of the line as you drag it; it shows you the midpoint of the line. Press the Option key and draw another line. Notice that this one is drawn from the center point out to the sides. Click the black pointer at

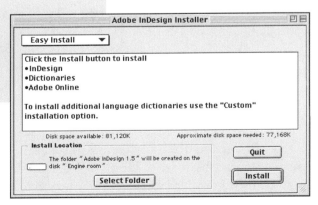

Figure 1.6
Easy Install supplies everything you need if you work in English.

the top of the toolbox to select it and then click one of the lines you drew. The line changes color to show that it's selected. If you drag the block on either end of the line, you'll make the line longer or shorter.

Now go to the Swatches palette and scroll down to the bottom. Click the blue square to change the stroke color to blue. If you look at the Gradient palette, you'll see that it shows a blue gradient, and there's a big hollow blue square at the bottom of the toolbox, too. If you draw another line, it will be blue.

Ah, but what does it all mean? How will this help you put together your annual report, your brochure, or even your garage sale flyer? In the next two chapters, you'll learn about these mysterious menus and palettes.

2

Adobe InDesign

Understanding the Pasteboard and Menus

In the previous chapter, you were introduced to the InDesign work area, which includes the pasteboard, menus, and palettes. In this chapter, you'll get to know the menus and the pasteboard better.

Working with the Pasteboard

Open a new single-page document, as you did in the previous chapter, by pressing Command+N and then clicking OK in the New Document dialog box to accept the defaults. (If you type Command+Shift+N, you bypass the dialog box and open a default page.) Now, click View and select Entire Pasteboard. Your screen should look something like Figure 2.1.

The pasteboard is the white area. When you import a picture or a story into InDesign, but aren't sure where to put it, you can just drop it on the pasteboard. If you lose something you think you brought in, zoom out and look at the whole pasteboard. It's there, unless you deleted it instead of dragging it off the active page.

You can also use the Navigator palette to show what's on the pasteboard. In Figure 2.2, I've placed a piece of text and a photo on the pasteboard next to,

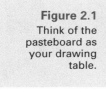

Figure 2.1
Think of the pasteboard as your drawing table.

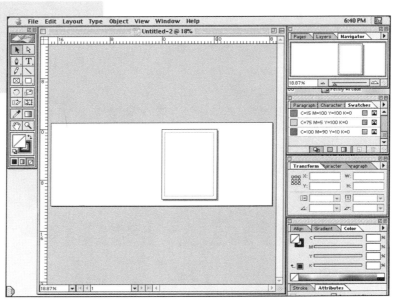

CHAPTER 2 • UNDERSTANDING THE PASTEBOARD AND MENUS   17

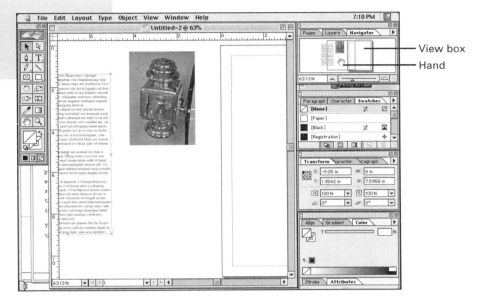

Figure 2.2
Use the hand to move the view box.

but not on, the page. Take a look at the Navigator palette in the upper-right corner of Figure 2.2. I've slid the view box to the left, so I can see part of the page and part of the pasteboard. You need to see at least a piece of the pasteboard in order to move items from the pasteboard onto the page. If you can't see them, you can't drag them.

> **TIP**
>
> You can also zoom out to see both the page and the pasteboard.

If you've attempted to paste a story that's too long for the page, you can store the extra lines on the pasteboard until you have a page on which to place them. (You'll learn how to place text in Chapter 5, "Creating Text and Graphics Frames.") You can also draw on the pasteboard, set type on it, and use it just as you would your non-computer work surface.

Exploring the Menus

InDesign has eight different menus. Some will be more familiar to you if you have worked in any Macintosh graphics application or word processor. Other menus will probably need some explaining.

The File Menu

Just like in any other piece of Mac software, InDesign's file-handling tools are on the File menu. Here you can open, save, close, print, and quit. Of course, you can also do all of these things with the standard key commands, and you probably will do so automatically. That's one of the great things about the Macintosh user interface—it's consistent. Adobe has done their best to make their document layout and graphics programs consistent as well. If you learn about menus, palettes, and commands using InDesign, and then you want to master Photoshop, you're already more than halfway there.

Of course, there are some menu items, even on the File menu, that you might not recognize. Take a look at the File menu, shown in Figure 2.3.

The New and Open Commands

New and Open are familiar commands if you have used any other Macintosh program. As you saw when you opened a new page, the New dialog box asks you to make some decisions about the size of your margins and the size and

Figure 2.3
What's on the File menu?

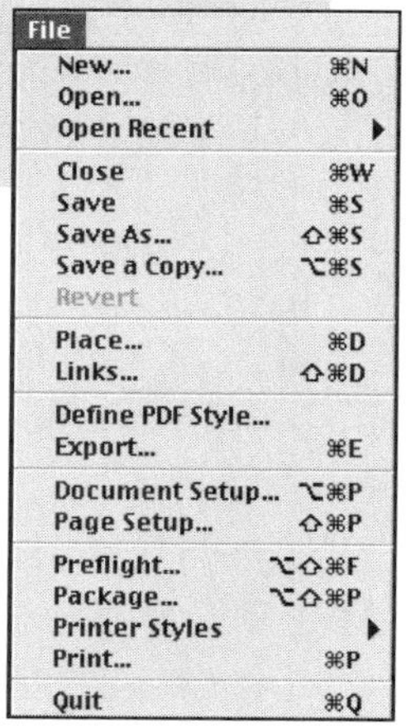

shape of your page. You'll learn more about this dialog box more in Chapter 4, "Opening and Saving Pages." The Open Recent option simply keeps a list of files with which you've recently worked, so you can find them more easily.

> **NOTE**
>
> The ellipsis after the menu item always indicates that the menu item opens a dialog box.

The Save Commands

The next thing you might notice is that there are three ways to save your work: Save, Save As, and Save a Copy. If this is the first time you have saved your InDesign page, it doesn't matter whether you choose Save or Save As. Either way, you'll have to give your page a name and tell InDesign where to save it. If you've already saved the file, but want to save it again with a different name, use Save As or press Shift+Command+S. If you want to save a copy of the current state of a file and continue working on the original file, use Save a Copy or press Option+Command+S. This feature is very useful if you're making changes you aren't sure you want to keep.

> **NOTE**
>
> You can use the Revert command to return to the last saved version of your document. Revert is only available after you have saved; otherwise, there'd be nothing to which to revert.

The Place Command

In my opinion, the single most important command for InDesign users is the Place command. This is how you bring stories and graphics into InDesign from your word processor or graphics program. True, it's not the only way. You can copy and paste, or drag from an open window, but using the Place command serves a very important purpose. It establishes a link from your original text document or piece of art to the InDesign document. If you go back and make changes to the original text document in your word processor, or decide to change the colors of a photo in Photoshop, the links will ensure that the changes are reflected in your InDesign file.

Clicking the Place command opens the Place dialog box, shown in Figure 2.4. Use the scroll bar to find the item you want to bring into InDesign, and then click Choose to copy it into your document. You use the same Place dialog box for graphics, text, and any other kind of files InDesign can read, including spreadsheet data and HTML (which is imported as plain text). After you click Choose, you'll see either the Place Graphics icon (a paintbrush) or the Place Text icon (a block of text). Figure 2.5 shows both of these icons.

The Document Setup Command

At this point, the only other important item on the File menu is Document Setup. If after opening a new document you decide you want to set up the document differently, use the Document Setup dialog box to make changes (see Figure 2.6). In this dialog box, you can change the number of pages and the page size and orientation, and choose whether interior pages face each other or not.

Figure 2.4 Use the pop-up menu and scroll bars to locate your files.

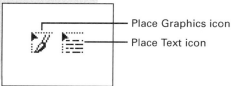

Figure 2.5 The Place Graphics icon and the Place Text icon

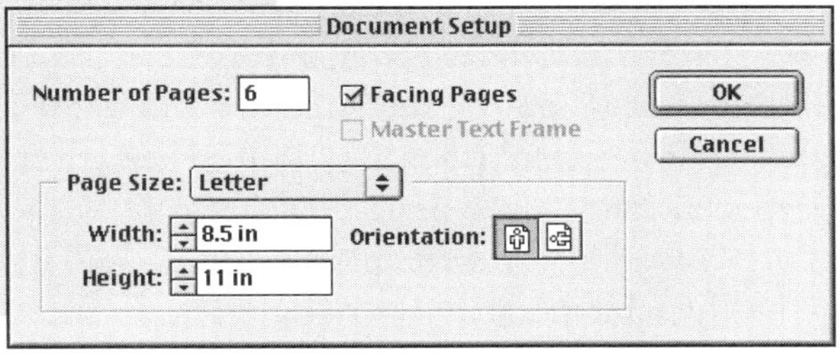

Figure 2.6
Want to make your catalog horizontal (landscape) instead of vertical (portrait)? Here's the place to do it.

The Edit Menu

Many of the commands on InDesign's Edit menu are identical to those on your word processor's Edit menu, including Undo, Redo, Cut, Copy, Paste, Select, Find/Change, and Check Spelling. Figure 2.7 shows the Edit menu.

The Undo Command

Take a close look at the Undo command at the top of the menu. It changes, depending on your most recent action. And, more important for those of us who change our minds often, you can undo multiple steps. Exactly how many steps you can undo is limited by the amount of RAM you have available, and by how long it has been since you last saved the file. Usually, though, you can expect to undo fifty steps or more with no problem.

Figure 2.7
There aren't too many surprises here.

The Paste In Place Command

Paste In Place is another useful command. You can use Paste In Place to paste a frame or imported graphic in the same position as the object that you originally copied. This is helpful when you want to keep the copy aligned with the original, or when you want to paste the copy at the same position on another page. Say you're working on a company brochure, and want to place the company logo on the same place in two pages: Paste In Place will do it. Select the first logo that you placed, and choose Copy or type Command+C. Then choose Paste In Place or type Option+Shift+Command+V.

The Step and Repeat Command

Step and Repeat is useful when you have an object you want to place many times. The Step and Repeat dialog box, shown in Figure 2.8, allows you to enter the number of repeats and offsets (how far apart the objects are placed). When you have entered your desired specifications, the copies of the object are placed according to your settings.

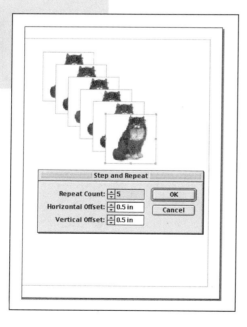

Figure 2.8
The Step and Repeat dialog box—a useful tool.

The Find/Change Command

Find/Change finds any word or string of words you enter and replaces matching text with a designated word or words. Suppose you have to do a sales brochure for a new piece of equipment. Then, at the last minute, someone in the home office decides to change the name of the gadget from "Atlas 2001" to "Acme 2001." With Find/Change, you don't have to redo the entire brochure. In fact, you don't even have to read it. Just enter the old name and the new one, click Change All, and you're done (see Figure 2.9).

There are a few other items at the bottom of the Edit menu that we'll come back to at the end of the chapter.

The Layout Menu

Every item in the Layout menu is important. Take a look at the options in the Layout menu, shown in Figure 2.10.

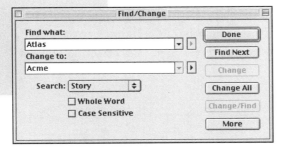

Figure 2.9 Changes are easy to make using the Find/Change option.

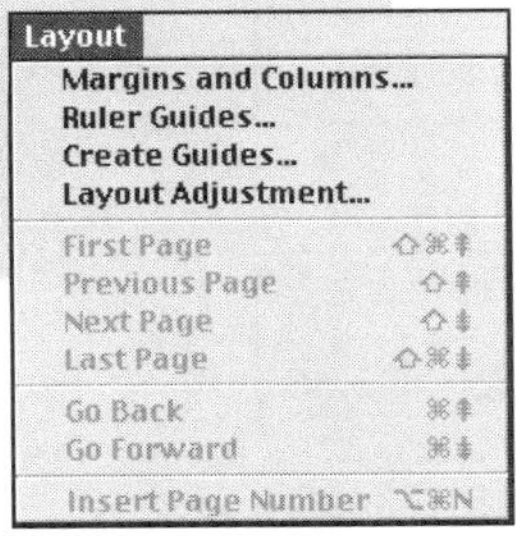

Figure 2.10 It's a short (but important) menu.

The Margins and Columns Command

When you start a new page, you're asked to enter the sizes of the margins and the number of columns per page. But let's face it, sometimes you need to make changes after you have already set up the page. Maybe the margins look too big after you put type on the page, or maybe a two-column layout doesn't look right and you want to try three. You don't need to go back and start from scratch. The Margins and Columns dialog box, shown in Figure 2.11, allows you to change these options simply by entering new values.

The Ruler Guides Command

Ruler guides are non-printing horizontal and vertical lines you drag onto the page. Use the Ruler Guides dialog box to change the color of the guides and the minimum page magnification at which you can see them. Changing the color of the guides is useful if you need to set a guide over a piece of art or a gradient.

The Create Guides Command

Gutters are the spaces between columns.

Use the Create Guides dialog box to set up evenly-spaced column guides (see Figure 2.12). Enter a number of columns per page and a gutter width. These column guides are different than the columns you set in the Margins and

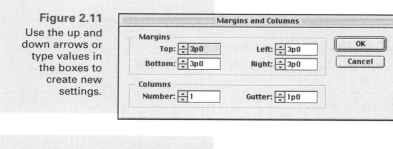

Figure 2.11 Use the up and down arrows or type values in the boxes to create new settings.

Figure 2.12 In the Create Guides dialog box, you can adjust column guides.

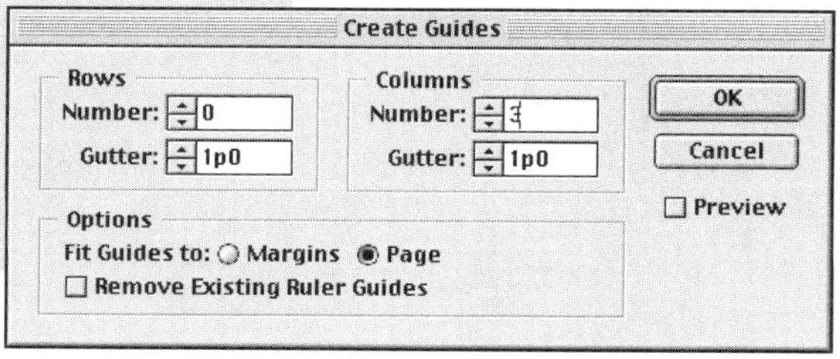

Columns dialog box. They are, in fact, guidelines for column spacing rather than actual columns. You can't pour type into them, unless you use the guides to draw a text frame. They are intended to help you visualize your layout.

The Layout Adjustment Command

Layout Adjustment is an ingenious feature that can save you time and energy. If you change an existing layout, you'll probably find that you need to slide things around to align them. Layout adjustment does that automatically, based on parameters you set in the dialog box (see Figure 2.13). Click the Enable Layout Adjustment check box, and check the appropriate options.

> **NOTE**
> Even with Layout Adjustment enabled, nothing will happen to your layout unless you change the page size, orientation, columns, or margins.

The Navigational Commands

The First Page, Previous Page, Next Page, and Last Page commands are simply navigational tools for your multi-page documents. You'll save yourself time if you memorize the keyboard shortcuts for these actions.

The Insert Page Number Command

The Insert Page Number command is the final item on the Layout menu. You must draw a text frame for the page number in order to activate this command.

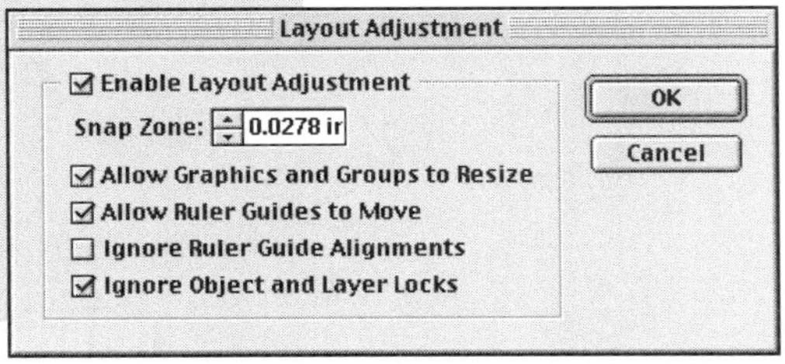

Figure 2.13
You must enable Layout Adjustment before you can change any of its settings.

The Type Menu

When you're setting type, you can use the commands on the Type menu to adjust font and size, or you can use the Character and Paragraph palettes. Figure 2.14 shows the Type menu. Click on Character or type Command+T to open the Type palettes.

The typesetting commands are fairly straightforward. The Font and Size options are self-explanatory—you've undoubtedly used them in your word processing program. However, to access the kerning, leading, and tracking commands, you must use the Type palettes.

The Story Command

Story is one of the less intuitive commands. It enables you to use optical margin alignment, which means that punctuation marks and wide letters like W and A can float into the margin. Though it seems contradictory, this actually makes the edges of the text frame appear more even. Figure 2.15 shows examples of both.

The Insert Character Command

The Insert Character command is a great timesaver if your work includes words in languages other than English. Most fonts include a variety of accented letters, as well as symbols such as trademark and copyright. The Insert Character dialog box, shown in Figure 2.16, allows you to access all the special characters in a font. In this respect it serves the same function as Key Caps. It is, however, much easier to use. Highlight the letter to be replaced, select its replacement in the Insert Character dialog box, and click Insert.

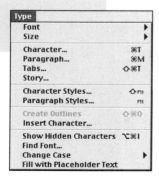

Figure 2.14
The Type menu

CHAPTER 2 • UNDERSTANDING THE PASTEBOARD AND MENUS   **27**

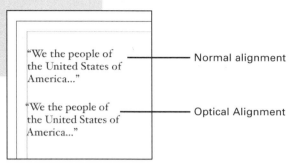

Figure 2.15 Normal alignment and optical alignment

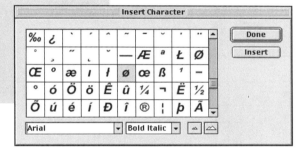

Figure 2.16 You can replace all the necessary characters, and then click Done in the dialog box.

The Fill with Placeholder Text Command

The Fill with Placeholder Text command is one that I use frequently when I am laying out pages. The command allows you to fill a text frame with placeholder text, so you can see how your page of type will look when you insert your own text. You can change the font, size, and other attributes as if it were real text and not mock Latin. Figure 2.17 shows an example of how placeholder text might be used.

The Object Menu

The Object menu lets you work with lines, blocks of color, graphics and text frames, and any other elements on your pages. You can group and ungroup objects; change the way they overlap; transform them by moving, scaling, rotating, or shearing them; and lock them in place or unlock them. Figure 2.18 shows the Object menu.

Figure 2.17
It looks like Latin, but it's called "greeking." Go figure.

> **TIP**
>
> The Transform tools can also be found in the toolbox.

Figure 2.18
The Object menu

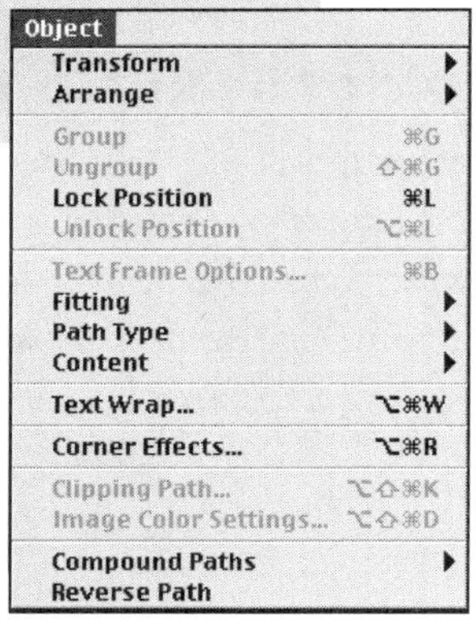

> A *pull quote* is an enlarged block of text that copies a piece of a story, usually a quote from a speaker. Pull quotes are used to attract attention, emphasize what's being said, or sometimes just to break up a page.

Selecting Text Frame Options opens a dialog box in which you can set specific options for a selected text block. The options you set in this dialog box will only apply to the text block you've selected, not the entire document. The Text Wrap option offers several ways to run text around pictures, or to set a pull quote.

The View Menu

The items on the View menu allow you to change the way you view a page (see Figure 2.19). You can zoom in and out, view the page at its actual size, or view the entire pasteboard. You can also choose the Fit Page In Window or Fit Spread In Window commands to view the entire page or spread in the window.

> **TIP**
>
> You can use the magnifying glass in the toolbox to zoom in or zoom out. Select the magnifying glass and click on the page to zoom in, and Option+click to zoom out. Or, you can use the Command++ and Command+× shortcuts to serve the same purpose.

Also on the View menu are commands to show or hide the edges of frames, the rulers, guides, and grids. The Snap to Guides and Snap to Document Grid commands have the effect of making these lines "magnetic" to a text or graphics element that is close to them. This can be helpful when you are trying to align several items, but it can be a nuisance if you are trying to place something not quite on a gridline or guideline. In such a case, turn the Snap to Guides and the Snap to Document Grid commands off by unchecking them. Then, you'll be able to place your object exactly where you want it.

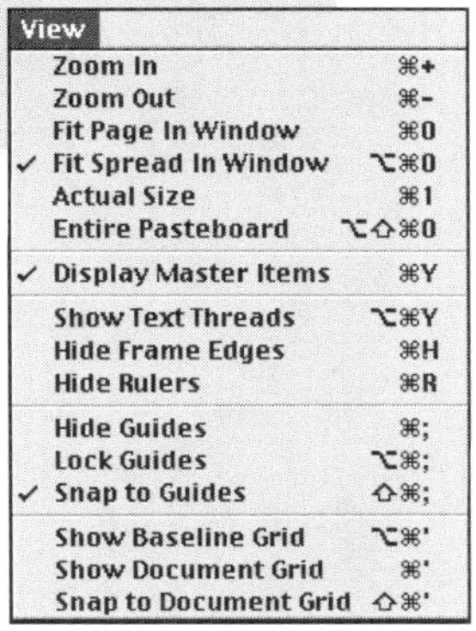

Figure 2.19
The View menu

View	
Zoom In	⌘+
Zoom Out	⌘-
Fit Page In Window	⌘0
✓ Fit Spread In Window	⌥⌘0
Actual Size	⌘1
Entire Pasteboard	⌥⇧⌘0
✓ Display Master Items	⌘Y
Show Text Threads	⌥⌘Y
Hide Frame Edges	⌘H
Hide Rulers	⌘R
Hide Guides	⌘;
Lock Guides	⌥⌘;
✓ Snap to Guides	⇧⌘;
Show Baseline Grid	⌥⌘'
Show Document Grid	⌘'
Snap to Document Grid	⇧⌘'

The Window Menu

You can use the Window menu to open palettes that aren't open on the screen. If you have pressed the Tab key with nothing selected, all of your palettes and the toolbox will disappear. You can use the items on the Window menu to bring them back. The palettes are listed in groups on the menu, and selecting one palette in a group will open all the palettes in that group. Figure 2.20 shows the Window menu.

The Swatch Libraries menu item gives you access to the many different spot color and limited color libraries supplied with InDesign. You can set your Mac to display the swatch set for Web-safe colors, Pantone Coated and Uncoated, Focoltone, or whatever spot color system your commercial printing company uses. Figure 2.21 shows the list of color libraries that come with InDesign.

The Help Menu

Help is something for which Adobe products are known, and InDesign is no exception. InDesign's Help window, shown in Figure 2.22, gives you three different ways to find the specific item with which you need assistance. You can look it up in the Help index, you can browse the Contents tab until you find a topic that describes your problem, or you can enter a single word in the Find tab and get a list of all Help topics that include that term.

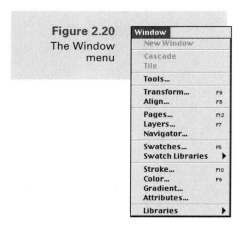

Figure 2.20
The Window menu

CHAPTER 2 • UNDERSTANDING THE PASTEBOARD AND MENUS

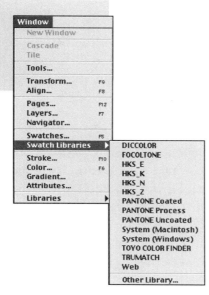

Figure 2.21
Each Swatch Library has several hundred color swatches.

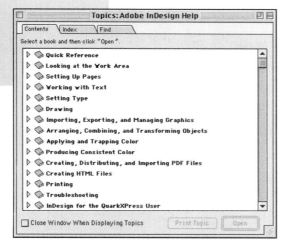

Figure 2.22
Use the contents or alphabetical index, or enter a search term.

The Help menu also gives you immediate access to Adobe's Web pages, which are full of interesting tips and tricks for all Adobe products, as well as galleries of art and illustrations that will get your creative juices flowing.

Using Shortcuts

Using the menus is simple enough, but it can be time-consuming. Many of InDesign's menu items can be accessed directly from your keyboard, either by using the F-keys or by using key combinations.

Using the F-Keys

If you're a "power user," you're already familiar with that row of keys at the very top of the keyboard. If not, take a look now. There are sixteen keys in all: F1–F12, plus Help, Home, Pg Up, and Pg Down. Many applications use F-keys, alone or with modifiers: Shift, Option, and Command. InDesign uses several F-key commands. However, some of these can be used only when a specific dialog box is open. For example, if you open the Find/Change dialog box, you can select a word in the text to be found and use Shift+F1 to enter it in the dialog box.

Unmodified function keys can open several of the palettes.

F-key	Opens
F5	Swatches palette
F6	Color palette
F7	Layers palette
F8	Align palette
F9	Transform palette
F10	Stroke palette
F11	Paragraph Styles palette
F12	Pages palette

> **NOTE**
>
> If you have a background application that uses any of the F-keys, those particular keys won't be available in InDesign. For example, my screen capture program uses F10 to capture the screen, so I can't use it to open the Stroke palette.

Exploring the Command Key Combinations

Most menu items can be opened either by the F-keys described in the previous section or by Command key combinations. Many of these combinations are shown on the menus next to the items they represent, but these combinations are just the tip of the iceberg. To see the full list of InDesign key commands, go to the Edit menu and select Edit Shortcuts. You'll see a dialog box like the one shown in Figure 2.23.

You can scroll through the lists and select items, and the appropriate shortcuts will display in the Current Shortcuts window. If you want to see the full list, click the Show Set button. This opens a complete alphabetical list of all defined and undefined actions in SimpleText. You can also use the Edit Shortcuts dialog box to assign shortcuts to items you use often. For example, if you have a favorite font in which all your text is set, choose a key combination to create a shortcut to apply that font.

Setting Preferences

InDesign's Preferences dialog box allows you to customize the way InDesign works for you (see Figure 2.24). You can access the Preferences dialog box by selecting the Preferences option on the Edit menu. Set your preferences before you start working on a new document, and they'll be saved with the document.

Figure 2.23
Select a menu to see what shortcuts are on it.

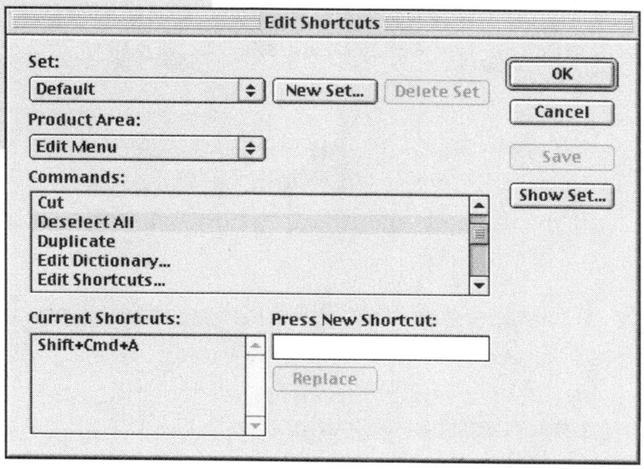

Figure 2.24
Click the double arrows to see the available options for each item.

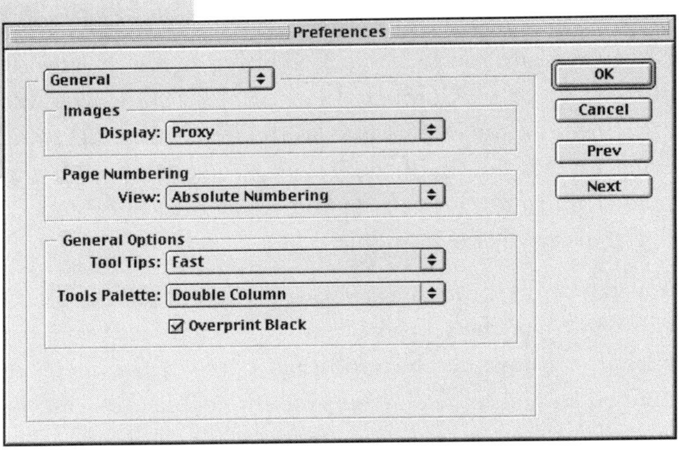

Adjusting Document Preferences

When you first open the Preferences dialog box, you will see that the General option is selected in the top pop-up menu. You can access other panes of the dialog box by selecting options from this pop-up menu, or by using the Next and Previous buttons.

> **NOTE**
>
> If you change preference settings while a document is open, the changes will apply only to that document. If you make changes when no files are open, the changes will apply to all subsequent files.

I won't tell you how to set your preferences—you know what you like. As you become more familiar with InDesign, you might want to change the colors of gridlines or the measurement units from inches to centimeters. It's all up to you.

However, I *will* tell you how to return to InDesign's default settings if you don't like the changes you have made. First quit the program, then open your System folder. Open the Preferences folder and locate the Adobe InDesign folder. Find the InDesign Defaults file and the InDesign SavedDatafile. Drag them out of the System folder (if you think you might want to put them back), delete them, or leave them there, but rename them (for example, olddefaults and oldsaveddata). Close the folders and restart the program. InDesign will create new defaults and saved-data folders, using the preset defaults supplied by Adobe.

Adjusting Online Settings

The Adobe Online Preferences dialog box is the last menu item on the Preferences submenu. It has two tabs: General and Application. The General tab is shown in Figure 2.25. If you have already configured your Internet settings, just click the Use Internet Config Settings check box. Otherwise, enter the appropriate information in the form. If you don't know the information, click the Setup button to open Adobe's Setup Assistant. It will walk you through the setup process one step at a time.

The options on the Application tab, shown in Figure 2.26, let you determine whether Adobe will send you periodic e-mails about InDesign, and whether you will connect automatically for downloads.

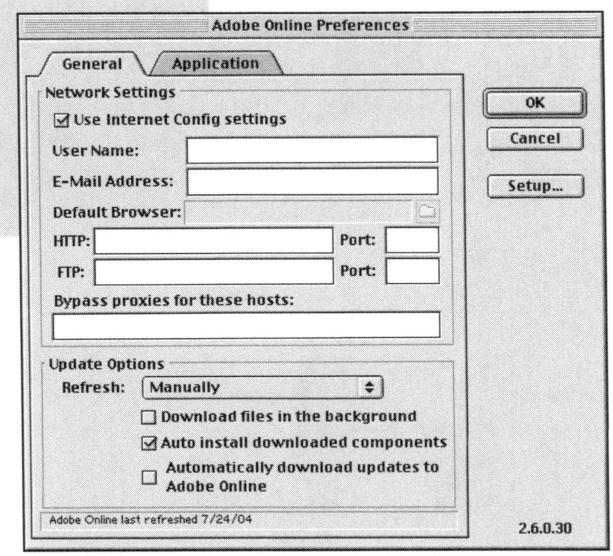

Figure 2.25
If your Internet connection works correctly, just check the Use Internet Config Settings box.

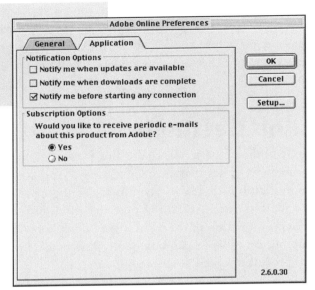

Figure 2.26
The Subscriptions Options put you on Adobe's e-mail list.

Adjusting Color Settings

The Color Settings dialog boxes are rather complicated, and are not very meaningful to you at this point in your exploration of InDesign. You'll learn about their purpose and meaning in Chapter 20, "Working with Color Modes and Color Models," and Chapter 21, "Applying Color." For now, leave the default settings unless you already know color management from some other application, and you know what you're changing and why. Default settings are there because they generally work well under any possible condition.

> **TIP**
>
> Whenever you open a dialog box in which you're *not* making changes, click Cancel rather than OK to close it. That way, you don't risk making an accidental change.

3

Adobe InDesign

Using the Tools and Palettes

If you have used any other Adobe graphics program, such as Photoshop, Illustrator, or even PhotoDeluxe, many of the tools in the InDesign toolbox will be familiar to you, as will the concept, if not the contents, of the palettes. Let's start with the tools.

Working with the Toolbox

Figure 3.1 shows the InDesign toolbox. Together with the palettes, it provides everything you need to place and manipulate text and graphics. Clicking the picture of an open book at the top of the toolbox connects you to Adobe Online, assuming you have a Web browser and an Internet connection.

To select a tool, just click it. Some tools have tiny black triangles in the lower-right corner of their icons, indicating that there are more similar tools on a pop-

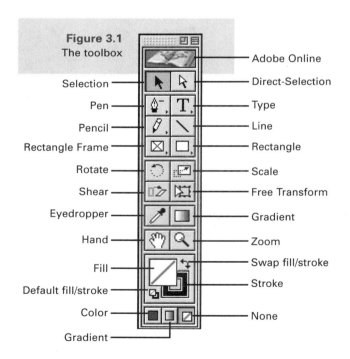

Figure 3.1
The toolbox

up menu. To reach these tools, click and hold the tool until the other tool choices pop up. You can also select tools by typing a single letter, if that suits your way of working. Of course, you have to memorize the letters, because there's no easy way to remember them all. Some of the letters are related to the tool name (for example, Text is T and Zoom is Z), but others are not. The Pencil tool is N, the Rectangle tool is M, and the Selection tool is V. Go figure.

Changing the Toolbox Layout from Two Columns to One

The default view of the toolbox places it in two rows down the left side of your screen. If you'd rather have a single row, either down the side or across the top of the screen, it's easy to change. There are two icons at the top-right corner of the toolbox that should be familiar to any Mac user. The one on the far right hides and reveals the window, and the one on the left changes the way the window is viewed. Click the left icon to toggle between a double row of tools, a single, vertical row, and a single, horizontal row.

Using the Selection Tools

The toolbox contains several different kinds of tools. The top two tools are selection tools. The filled arrow is called the Selection tool, and you can apply it either by clicking on it to select it, or by typing V. The unfilled arrow is the Direct-Selection tool. What's the difference? The Selection tool is used for general selection tasks, such as moving an object or dragging a handle to resize an object. The Direct-Selection tool is used when you need to work with a path, frame, or frame contents. The Direct-Selection tool can drag anchor points on a path, allowing you to reshape the path.

So how can you tell if you've properly selected an object to perform a specific task? Simply look at the blocks on the corners of the object you are selecting. Hollow blocks are anchor points, which indicate that you've selected a path or frame; use the Direct-Selection tool with these. Filled blocks are handles, which indicate that you have selected a bounding box; use the Selection tool with these. Figure 3.2 shows examples of both.

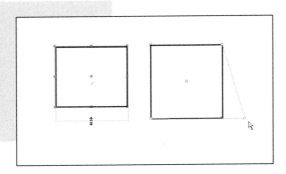

Figure 3.2
A square frame selected and moved with the Selection tool (left) and with the Direct-Selection tool, (right).

Using the Path Tools

InDesign has a set of five path tools that should be familiar if you have used any kind of vector-drawing program. These path tools, shown in Figure 3.3, appear when you click and hold the mouse button on the Pen tool.

The Pen tool is the one you'll use the most—it draws paths, which can be open or closed. Paths themselves are invisible on the printed page. To make them visible, you must stroke and/or fill them. Stroking a path applies a line to it. Filling it, logically, fills it with a color, pattern, or gradient of your choice. Both open and closed paths can be filled as well as stroked. Figure 3.4 shows some examples.

The other path tools allow you to add or remove points from a path, to reshape the path, and to split a single path into two. You'll learn to work with all of these tools in Chapter 6, "Working with Frames and Lines."

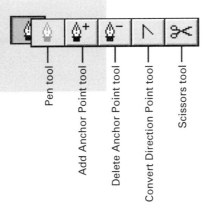

Figure 3.3
Click and hold the Pen tool to display the other path tools.

Pen tool
Add Anchor Point tool
Delete Anchor Point tool
Convert Direction Point tool
Scissors tool

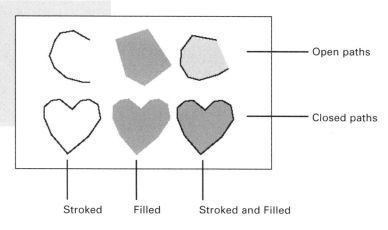

Figure 3.4 Above, open paths—stroked, filled, stroked and filled. Below, closed paths given the same treatment.

Using the Type Tools

There are two type tools, as you can see in Figure 3.5. The Type tool, which looks like a vertical T, sets type in normal fashion, in a text frame. The Type Path tool, which looks like a slanted T, sets type on a path. To use the Type tool, click it or type T, then position the cursor at the point where you want the type to start. To draw a text frame box, drag the tool on the document. In the resulting text frame box, you can enter text using the keyboard or place text from a source outside of InDesign.

If you want to move or change the size of the text frame, use the Selection arrow. If you want to reshape the frame, use the Direct-selection arrow, because you're only moving part of the frame.

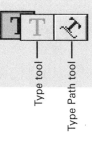

Figure 3.5 Click and hold the Type tool to reveal the Type Path tool.

> **NOTE**
>
> If you click the Text tool inside any frame, shape, or path that you've drawn, the frame becomes a text frame.

To set type on a path, you must first create the path, using the path tools. A path, as you saw previously, can be a shape or a line. After you prepare the path, you simply click the Type Path tool at the point where you want the words to begin, and type or paste as needed. Paths only accept one line of type; if you need several lines, duplicate the path and flow the text from one line to the next.

Using the Line Tools

There are two line tools. The Straight Line tool, which looks like a diagonal line, draws straight lines. If you hold down the Shift key as you draw, you can constrain your line to vertical, horizontal, or a 45-degree angle. The other line tool is the Pencil tool, which draws paths that can be reshaped or edited just like lines drawn with the Pen tool. The difference is that as soon as you deselect a path drawn with the Pencil tool, it becomes a line in whatever color and weight were selected before you started to draw. You can change the color and weight by reselecting it with the Selection tool.

Using the Shape Tools

InDesign has three kinds of shape tools: Rectangle, Ellipse, and Polygon. The Ellipse and Polygon tools appear when you click and hold the Rectangle tool, or you can cycle through all three by typing Shift+M three times. These tools are shown in Figure 3.6. Don't confuse them with the frame shape tools, which draw frames as placeholders. The frame shape tools each have a large X through the appropriate icon; the shape tools do not.

To change the number of sides in a polygon (either a polygon shape or polygon frame), double-click the appropriate tool. A dialog box will ask you to set the number of sides and, if you want a star shape rather than a straight-sided polygon, to set a percentage to inset the spikes. Figure 3.7 shows some stars with different inset values.

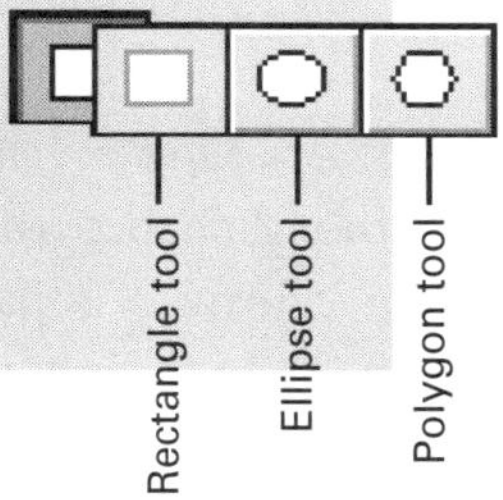

CHAPTER 3 · USING THE TOOLS AND PALETTES 43

Figure 3.6
Select the shape you need, and drag its tool to place the shape on the page.

Figure 3.7
From left to right: 20, 50, 80, and 100% inset.

To draw a shape with any of these tools, click on the page where you want the upper-left corner of the shape or frame to begin, and drag until the shape is the right size. To draw a shape outward from its center, press and hold the Option key while you drag. The shape will then expand outward from its center point. Draw perfect circles and squares by pressing the Shift key as you drag the cursor to draw the shape.

Using the Transform Tools

The toolbox includes four tools for transforming shapes and frames. They are the Rotate, Scale, Shear, and Free Transform tools. Figure 3.8 shows these handy tools.

The Rotate tool turns a shape or frame when you drag a corner of the object. The Scale tool enlarges or reduces the shape or frame. Shear tilts the shape or

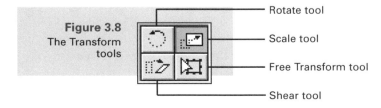

Figure 3.8
The Transform tools

frame on one axis only. Free Transform lets you do all of these things at once, if you desire.

Because you can use these tools on frames as well as on shapes, you can rotate graphics, set text on an angle or in a diamond shape, resize pictures, and tilt both words and pictures. Transformations can make a page more interesting and dynamic, or can make it totally chaotic. Use these tools wisely.

If you are rotating a text frame (for instance, to make a diamond instead of a square), and want the text to remain horizontal with respect to the page, rotate the frame first. Then add the text. If you want the text or graphic to rotate, add it to the frame, and then apply the transformation. See Figure 3.9 for an example of both methods.

All transformations happen in relation to a fixed point on or near the object being transformed. This point is called the point of origin and is marked, when the transform tools are active, by a sort of target with crosshairs. The upper-left corner is usually the point of origin for an object because that is the point from which it is drawn. A line's point of origin is the midpoint of the line. You can change the point of origin by selecting and dragging it. Why would you want to? Well, suppose you have a circle, and you want to scale it. The circle's point of origin, by default, is actually outside the circle itself, at the upper-left corner. If you drag the circle to enlarge it, it will move down and to the right. If you move the point of origin to the middle of the circle, when you scale it, it will grow outward in place instead of moving. Figure 3.10 illustrates this point.

Scaling and rotating are fairly obvious concepts. Shear, however, may take a little explaining. When you shear an object, you skew it or slant it. Shearing is useful to indicate certain kinds of perspective, to cast a shadow by shearing a copy of an object, or to slant a text frame. I've created some examples in Figure 3.11.

Figure 3.9
Rotate the text frame, before or after placing the text.

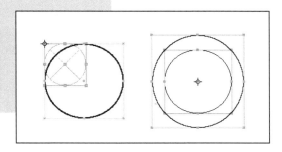

Figure 3.10
In the figure on the right, I've moved the point of origin to the center of the circle.

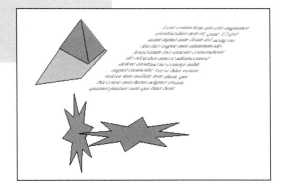

Figure 3.11
Various sheared objects

Free Transform does exactly what it sounds like; it lets you scale, stretch, skew, and rotate all at once. Just grab a handle and drag until you have achieved the look you want. Figure 3.12 illustrates what can happen when you apply Free Transform to a text block.

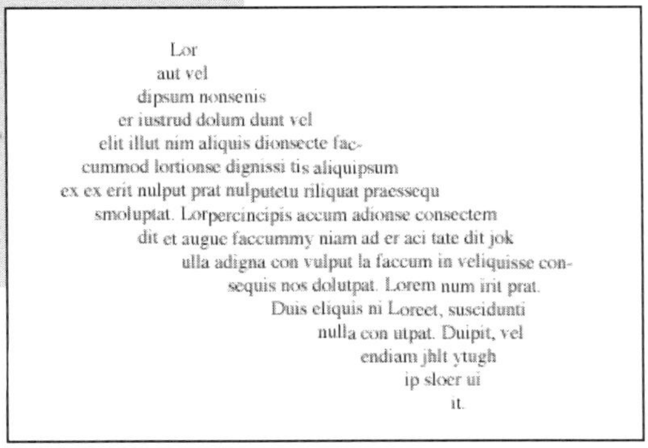

Figure 3.12
Using Free Transform, you can stretch and skew a text block into an interesting shape.

Using the Eyedropper Tool

If you've worked with graphics, you may think you know the Eyedropper tool. It picks up a sample of color and makes it the active color on your palette, right? Well, that's part of what it does. In InDesign, the Eyedropper tool can also sample and place text and paragraph styles, and fill and stroke attributes.

To copy text attributes with the Eyedropper tool, select the tool and click the text from which you want to copy text attributes. (The text can be in the same document or in another open InDesign document.) The Eyedropper tool reverses direction and appears full, to indicate that it's loaded with the attributes you copied (see Figure 3.13). When you position the Eyedropper over another text block, an I-beam cursor appears next to the loaded Eyedropper. Drag the I-beam cursor to select the text you want to change. The selected text then takes on the type attributes loaded in the Eyedropper. As long as the Eyedropper tool is loaded, you can select other text characters and apply the loaded formatting to them. By default, the Eyedropper tool copies all attributes of a type selection.

Use the same technique to copy attributes of a line or shape. Click to fill the Eyedropper, and then click with the full Eyedropper on an object to be changed.

Copying a color with the Eyedropper is very simple. Just click on the color you want to copy, and it will appear as the fill color. You can use the color palette as a source for colors, or use a photo or piece of art you have brought into InDesign. Using colors from your images helps guarantee that your layout colors will coordinate with your photo colors.

Figure 3.13
An empty Eyedropper on the left, and a filled Eyedropper on the right

Using the Gradient Tool

The Gradient tool creates and applies various kinds of gradients. You can put a tint behind your text to make it stand out, or you can create a shaded object. You can even apply a gradient to type. An example of gradients applied to objects and text is shown in Figure 3.14.

Using the View Tools

The Zoom tool and the Hand tool are the two view tools. Zooming in and out lets you see more or less of your pasteboard. Zooming in is very helpful when you're trying to kern type or align things manually, and zooming out lets you see what parts of your project you might have dumped on the pasteboard and forgotten. The Zoom tool looks like a magnifying glass. You can zoom in by clicking on the page with the Zoom tool selected. To zoom out, press the Option key as you click the Zoom tool.

The Hand tool looks like a hand, and works like one, too. It slides the visible section of your document in the open window. You can also use the Hand tool in the Navigator palette to change your view of the page.

Using the Stroke and Fill Tools

The larger squares toward the bottom of the toolbox represent stroke and fill. Stroke, as you learned earlier, is how you apply color and weight to a line or path. Fill applies color inside a drawn shape, frame, or path. If you see a white

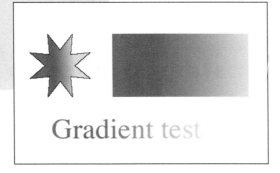

Figure 3.14
You can adjust the colors of the gradient by using the Gradient palette.

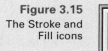
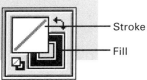

Figure 3.15
The Stroke and Fill icons — Stroke — Fill

square with a red line through it, it means that no color is selected. A box drawn with no stroke and no fill is invisible. To save time, set your stroke and fill colors before you begin to create shapes or paths.

Clicking the two little squares at the bottom left of the Stroke and Fill icon (see Figure 3.15) resets the default colors, black for stroke and none for fill. Clicking the double arrow at the top right of the icon (or typing X) swaps the fill and stroke colors.

The small swatches at the bottom of the toolbox are simply shortcuts. Clicking the Color swatch applies the last selected color to the selected object. The Gradient swatch applies the most recently used gradient, and the None swatch removes any color fill or stroke from a selected object.

> **TIP**
> Whenever you're not sure what a tool or icon does, just move your cursor over it and wait a couple of seconds. You'll see a tool tip telling you the name of the tool and what key or combination (if any) you can type for its shortcut.

That covers everything on the left side of the screen; on the right is a set of palettes. Palettes help you manage your documents, and provide many shortcuts and controls for working with the tools.

Using Palettes instead of Menus

Much of what you'd use the palettes for can also be accomplished by using menu commands, and for some people, the commands are the best way to work. If you memorize the key commands for the menu items, your fingers never have to leave the keyboard. However, if you're more comfortable using a mouse, the palettes might work better for you.

Docking Palettes

Each palette has several tabs, indicating other palettes docked within the same box. You can bring a different palette forward by clicking the tab. If there are some palettes you use a lot, you can dock them together by dragging the tab from one box to another. I like to keep the Color palette available, so I've dragged it into the box with the Navigator, Layers, and Pages palettes.

Most palettes can be turned on and off from the Window menu, with the exceptions being the Character and Paragraph palettes, which can be reached from the Type menu.

Using the Palette Menus

In addition to the options available on each palette, most have flyout menus, indicated by a black triangle in the upper-right corner. The menus give you access to even more options and commands. The Layers palette and its flyout menu are shown in Figure 3.16.

Working with Palette Options

You have some options on the Layers palette (and typically on other palettes as well) that aren't duplicated elsewhere in InDesign. However, you can access the most frequently used options in several ways. For example, you can use the flyout menu to start a new layer on your page, or you can click the New Layer icon at the bottom of the palette. To delete a layer, you can use a menu command or simply drag the unwanted layer to the Trash can icon.

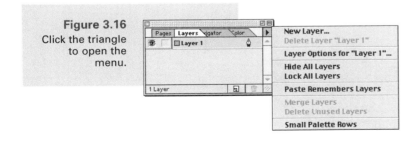

Figure 3.16
Click the triangle to open the menu.

Exploring the Pages, Layers, and Navigator Palettes

Before we go any further, let's stop and take a look at each palette. Figure 3.17 shows the Pages palette. You can see that I've set my document up as a four-page newsletter. You can see an inside double-page spread and front and back pages. To go to the page on which you want you want to work, click on it. The icons in the top section of the Pages palette represent the master pages. You'll learn more about working with master pages later on.

The Layers palette lets you add layers to your pages, allowing you to place one item over another more easily. Layers are like sheets of cellophane. You can paste things on them, create text frames or graphics frames on them, and merge them when you're done working on your layout.

The Navigator palette shows you, in a thumbnail version, what's visible on your screen and what isn't. Use the Hand tool to slide the large frame around inside the palette. This changes the area seen in the program's window. In Figure 3.18, I'm looking at the first page of my four-page brochure.

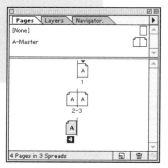

Figure 3.17
To apply a master page, drag it to the document pages.

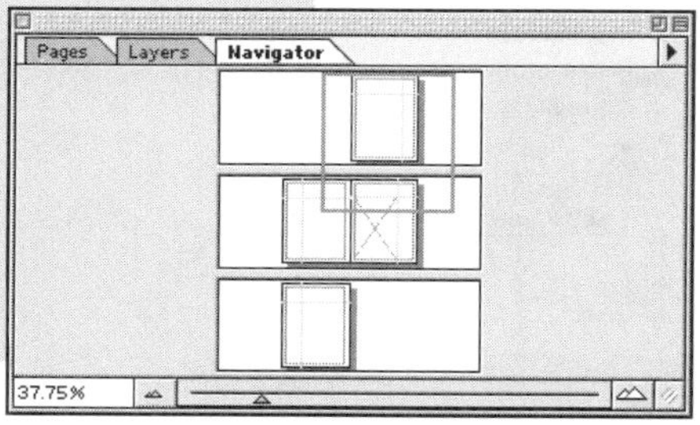

Figure 3.18
The Navigator palette shows what's visible on your screen, making it easy to move from one page to another.

Exploring the Transform and Align Palettes

You have already learned about using the Transform tools to change an object's shape or size. If you use the Transform tools and the Transform palette together, you can make precise changes instead of approximate ones. Figure 3.19 shows the Transform palette, along with its flyout menu. To make a precise adjustment to an object, such as a 45-degree rotation, enter the appropriate numbers in the boxes. To change an object's point of origin, click one of the nine squares in the upper-left corner of the palette, and the object's point of origin will change to reflect your selection.

The Align palette both aligns objects and distributes or evenly spaces them. It's shown in Figure 3.20, and it is one of the more intuitive palettes. The small icons show you exactly how your selected objects will align, and you can use the Use Spacing check box and window to distribute objects evenly across or down the page.

Exploring the Stroke, Gradient, Attributes, and Color Palettes

The Stroke palette appears at first to be a simple palette that only asks for stroke weight, but if you select Show Options from the flyout menu, you'll see the full palette, as shown in Figure 3.21. Here you can choose arrows, circles,

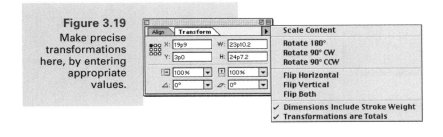

Figure 3.19
Make precise transformations here, by entering appropriate values.

Figure 3.20
Choose an alignment method by clicking on the appropriate icon.

or other symbols to start and end the line. You can choose multiple lines of different weights, and you can determine how a line ends, how a shape is drawn, and how corners and miters are handled.

The Gradient palette, shown in Figure 3.22, also appears very simple until you look at its options. InDesign can create both linear and radial gradients, and the Gradient palette adjusts the blend of the gradient from one color to another. You're not limited to a two-color gradient. You can add as many colors as you want, but it's a good idea to place the gradient wherever you're using it before you get too fancy. That way you can see the modifications as you make them, and undo what doesn't work. To remove extra colors from the gradient, simply select their tabs at the bottom of the gradient bar and slide them to the right until the colors disappear.

The Attributes palette really is as simple as it looks. There are no options beyond the Overprint Fill and Overprint Stroke checkboxes. Understanding what these two options mean is a little more complicated. These two options refer to color printing and to the process of color trapping. Overprinting means that the color is printed on top of whatever else is already there, instead of knocking out the color behind your chosen line or shape so that it prints on white. If this is clear as mud, don't worry. It will all make sense when you learn about printing in Chapter 23, "Service Bureaus."

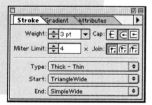

Figure 3.21
The stroke options are hidden until you select Show Options.

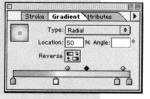

Figure 3.22
Click the Reverse button to make the gradient shade in the opposite direction.

Using the Color palette is one of several ways you can select colors. You can set the palette to one of three color modes, using the flyout menu. You can show only RGB colors (the kind your monitor displays), CMYK colors (the kind your printer uses), or LAB color, a third and possibly more accurate way of describing colors. The color mode in which you choose to work depends on the final purpose of your document. If your document is going on the Web, stick with RGB. If it's going into print, using CMYK may give you slightly less accurate color onscreen, but you can be sure your colors will be printable. I prefer to do all my work in RGB, and then convert to CMYK when I'm getting the files ready to print.

Take a look at the Color palette, shown in Figure 3.23. At the top left are copies of the Stroke and Fill swatches. Click whichever one you want to make active. To change the color of the Stroke or Fill swatch, move the cursor over the spectrum at the bottom of the palette. The cursor turns into an eyedropper, which you can use to select a color. You can also change a color by moving the RGB sliders or by entering new values in the boxes. At the left end of the spectrum is a "no color" box. At the right are black and white patches. Clicking any of these will change the stroke or fill accordingly.

Exploring the Swatches Palette

Using the Swatches palette is yet another way you can keep track of the colors you use. You can control all the document's colors and gradients from the Swatches palette, if you wish. You can store colors and gradients for instant access and you can even create colors on the palette.

If you look at the Swatches palette in Figure 3.24, you can see the default colors, plus one that I added. Colors can be named by the amounts of CYMK or RGB, or can be given names. You can also select spot colors and list them by

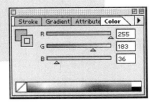

Figure 3.23
This is set for RGB color.

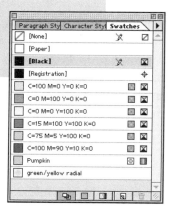

Figure 3.24
Use the scrollbar to view the rest of the palette.

number, such as Pantone CV413. Spot colors are designated by an icon with a spot in the middle. Pumpkin, in the example, is a spot color. The process colors have an icon with gray dots. CMYK colors have a second icon, which is a combination of four (cyan, magenta, yellow, and black) triangles. RGB colors have an icon with bars of red, green, and blue.

When a selected object's stroke or fill color is one you have assigned from the Swatches palette, the applied swatch is highlighted. A percentage value next to a swatch indicates that there is a tint in that percentage of the swatch color. Thus, "Pumpkin 25%" indicates a very light tint of orange. To change a tint percentage, drag the slider on the color palette or enter a percentage in the box.

There are some swatches that you can't edit or remove, specifically None and Black. An icon of a pencil with a line through it designates these. The None swatch removes the color from an object, while black is a built-in process color defined with the CMYK model.

Registration is another built-in function that prints registration marks when you prepare color separations for printing. Registration marks help assure that the separate printing plates for the process colors line up, making the colors register properly when printed.

Paper can be set to any color. This feature is intended to let you see what your layout will look like if printed on colored stock. If you are using colored stock and spot colors, this is a way to make sure they harmonize. To set a paper color, double-click the Paper icon to open the Swatch Options dialog box shown in Figure 3.25. Look at the small square on the left side of the dialog box and

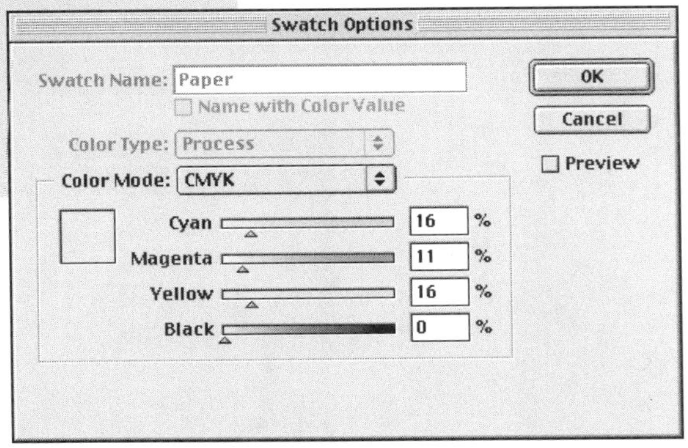

Figure 3.25
Click the Preview check box to see your color on the page.

move the sliders until you have matched the paper color as closely as possible. If it's easier, check the Preview check box to see the paper color on the page, and hold your paper up to the screen while you adjust the sliders for a perfect match.

You can also open Swatch libraries from the Window menu. These are libraries of spot colors arranged by color family. The available swatches include Pantone, DIC Color, Focaltone, Toyo, Trumatch, and several others. You can have several Swatch color libraries open at once. They'll appear on the same palette window but with different tabs identifying their source. To import a color from a Swatch library, just double-click the color you want. To add several swatches, select them in the palette, holding down the Shift key as you click to make multiple selections. Use the Add to Swatches command on the flyout menu to move them all into your working Swatches palette.

To apply a swatch color to an object or line, select Line or Fill as appropriate, and click the swatch color. The object will change color immediately.

So, there is a brief introduction to the tools and palettes. Poke around in their menus and see what's there. In the next chapter, we'll start putting them to use.

4

Adobe InDesign

Opening and Saving Pages

Now that you have had a chance to look at the menus and tools, it's time to put them to work. In this chapter you'll learn about pages. The page is where you place your text and pictures, just as if you were doing an old-fashioned paste-up on a piece of illustration board.

Starting a New Document

Creating pages is easy. From the File menu, choose New or type Command+N. The New Document dialog box opens, as shown in Figure 4.1. Decide how many pages your document should have, and what size they'll be. If you don't know how many pages you'll need, just make a guess. You can always add or subtract pages later. Enter the appropriate numbers in the windows, and be sure to check Facing Pages if your document will be printed on both sides of a page.

> Facing pages are called *spreads*.

In the example shown here, I've set up a simple four-page, letter-sized newsletter, with three columns per page. I'm not stuck with this format; I can change individual pages as much and as often as I need to, but this gives me a basic framework for my project.

The Gutter entry in the New Document dialog box determines the amount of space between columns. The current default is an eighth of an inch, but you can increase this amount as much as you want. I wouldn't recommend decreasing the setting, because your columns could end up looking squashed together.

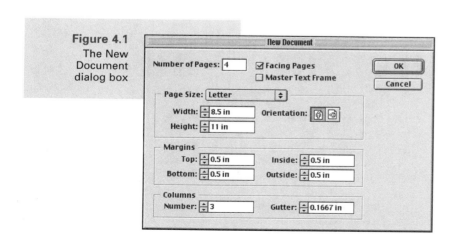

Figure 4.1
The New Document dialog box

CHAPTER 4 • OPENING AND SAVING PAGES

> **NOTE**
>
> I prefer to keep measurements in inches. If you find it easier to think in points, picas, centimeters, or even ciceros, use the Preferences dialog box to change the measurement method. In case you've forgotten, the Preferences option is at the bottom of the Edit menu.

When you finish entering the required information, click OK. Figure 4.2 shows my newsletter page, all ready for type and pictures. The guidelines I set define the margins and columns.

Opening Existing Pages

Not surprisingly, InDesign works like every other Macintosh program. To open a page when InDesign is already running, use File, Open to locate the desired document, or—if you know where the document is—double-click its icon. If InDesign isn't open, double-clicking on an InDesign document will launch InDesign and open the document.

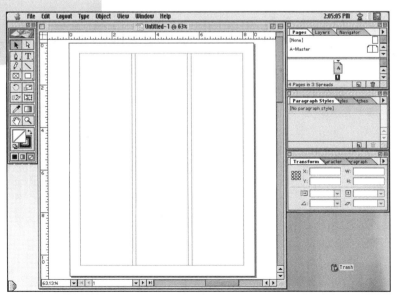

Figure 4.2
The front page of my newsletter

Making Changes to Your Document

Nobody gets everything right the first time, so it's good that InDesign lets you change your mind, and your layout, as much as you want. You might think a three-quarter inch margin sounds good, but until you have seen the page full of type, you won't know for sure if half an inch, or even a whole inch, might be better. Trial and error has been part of the process since the beginning. Just keep trying things until they look right.

Resizing Margins

As I look at my page, I realize that the margins are too small. No problem. To change the margin amounts, select Margins and Columns from the Layout menu, as shown in Figure 4.3. This opens the Margins and Columns dialog box, shown in Figure 4.4. Here you can enter different settings for the margins or change the number of columns.

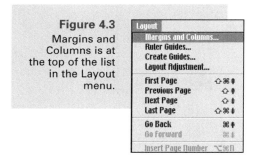

Figure 4.3
Margins and Columns is at the top of the list in the Layout menu.

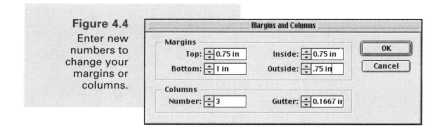

Figure 4.4
Enter new numbers to change your margins or columns.

Changing the Default Margin Settings

If you know that you'll always want to use a certain margin setting, such as a larger margin, a wider gutter, or two columns, you can make these settings the defaults by changing the appropriate dialog box entries when no pages are open.

To change the default settings, open InDesign, but don't open a publication. Open the Margins and Columns dialog box and change the values to the desired settings. To change other defaults, open the appropriate dialog box and make the desired changes. (Don't use the New Document dialog box when you want to change defaults. Settings you change there relate only to the new document that you are creating.)

Adding Pages

There are several ways to add pages to your document. The first, and simplest, method is to use the Document Setup dialog box to change the number of pages (see Figure 4.5). Select Document Setup from the File menu and enter the desired number of pages in the dialog box. Pages are added after the last page.

You can also use this dialog box to change the size of the pages and their orientation. Among the page size options are Letter, Legal, and Tabloid, as well as common European sizes and CD inserts. There's also a setting for Custom, which lets you enter any page size you want to use. This is where you'd set up a square catalog, a long four-fold brochure, or other nonstandard pages.

The second way to add pages is to use the Pages palette, shown in Figure 4.6. Click the Page icon at the bottom of the window to add a page after the current page. Click twice to add two pages.

Figure 4.5
European pages (A3, A4, A5, and B5) are available on the Page Size pop-up menu.

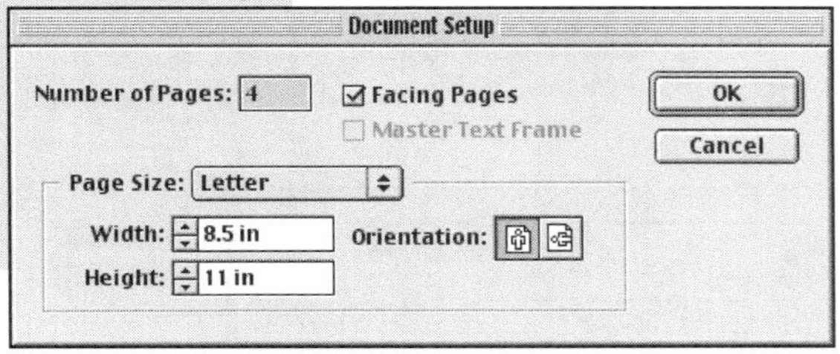

Figure 4.6
Pages are added after the last page.

Adding Pages to the Middle of a Document

There's still another way to add pages, if you want them to appear somewhere other than after the last page. There's a flyout menu on the Pages palette, shown in Figure 4.7. Click on Insert Pages to open the Insert Pages dialog box, shown in Figure 4.8. The Insert pop-up menu gives you several options for placing your new pages. This can be extremely helpful. Suppose you have already set up the front and back pages of your four-page newsletter, and then you discover that you have twice as much news as will fit. Rather than redoing pages one and four, you can add four more pages after page one, before page four, or between pages two and three.

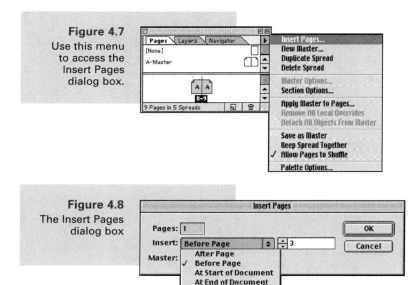

Figure 4.7
Use this menu to access the Insert Pages dialog box.

Figure 4.8
The Insert Pages dialog box

Adding Pages to a Spread

You can also create spreads, in which two or more facing pages are composed and treated as one. If you are using a gatefold or accordion foldout, so that the reader sees three or four pages at once, it's called an island spread. Spreads are shown as double page icons on the Pages palette. Island spreads are shown with multiple pages. Figure 4.9 shows an example of a single page, two spreads, and an island spread.

To add pages to a spread, use the Keep Spread Together command. It's on the flyout menu on the Pages palette. Then drag the page icons to merge them into a spread. To change the order of pages, use the Pages palette. Click on the page you want to move, and drag it to its new position. As you drag, a black vertical bar will appear to show you where the page will be when you drop it. If the black bar touches an island spread, the page you're moving will be added to the spread. Otherwise, the pages in the document will be redistributed as necessary to make facing pages line up.

Removing Pages

To remove pages, click the Trash Can icon after selecting the page(s) you want to remove. You'll be asked to verify your action. To avoid the "Did you really want to do that?" dialog box, hold down the Option key while you click the Trash Can. You can also drag a page or spread to the Trash Can, or select the page(s) and choose Delete Page or Delete Spread from the flyout menu.

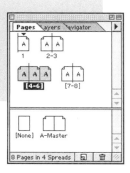

Figure 4.9
Island spreads have their page numbers enclosed in square brackets.

Saving Pages

Saving your InDesign documents is also simple, and follows Mac conventions. Choose File, Save As and give your document a title. After that, you can use Command+S to update your work. Save often; every time I do something I like, I save.

Setting Up Guidelines and Grids

Go back and look at the page you set up earlier, shown in Figure 4.10. If you're looking at this page onscreen, the margins are shown in pink, and the column guides in purple. I've set the rulers to measure inches, but if you prefer to work with some other measurement system, you're welcome to change it in the Preferences dialog box. You can also set the vertical and horizontal rulers each to different measuring systems. Many users find it convenient to measure column height in inches, but set the width measurement to picas to match standard newspaper columns.

If you want to place things at specific points on the page, the easiest way is to place guidelines for them. To place a horizontal guideline, click the ruler at the top of the page, and drag a line down the page to the appropriate spot. (If

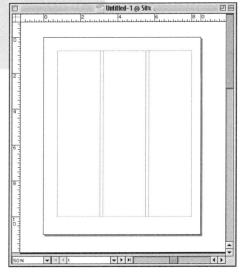

Figure 4.10
Your page, waiting for some content

Rulers aren't turned on, go to the View menu and turn on Show Rulers, or just type Command+R. (Type Command+R again to turn them off.) You can see exactly where your line is located by watching the left (vertical) ruler. Dotted lines on the ruler show the position of the cursor.

Because I originally set up the page for three columns, there are three sets of purple column guides in my sample page. Columns are created equal, but if you want them to be unequal, drag the column guides left or right as needed to adjust the column widths. The two guides will move as one, maintaining the set gutter distance between them.

Changing the Zero Point

Sometimes it's helpful to move the zero point of the ruler. You can reset it by placing the cursor at the upper-left corner of the page where the rulers intersect, and dragging the zero point to wherever it needs to be. You can also use it, appropriately enough, as a measuring tool. Suppose your flyer has a tear-off postcard that must be exactly three by four inches. Drag the intersection point down the page to locate the upper-left corner of the postcard, and then you can place lines to show where to tear out the postcard. Figure 4.11 shows what this would look like. To reset the zero point, double-click the crosshairs at the intersection of the rulers.

> The intersection point, or *zero point,* is the point at which the zero marks on the vertical and horizontal rulers intersect.

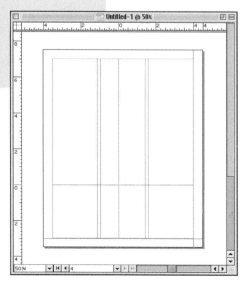

Figure 4.11
Don't forget to move the zero point back when you're done.

Using a Grid

Any time that you have many elements to place on a page, or you're setting up many similar pages, a layout grid will save you time and effort. A grid is a pattern of nonprinting lines, which you can use to align text blocks or illustrations. You can place your own gridlines by dragging them from the rulers, or you can use the grids that InDesign places for you. There are two kinds of grids available. Baseline grids help you align type, and document grids help you position objects accurately. Baseline grids look like ruled paper, and document grids resemble graph paper. To set grid features, click Edit, Preferences, Grids. The Preferences dialog box for grids is shown in Figure 4.12.

Set document grid spacing in this dialog box by specifying values for horizontal and vertical gridlines. For example, you could enter gridlines every one inch, and then specify a smaller value for subdivisions between the gridlines. Figure 4.13 shows a page with guidelines and gridlines in place. If you don't see the Document and Baseline grids, make sure they are selected under the View menu.

You can also set baseline grid spacing in the same dialog box. Choose a color for the baselines, and an appropriate spacing. Because I am using 12-point type, I've set the baseline to an eighth of an inch (.1667 in decimals). Remembering that there are 72 points to a vertical inch, the height of the 12-point type with its leading is approximately an eighth of an inch.

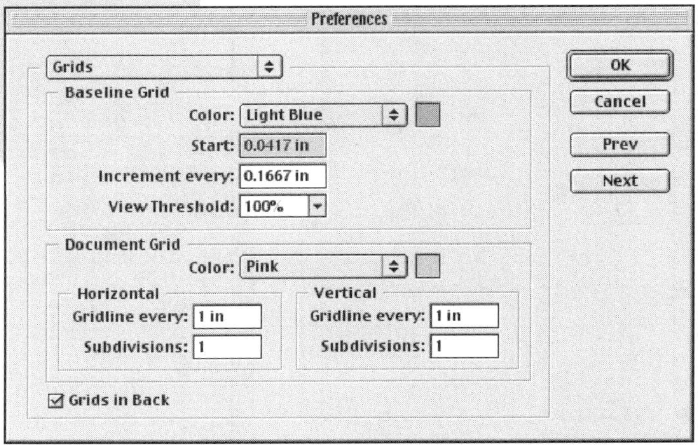

Figure 4.12 Use this dialog box to adjust the spacing of gridlines.

Figure 4.13
The gridlines help you place text and photos.

> **TIP**
>
> This is one case where it may be easier to change the measurement system to picas or points instead of inches. Go to the Edit menu and open the Preferences dialog box. Choose the Units and Increments page and reset the measurements. You can set them back to inches at any time.

Creating Templates and Stationery

If you have to lay out the same pages over and over again with only minor changes, such as in a newsletter or a series of similar brochures, you can save a great deal of time by setting up your grids and guidelines, logos, and any text that doesn't change in a document template. If you search the Internet, you can also find pre-made templates that other artists and designers have made available. Remember that InDesign can convert and use both PageMaker 6.5 and Quark templates.

> **NOTE**
>
> PageMaker and Quark documents are opened in the same way as InDesign documents. When the PageMaker or Quark page opens, InDesign converts the documents. Text is converted to InDesign text frames, and styles are added to existing InDesign styles. InDesign preserves links to text and graphics files, but will not convert embedded graphics (those that you put in with the Paste command, rather than the Place command). Grouped objects remain grouped, and colors translate to their InDesign equivalents.

If you decide to make up your own templates, set up the page size, columns, gridlines and guidelines, and number of pages, and place logo graphics, newsletter banners and mastheads, column heads, and whatever else is consistent from one issue or job to the next. (After you learn about style sheets in Chapter 13, "Using Styles and Style Sheets," you'll want to include those, too.)

Now comes the (not very) tricky part. Although these documents are called templates and are saved as such on the PC platform, on a Macintosh they're known and saved as stationery. To save a document as stationery, click File, Save As to open the Save As dialog box. Enter a name that will help you locate your file. Use the Format pop-up menu to open the Stationery Option dialog box, as shown in Figure 4.14. Click the Stationery option, then click OK to close the dialog box. Save your file by clicking Save in the Save As dialog box.

Figure 4.14
Use the Format pop-up menu to open the Stationery Option dialog box.

Even though the Save As dialog box will still say InDesign 1.5 document, it will be saved as stationery. How can you tell? It's simple. The icon for a normal document looks like a single page, with the upper-right corner folded over. The icon for stationery has multiple pages and a bottom corner turned up. Figure 4.15 shows the difference. These icons appear on the desktop or in the folder where you save your work.

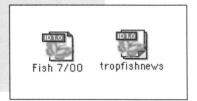

Figure 4.15
Give your files names that will help you remember what they are.

Now you know how to open pages, how to start new pages, and how to save them. If you remember only one thing from this chapter, let it be this: Save your work often! Things do go wrong. Computers freeze. The power goes off without warning. The cat jumps on the keyboard and lands on the Delete key. If you've saved recently, you won't lose much. If not, you could find yourself starting from scratch.

Adobe InDesign

PART II

Understanding Frames and Lines

5 Adobe InDesign

Creating Text and Graphics Frames

I've always liked this definition of a yacht: A hole in the water, surrounded by wood, into which one pours money. You could define a frame more or less the same way: A hole in the page, surrounded by an invisible box, into which one pours something, either text or pictures.

The concept that the frame itself is invisible is somehow a difficult one to grasp. When you draw a frame with the Shape tool or the Text tool, you can see it. It has an outline and handles. But if you were to draw a frame and then print the page, you'd have a blank page. To make a frame visible, you must stroke it with a line, and then it becomes an object. An object is any printable element on the page or pasteboard. If you don't stroke the frame, it won't print as a box or shape.

Sometimes you want a frame to print, as a box around your text or as a line around your picture. That's when you'd select the frame and stroke it, using the Stroke palette to specify a line type and weight.

Creating Frames

There are several ways to make frames. Of course, InDesign is an Adobe product and all Adobe products give you several ways to do almost anything. In Figure 5.1, I've created some frames in different ways, and filled them. The first one, in the upper-left corner, is a rectangular shape, stroked, filled with text, and then sheared to the right. The next is a hand-drawn path, drawn using the Pen tool, and then filled with a photo. In the lower-left corner, I used the Polygon Shape tool, and filled it with a photo. Finally, the lower-right frame was drawn with the Text tool and filled with placeholder text.

Working with Text Frames

First, let's clear up the difference between text and type. Text refers to the words in your document, whether it's a headline, a story, or a bulleted list of sales features. Words are made up of type. When you work with type, you change the size, shape, or appearance of the letters. When you work with text, you edit it or check the spelling.

Figure 5.1
Frames of all kinds

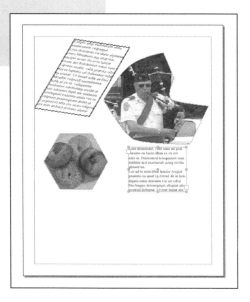

All text must be placed in a text frame. Like graphics frames, text frames can be moved and resized as necessary. You can, as you've seen, turn any shape into a text frame. You can also use the Text tool to draw a text frame. To draw a text frame with the Text tool:

1. Select the Text tool from the toolbox by clicking it, or by typing T. The text insertion cursor appears, surrounded by a dotted square.

2. Place the tool on the page, at the point where you want the upper-left corner of the text block. The cursor changes to crosshairs, as shown in Figure 5.2.

3. Hold down the mouse button and drag the frame until it's the correct size and shape. When you release the mouse button, the cursor again becomes a text insertion cursor at the top-left corner of the frame, waiting for you to enter, paste, or place your text.

If you attempt to place text without first drawing a text frame, InDesign will draw one for you, starting at the point where you click to place the text, and filling the entire column.

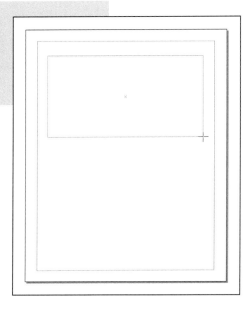

Figure 5.2
Notice the crosshairs at the bottom-right corner of the text frame.

Setting Text Frame Properties

The first property of a text frame is that it holds text. If you create a frame in some way other than using the Text tool, you make it a text frame by clicking the Text tool inside the frame. If you create a text frame, and then decide you would rather put a picture in that space, no problem. Here's how to change it to a graphics frame.

1. Select the frame.
2. Go to the Object menu and choose Content.
3. Choose Graphic from the submenu.

If you're not sure how you want to use the frame, choose Unassigned instead of Graphic. The frame will then convert itself as needed to fit whatever you place there.

Sometimes a block of text looks better with an extra margin around it inside the text frame. This is called an *inset*. You can use Text Frame Options to create space between a frame and the text in the frame. The Text Frame Options dialog box is accessed via the Object menu. It's shown here in Figure 5.3.

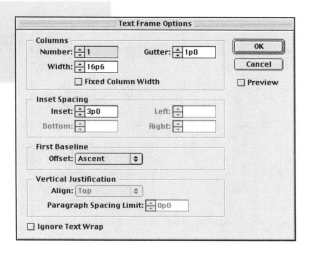

Figure 5.3
The Text Frame Options dialog box

Instead of specifying one amount for the inset on all four sides, you can enter different amounts for each side, assuming that your frame is rectangular. If it's odd-shaped, the Bottom, Left, and Right options are dimmed, and you enter the amount in the Inset box. In Figure 5.4, I have created two text blocks. The hexagonal one has an inset of three points all around, while the rectangle has an inset of two points at the top and bottom and three points on the sides. Insets look best with justified type.

Justified type is set so it fills out the lines from one margin to the other.

You can even set the inset text in two or more columns. In Figure 5.5, I've set two pages of text. The left one uses the full page, while the right one uses insets and places the text in two columns.

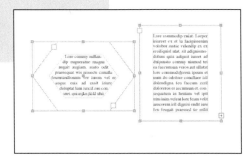

Figure 5.4
Insets can add emphasis to text.

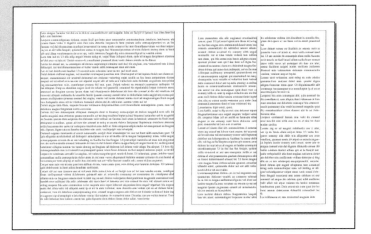

Figure 5.5
I know which page I'd rather read.

If you set text in multiple columns, you also have to specify a margin between the columns or else the words will run into each other and the page will be totally illegible. The margin between columns is called a gutter. Gutter width is a matter of personal taste. I believe that narrow gutters belong with narrow margins, and that wider gutters demand wider margins. Figure 5.6 shows examples of both. Which do you like?

There are even options in the Text Frame Options dialog box that allow you to place type in relation to the top inset of the text frame. You can specify an

Figure 5.6
The upper sample has a one-pica gutter; the lower has a two-pica gutter.

arbitrary offset for the baseline of the first line of text. From the Offset pop-up menu, select one of the following:

- **Ascent**. Select this option if you want the tallest character in the font to fall below the top inset of the text frame.
- **Cap Height**. Select this option if you want the top of uppercase letters to just touch the top inset of the text frame.
- **Leading**. Select this option to use the text's leading value, the amount of space between lines, as the distance between the baseline of the text and the top inset of the frame.

The results of each of these options are shown in Figure 5.7.

Aligning Text Frames to a Grid

In the previous chapter, you learned when to use grids and how to draw them. Now, let's look at applying text frames within a grid.

First, set up your grid. In Figure 5.8, I've drawn a simple grid. Now I am ready to place my first text frame. Notice that the Text tool starts to draw the frame from the small crossbar on the tool, not from the dotted box. As soon as you start to drag, the cursor changes to the crosshairs.

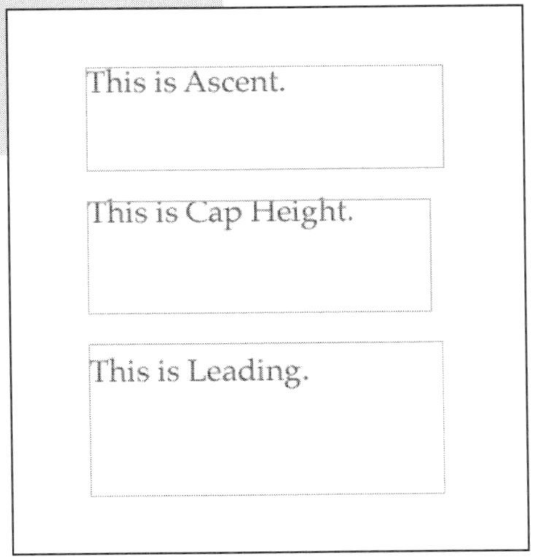

Figure 5.7
The Ascent, Cap Height, and Leading options

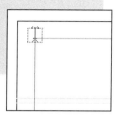

Figure 5.8
Dragging the Text tool draws a text frame.

When you are placing text frames, remember that you can't put one inside another—InDesign won't let you. So, if you try to draw a text frame and you get the text placement cursor instead of the Text Frame tool, you'll know that you are trying to place a frame inside an existing frame. To locate your frames, click either of the Selection Arrows, and type Command+A, for select all. All the frames will appear, with their handles (see Figure 5.9). In this example, there are four text frames and a graphics frame. In each case in the figure, the number is next to the center point of the frame. You can tell the graphics frame from the text frames, because it has an X through it. Graphics frames always have an X, and text frames don't.

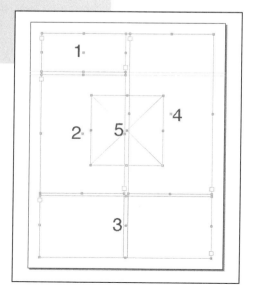

Figure 5.9
Number 5 is the graphics frame.

CHAPTER 5 · CREATING TEXT AND GRAPHICS FRAMES

Figure 5.10
Now it looks more like a real page.

To make it easier to see what's going on, I've taken the same layout and added text and a photo (see Figure 5.10). Notice, in frame 3, that you can add a subhead and body type in different fonts and styles within the same frame.

Drawing frames against a grid is even easier if you turn on the Snap to Guides command on the View menu, or type Shift+Command+; to turn on this option. You can also use the View menu to show or hide the guides, grid, and the frame edges. It's often easier to see how a page will look if you turn off the frame lines.

Moving and Resizing Frames

It would be unusual if everything worked the first time you did it. Placing frames is no exception. No matter how carefully you try to judge the size of the headline or photo, it usually needs to be adjusted, either for size or for position.

The main thing to know about moving and resizing frames is which of the two selection tools to use. Clicking on the frame or inside it with the Direct-Selection tool (the hollow arrow) moves the entire frame and its contents, if any. Clicking on a frame handle with the Selection tool (the black arrow) allows you to move that edge. The cursor becomes a double-pointed arrow showing the direction that you can move the handle. Holding down Shift as you drag the Selection tool maintains the original proportions of the frame or object.

Clicking a corner handle turns the arrow into a diagonal double-pointed arrow, indicating that you can move the two adjacent sides at once, making the frame either larger or smaller. Clicking inside the frame with the Selection tool also allows you to move the frame without resizing it. In Figure 5.11, you can see the anatomy of a frame.

Figure 5.6 shows frame handles and corner handles. Because it's a text frame, you can also see empty white squares at the top and bottom of the frame. The top square is called an in port and the bottom square is called an out port. An empty in or out port indicates the beginning or end of a story. In this example, both ports are empty because I haven't placed any text yet. A red plus sign (+) in an out port indicates that there is more text in the story to be placed, but no remaining frame space in which to place it. This remaining unseen text is called *overset* text.

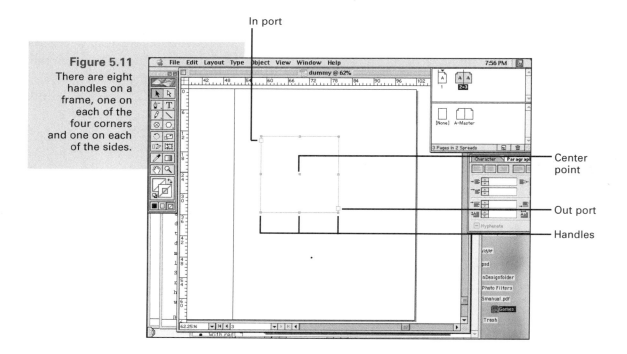

Figure 5.11
There are eight handles on a frame, one on each of the four corners and one on each of the sides.

CHAPTER 5 • CREATING TEXT AND GRAPHICS FRAMES

> **NOTE**
>
> An arrow in a port indicates that the frame is *linked* to another frame, meaning that the text flows from one frame into the next. Changes in one linked frame will affect those that follow.

When you move a frame, you can drag it anywhere on the pasteboard. You can also drag a frame and its contents from one open document to another, as long as both windows are visible. The second document will display a copy of the frame, while the original will remain where it was. If you want to make a copy of a frame and keep it in the same document, press the Option key as you drag. This is a very convenient way to duplicate an object, piece of text, or photo. You can also drag a copy off the page to the pasteboard to experiment with cropping, resizing, or manipulating it without destroying the original. You can even flip a photo or make mirror text by dragging one handle across the frame and beyond the opposite corner or edge. Figure 5.12 shows some mirrored frames.

If you want to move a frame vertically or horizontally, or at a precise 45-degree angle, hold down the Shift key while you drag the frame with the Selection tool, to constrain the motion.

Sometimes all it takes to put the frame or object in the right place is a little nudge. You can use the arrow keys to move any selected object. By default, each nudge is 1 point. To give an object or frame a bigger nudge, hold down the Shift key as you nudge with the arrow keys, and the object will move 10 points at a

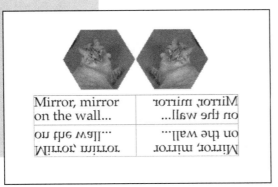

Figure 5.12 Frames flipped by being dragged across themselves. It's as if each were printed on transparent cellophane and viewed from behind.

time. You can change the nudge distance by choosing File, Preferences. Open the Units and Increments dialog box and change the Cursor Key field. InDesign uses the notation 0p1 to represent zero picas, one point. Enter a different number of points, using the same notation. Two points would be 0p2, and so on. Figure 5.13 shows the Preferences dialog box for Units and Increments.

> **NOTE**
>
> The shift nudge is 10 times larger that the cursor key nudge.

Creating Graphics Frames

You've spent a lot of time learning about text frames. But what about graphics frames? The bottom line is, any tool that creates a text frame can also create a graphics frame—yes, even the Text tool. You already learned how to do that earlier in this chapter, by using the Contents submenu. If you accidentally draw a frame using the Shape tool instead of the Frame tool, you can use the same submenu to convert it to either a text or graphics frame as needed.

Sometimes the frame itself becomes a graphics element. Stroking a frame makes it visible by adding a printable line (or multiple lines) and letting it be a frame for the picture. Figure 5.14 shows a photo, with and without a stroked frame. Notice how much more finished the framed picture looks.

Figure 5.13
I've changed the default nudge to two points.

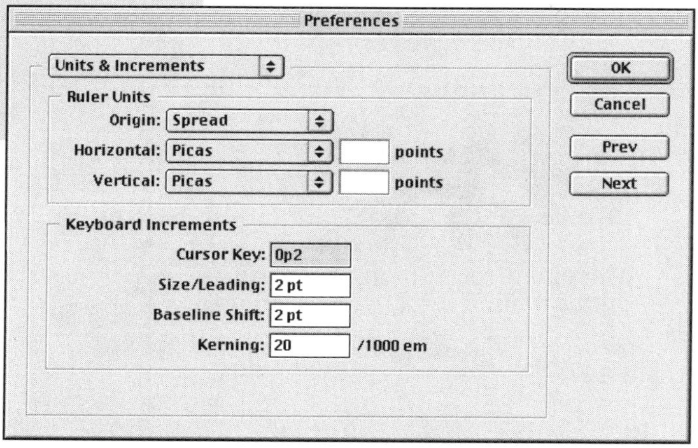

CHAPTER 5 · CREATING TEXT AND GRAPHICS FRAMES 85

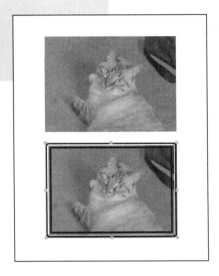

Figure 5.14
The frame adds a sense of completeness.

Figure 5.15 shows the Stroke palette for the frame in Figure 5.14. I used the rounded corners option. Because there are multiple lines, the line weight refers to the entire stroke width, not the width of each line.

A graphics frame can serve another function, which you'll frequently find helpful. After you have placed a picture or drawing inside the frame, you can use the frame as a cropping tool to change the size and shape of the picture. Figure 5.16 shows the same photo, placed and cropped by moving the frame.

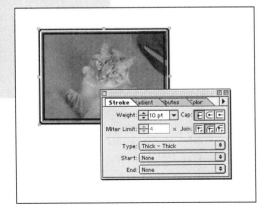

Figure 5.15
There are eight different kinds of strokes available to you in the Stroke palette.

Figure 5.16 Cropping usually improves a picture.

Deleting Unwanted Frames

Because it's so easy to draw frames, it's easy to get carried away and draw more than you need. Fortunately, it's equally easy to get rid of them. If you think you might possibly want to save a block of text or a graphic, but you don't want it on the page where you are working, just drag it off the page to the pasteboard. It will be saved with the rest of the document, and you can go back and find it for another use, or you can drag it onto a different page whenever you want. If you know you don't want that frame (or its contents, if any), just select it and press the Delete key, and it's gone. If you then say, "Oops, maybe I should have kept it," just Undo (Command+Z). It's back, as long as you haven't saved the change. Undo/Redo resets itself when you save, and changes made prior to the save aren't available.

Drawing Shapes

The main difference between shapes and frames is that shapes are automatically stroked when you draw them. Frames, of course, aren't. Shapes can be drawn in either of two ways. You can use the shape tools to create rectangles, ellipses, and polygons, and you can use the pen tools to draw paths that can be filled and stroked to make freeform shapes.

Drawing Filled Shapes

To draw a filled shape, first select a color or gradient fill for the shape. Use the toolbox swatches to specify the fill or stroke of the object. To change colors, use the Swatches palette, or select a color by clicking on it on the Color palette. (If the Color palette is not open, you can access it by pressing F6.) Select a stroke color and weight if one is to be used, and then select a shape tool and draw the shape by clicking and dragging the mouse on the page. As you draw, a blue line indicates the current size and shape of the object. You can draw a perfect circle or square by holding down the Shift key as you draw the shape. Using the Shift key while you drag a polygon gives you an equal sided one. You can make wide shapes, narrow shapes, and flat or tall ovals. Double-click the Polygon tool to open the Polygon Settings dialog box (see Figure 5.17), which allows you to change the number of sides of the polygon, and to specify an inset amount if you want to use the tool to draw stars. Remember that an inset of 100 percent gives you a star made of lines.

To use a gradient stroke or fill, double-click the small gradient swatch at the bottom of the toolbox to open the Gradient palette. Change colors by clicking the small squares under the Gradient ramp to select them, and then clicking the color you want to use.

After you have drawn a shape, you can modify it using the path tools. You can overlap two shapes to make a third, and you can combine several different shapes to form objects. In Figure 5.18, I used the shape tools to draw some fruit.

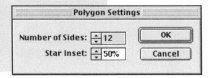

Figure 5.17
Enter a number of points and an inset.

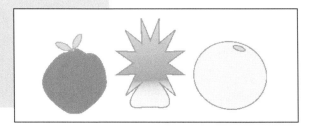

Figure 5.18
The pineapple started as a star, with its bottom points cut off and the base reshaped.

Working with Corner Effects

The Rectangle and Polygon tools draw lines that meet at corners. The ellipse obviously doesn't, and isn't part of this discussion. Whenever you have a corner, you have to deal with the way the two lines meet. There are two factors that influence this: miters and joins. You can address both in the Stroke palette.

Miter limit determines when a corner point stops being mitered or squared off, and becomes beveled. You can select any point between one and five hundred. The default setting is four, which means that when the miter extends from the adjoining corner lines by at least four times the weight of the stroke, the corner switches from miter (pointed) to bevel (squared off). You won't need to apply this unless you have a shape with thick lines joining at a fairly sharp angle.

There are three corner treatments you can apply from the Stroke palette. Your choices are square, rounded, or beveled. Figure 5.19 shows examples of all three.

You can also go for really fancy corners, by using InDesign's Corner Effects option. To open the Corner Effects dialog box, go to the Object menu and choose Corner Effects, or type Option+Command+R. The dialog box, shown in Figure 5.20, contains a pop-up menu with five different choices for corner effects (six if you count None as an effect).

Figure 5.19
From left to right, squared, rounded, and beveled corners.

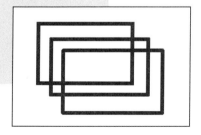

Figure 5.20
Choose an effect from the pop-up menu.

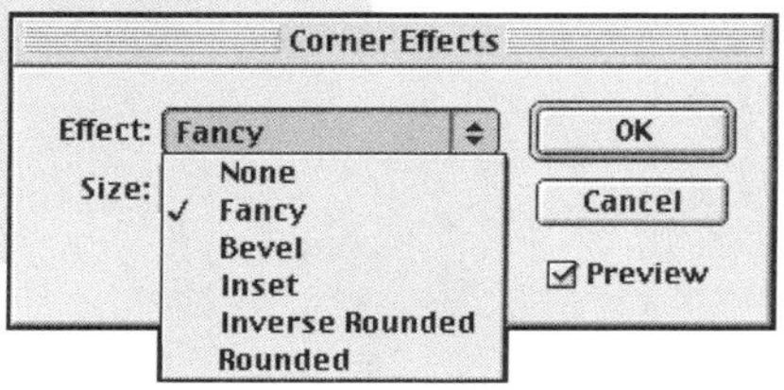

Of the five effects, Rounded and Bevel are probably the most useful. I have used both on buttons for Web pages, and they're very effective as containers for inset text blocks. I like Fancy for creating certificates and diplomas, and Inset and Inverse Rounded work well for logo design or for surrounding a title. All five effects are shown in Figure 5.21.

As with fancy fonts and other special effects, corner effects must be applied with restraint. They're great for certificates, for coupons, and for making a photo stand out, but they're not for use in all of your InDesign documents, and you probably won't want to apply more than one per publication.

Now that you know more about frames and shapes, you're ready to go on to drawing shapes from scratch with the pen tools, and putting your frames, shapes, and lines to work on the page.

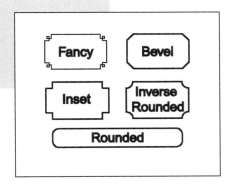

Figure 5.21
Vary the look of the corners by changing the stroke width.

Adobe InDesign

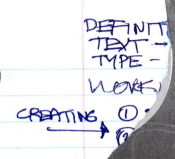

Working with Frames and Lines

Frames with nothing in them are just empty boxes. Unless you have stroked the edges of a frame, it's not even visible. Later on, you'll place text and graphics in frames. Right now, take a look at how to fill them with tints and gradients.

Adding Fills and Gradients to Frames

A frame can only hold one item, but frames can be placed on top of other frames. If you want a block of text (perhaps a pull quote) set over a different color background, create the background frame first, fill it with an appropriate color, and then place the text frame on top. Or, you can place a fill directly into a text frame. Either way, it's simple and effective.

Adding Fills

Fills can be a solid color, a tint, or a gradient, and can be placed in any frame, whether it has been stroked or not. Figure 6.1 shows three filled frames. The upper one has a three point black stroke around the frame. The second has a fifty percent gray stroke against a thirty percent gray fill. I think it adds a little more definition to the box, without being too obvious. The bottom example is unstroked. All three frames are filled with 30 percent gray. You can set gray fill percentages in the Color palette, by entering a number or clicking on the color ramp.

Obviously, if something is going to go over a filled frame, the fill needs to be very light, or have the text or drawing reversed out of it. Reversed type means that the type is a light color or white against a dark background. Used for a

Figure 6.1
You can make the stroke darker or lighter by changing the stroke color.

pull quote, a title, or a company logo, reversed type really makes the words stand out, as shown in Figure 6.2.

Working with Color Fills

Filling frames and objects works just as well in color. (You'll have to use your imagination, because this book is black and white.) In Figure 6.3, the star is a rich royal blue and the lettering is gold. If there's a possibility that your color work will be seen in black and white, always check a grayscale version of it before you assume you're done. The easiest way is to switch your monitor temporarily from color to grayscale. This will let you see if there's enough contrast between the letters and the background.

InDesign gives you several different ways to apply colors or tints to a frame, including using the toolbox, the Swatches palette, or the Color palette. The three swatches at the bottom of the toolbox represent Color, Gradient, and No Color. If you select a shape or a frame and click on Color, the object will fill

Figure 6.2
Romance, drama . . . what do you want to suggest?

Figure 6.3
Blue and gold, believe it or not.

with the selected color. Because the default for the Color swatch is black, you'll probably want to change the color before you apply it.

If you double-click on the Color swatch, you will open the Color palette, shown in Figure 6.4. By default, it shows a grayscale bar that Adobe calls the tint ramp. It makes sense—gray *is* a tint of black. When you move the cursor over the ramp, the cursor changes to an eyedropper, which means you can click any shade of gray in the box and apply it to the selected frame or object.

Applying Spot Colors

> A *spot color* is a special, pre-mixed ink in a specific color that is used instead of, or sometimes in addition to, CMYK process inks.

Use spot color when color accuracy is critical, or when your publication has only black and up to three spot colors. Each spot color you use generates an additional spot color printing plate, which raises your printing costs accordingly. If you think you might require more than three colors plus black, you might as well use process colors. That said, spot color inks can accurately reproduce colors that are outside the gamut of process colors. Occasionally, there might be times when you'll need to use both.

When you want to apply a spot color, go to the Swatches palette and the Swatch libraries. There are default swatches for cyan, magenta, yellow, red, green, and blue. If you want to apply any of these colors, just click the colored block. If you want to apply a tint of any of these colors, select New Tint Swatch from the flyout menu on the Swatches palette. The New Tint Swatch dialog box is shown in Figure 6.5.

Choose the color before you open the dialog box. You can move the slider at the bottom of the box to select a tint percentage, or you can simply type a percentage into the box. When you click OK, the tint will be applied, and also entered on the Swatch menu.

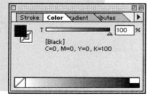

Figure 6.4
Notice the black, white, and no color blocks at the ends of the tint ramp.

Figure 6.5
The New Tint Swatch dialog box

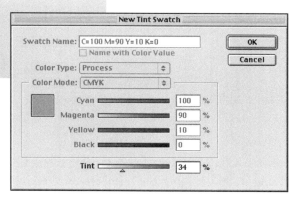

Using the Swatch Libraries

The Swatch libraries are intended for use with spot color printing. Each spot color needs to be on a separate printing plate when you print to a printing press. (Home inkjet printers don't care.)

If printing costs are a factor, try to minimize the number of spot colors you use. Before you start to work with spot colors for a printed piece, check with your print shop or service bureau to find out which color matching system they use. There's no point in finding the perfect Trumatch shade if the print shop uses Pantone inks. Figure 6.6 shows a swatch library, which you can access via the Window menu.

Figure 6.6
The Tint Swatch library palette

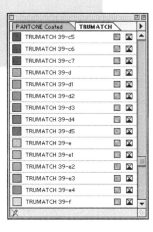

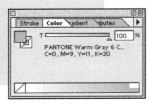

Figure 6.7
Warm gray uses both magenta and yellow, with some black.

You can find the CMYK values for any color by adding it to the Swatches palette, clicking it, and reading the numbers on the Color palette. Figure 6.7 shows the values for Pantone Warm Gray 6 Coated. Just double-click on the color to add it to the Swatches palette.

Knowing the CMYK values can sometimes help you find a match from a different library, although similar colors can be made with very different ink percentages. Matching colors is a job that is really best done by eye.

Adding Gradients

Gradients are blends of two or more colors that shade from one to another across a frame. You can set stops in the Gradient palette to affect the smoothness of the blend. Gradients can include process colors or spot colors, but will be difficult to print if you mix the two kinds of color.

Gradients are defined by blends of colors in the gradient ramp. By default, a gradient starts with two colors and a midpoint at 50 percent. You can create and apply gradients from the Swatches palette. Use the flyout menu to open the New Gradient Swatch dialog box, shown in Figure 6.8.

You can give your gradient a distinctive name, like "yellow to blue" or just identify it by the appearance of the swatch. The gradient type is either linear or radial. Linear gradients move from one color to the other in a straight line, while radial gradients move out in a circle, like a sunburst. Figure 6.9 shows examples of both.

In order to make matters confusing, a gradient starts and stops with *stop colors*. The color stops are those little pointed things underneath the gradient bar. A stop is the point at which a gradient changes from one color to the next. Make sure that the left stop is at 0% and the right one is at 100% for a

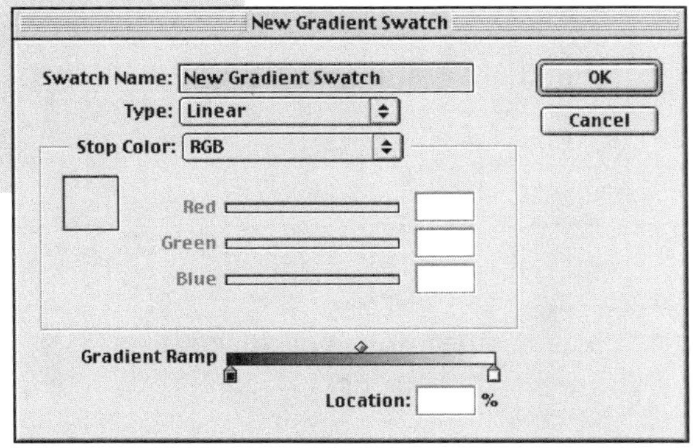

Figure 6.8
This dialog box helps you create gradient swatches.

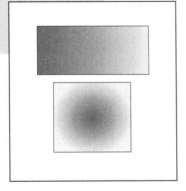

Figure 6.9
Can you guess which is which?

full-scale gradient. You can check by clicking them and reading the percentage in the Location field at the bottom of the dialog box.

To set the left stop, you can choose a color that's already in the Swatches palette, or you can mix one. To choose a color from the Swatches palette, choose Named Color from the Stop Color pop-up list and select a color from the list. To mix a new color for the gradient, choose a color mode (LAB, CMYK, or RGB), and enter color values or drag the sliders. To change the second color in the gradient, select its color stop, and choose another color as described previously.

The diamond on top of the gradient bar shows the point in the blend that is a given distance from the start of the gradient. The default amount is 50%. You can slide it left or right so your gradient has more of one color than the other.

In addition, you can drag the stop points so that the blend begins at a different point along the bar. As an alternative to dragging, you can enter percentages in the Location field (see Figure 6.10).

> **NOTE**
>
> Although the Swatches palette is the recommended palette for creating and storing gradients, you can also work with gradients using the Gradient palette. The Gradient palette is useful when you want to create a quick gradient that won't be used often. You can add the current gradient to the Swatches palette at any time, by opening the New Gradient dialog box. It opens with the current gradient, so you can just click OK to save it.

So, there's your perfect gradient, showing up as a swatch, or waiting to be applied from the Gradient palette. Now what? If you select the gradient and draw a frame, it will contain the gradient. If you draw a frame first, or have an empty frame waiting, select the Gradient tool from the toolbox, and drag a line across the shape in the direction you want the gradient to go. You're not limited to vertical or horizontal; diagonals work well, too. If the gradient is shading in the wrong direction—from light to dark, when you intended dark to light—fix it by redrawing it with the line starting on the opposite side from where you drew it the first time. You can even apply the same gradient across a page so selected frames will show parts of it. Figure 6.11 shows this effect.

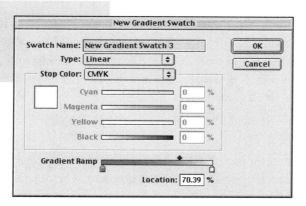

Figure 6.10
InDesign can deal with precise percentages.

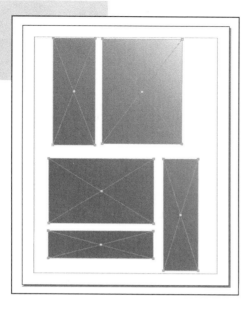

Figure 6.11
Each frame shows a section of the gradient.

To add extra colors to a gradient, select an additional color from the Swatches palette or from the Color palette, and click below the gradient bar to place a new color stop. The new color stop is automatically defined using the color values at that position along the existing gradient. Figure 6.12 shows a two-color gradient and a four-color gradient. You can remove colors by dragging their stops to the right, off the bar.

Figure 6.12
Gradients can use as many colors as you like.

Drawing with the Pen Tools

If you have used Illustrator, Photoshop, or Macromedia FreeHand, you already know how to use the Bézier-based pen tools. The pen tools draw straight lines, freeform lines, and Bézier curves. Bézier curves, named after Pierre Bézier, were developed in the 1960s, under the sponsorship of the Renault Automobile Company, as a way to draw and define in computer language the sleek curves of the Renault Dauphine.

A *Bézier curve* is a curve defined by four points: two at the ends of the curve and two outside the curve at the ends of handles that you can use to change the angle and direction of the curve. These are called control points. Figure 6.13 shows the parts of a Bézier curve.

If you haven't used these kinds of tools before, you should know right up front that it takes a little practice, but the payoff is worth the effort. In addition to the standard pens that draw lines and add or remove points on a line, InDesign gives you two more handy tools. The Scissors tool cuts a path or line into segments, and the Convert Direction Point tool reshapes curves and lines.

Now would be a good time to do some practicing with the pen tools. Open a new page in InDesign and select the Pen tool. To draw a straight line, move your cursor and click somewhere else. (Don't hold the mouse button down!) The second point is called a corner point. Moving the pen and clicking again gives you a line at an angle to the first, forming a corner, hence the name. The little empty block in the middle of a line is its midpoint. Two or more lines define an object vertically and horizontally, and the middle of that object is also indicated with an empty block (see Figure 6.14).

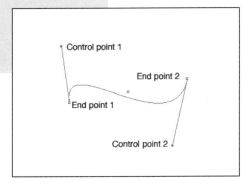

Figure 6.13
Move the control points to change the curve.

Figure 6.14
Just a few clicks create corner points and straight lines.

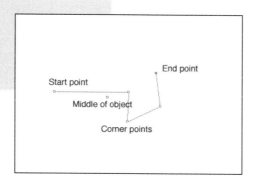

To create a path with a curved line, move your cursor to the bottom of the window and then click and drag left. You'll see a curve immediately appear and change as you drag it (see Figure 6.15). You've just created a *smooth point*, which means that InDesign created a smooth curve where two curved line segments meet. Click and drag again to add a second curve.

Notice the middle point you just created. It creates a nice smooth curve between the two curved lines. That's why it's called a smooth point. Smooth points and corner points are collectively called *anchor points*. You can draw paths using any kind of anchor point. If you later decide that a corner point should have been a smooth point, or vice versa, use the Convert Direction Point tool to change it.

Figure 6.15
Click and drag for a curve.

As you have no doubt noticed, creating smooth points also results in the appearance of two handles for each point. These handles can be used to change the angle and direction of a curve after you've initially established it. Use the Direct-Selection tool for editing path segments. Clicking and dragging a handle changes the shape of the curve, while clicking and dragging a point stretches the line in the direction you drag. In Figure 6.16, I've dragged a handle following the direction of the arrow. The original curve segment and new one are labeled.

Drawing Compound Paths

As the name suggests, compound paths are made up of several segments. They can be either closed or open. If you decide to close a path, position the pen point over the hollow square at the first end point, after you have drawn the next-to-last segment. A small loop appears next to the pen point when it is correctly placed. Click to close the path. Figure 6.17 shows a before and after view.

Compound paths can contain both corner and smooth anchor points, even when a corner point joins two curves, as in the bottom example in Figure 6.18. This type of curve is called a *sharp curve*.

To draw a sharp curve, begin the path with an initial point. Create a smooth point as you normally would, making one curve. Move the pointer so that it's exactly over the smooth point you just created. Hold down the Option key

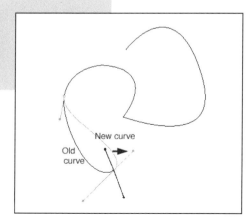

Figure 6.16
It's fun to watch the curves change as you drag.

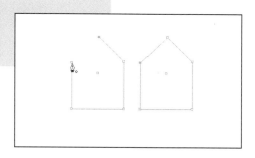

Figure 6.17
Before and after closing a path

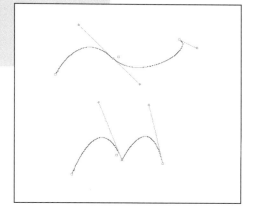

Figure 6.18
A smooth curve and a sharp curve

while you click and drag the mouse in the direction of the bump in the new curve. Release the Option key and mouse button, and (here's the tricky part) move the cursor to where you want the line to end. Then click and drag in the opposite direction from the one you just dragged. Voilà!

Using the Scissors Tool

Say you have created a complex path that's a little *too* complex. You can use the Scissors tool to cut apart sections of the path. You can delete the sections you don't want, and use the Direct-Selection tool to move the others around. Click where you want to cut, and then use the Selection tool to drag away the parts you don't want. In Figure 6.19, I've cut a couple of bumps off my abstract shape. I can then click on the open ends to connect them with a new segment.

Figure 6.19
Move the cut pieces out of the way.

Stroking Lines

Remember, a line isn't a line unless it's stroked. Ordinarily, when you draw with the pen tools, you'll set the stroke and fill in the toolbox to the line color and fill, if any, that you need. If you goof occasionally, and draw lines with the toolbox incorrectly set, all you need to do is to select the line and change the settings. The object changes accordingly.

Drawing Lines with the Line Tool

When you need curved lines, the Pen tool is the right choice. If you need a straight line, it's easiest to use the Line tool. Just click where you want the line to start and drag to where it should end.

> **NOTE**
> Diagonal lines may look jagged on the screen. Don't worry. They print smoothly on your PostScript printer.

Changing the Weight of a Line

One of the nice things about desktop publishing, as opposed to the old-fashioned method, is that changes are easy to make. If you draw a line that you think is right, and you later realize it's too thick or too thin, it's easy to fix. Select the line and go to the Stroke palette, shown in Figure 6.20. There's a pull-down menu of point sizes, or you can enter your own value. You'll see the changes as soon as you make them, so you can fine-tune your page.

Starting and Ending Lines

Most people don't often think about how a line starts or ends—it's just there. If anything, the ends are cut off square, like a carpenter trimming a two-by-four. That's not the case with InDesign; you have lots of options. You like arrows? Circles? Blocks? Figure 6.21 shows the pop-up Start and End menu on the Stroke palette, and lines to which each end cap treatment has been applied. Some treatments need to be applied to lines that are at least two points wide in order to look right.

If you don't want anything this fancy, you can still choose a straight or rounded end for your lines. Just click the appropriate icon in the Stroke palette.

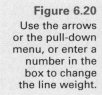
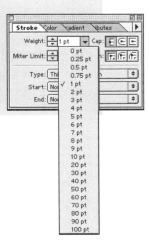

Figure 6.20
Use the arrows or the pull-down menu, or enter a number in the box to change the line weight.

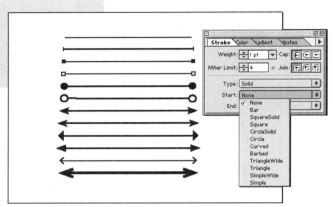

Figure 6.21
You have the same choices for line ends as for line starts.

Moving and Resizing Lines

Okay, so your line is the right weight and it has the right ends, but it's not quite in the right place. Use the Selection tool to select and move it. If you drag the left or right endpoint, the line will stretch. If you click anywhere else on the line, you can then drag it to a new location.

Use the Align palette to make two or more lines "line up." You can space them equally, too, and using the Align palette is much quicker and easier than trying to move each one into place against a grid. Figure 6.22 shows the Align palette.

Changing Colors

Black is boring? Change the line to a spot or process color by clicking on a color in the Swatches palette. If you're printing with CMYK inks, choose any color you like from the Color palette. Just select the line, and click the color to apply it.

Now, you understand all of the elements that go into a page. In the next chapter, you'll start to put together some pages and master pages.

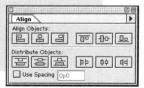

Figure 6.22
You can align centers, sides, tops, or bottoms.

Adobe InDesign

PART III

Document Basics

7

Adobe InDesign

Using Master Pages

If you think of building a publication as something like building a house, the master pages are the foundation. Master pages are preconstructed layouts that you can use to assemble multi-page documents. Suppose you have a booklet that has a page number in the upper corner of each page, a vertical rule half an inch from the edge of the page, and maybe a small company logo at the bottom of each page. For a 12-page brochure, you could set this 12 times, or you could set up the page once as a master page, use it as the background for all the pages, and then move on to the more interesting parts of the project.

Creating Master Pages

Actually, you don't have to "create" master pages. By default, they are part of the document as soon as you create it. You can ignore the master page and just go ahead and set up your pages, if you want. If you're creating a single sheet, like a poster or flyer that's a one-of-a-kind item, it's silly to waste the time on a master page. But if your document contains items that will appear in the same place on each page, then starting with a master page can save you a lot of work. Master pages also ensure that your design is consistent from one page or section to the next.

Whenever you're working with master pages, or with any multi-page document, you'll want to have access to the Pages palette. In Figure 7.1, I've opened a simple four-page newsletter.

As you can see, the palette displays icons for the first and last page, and a double icon for the inside two-page spread. You can also see the master pages, right and left. The document pages are labeled A, indicating that they are

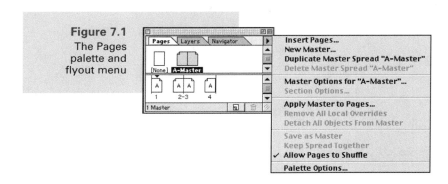

Figure 7.1
The Pages palette and flyout menu

linked to the A master. There's another icon labeled None. If you click and drag from None to the first page, the A disappears, showing that the page is no longer linked to a master, so you can set it independently, without having to remove or relocate any of the master page items. This flexibility is one of the things that make master pages so helpful.

The flyout menu contains commands you might need when working with master pages. Looking again at the Pages palette in Figure 7.1, notice that one of the icons is shaded. That represents the page that's currently active on the pasteboard (see Figure 7.2). In this case, it's page one.

If you scroll down in the main window, you can see the other pages in your document. Clicking on a page makes it active, and the shaded icon in the Pages palette changes accordingly. The Pages palette has icons at the bottom of its window that you can click to create additional pages or to discard pages, along with a reminder of how many pages and spreads are in your document.

To work on master pages instead of document pages, double-click the master page icon. It changes to a shaded icon, indicating that your master pages are active.

Figure 7.2
Page one is displayed on the pasteboard.

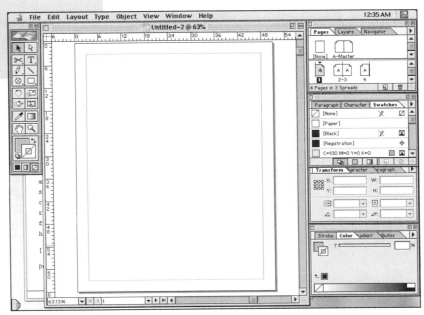

Deciding What to Include on a Master Page

Any element or setting that's going to be used on multiple pages can go on a master page. Your master pages will probably have margins and columns set for the entire document, or at least for sections of it. A master page might have page numbers or a header, if your document uses one. Design elements that repeat, such as decorative rules, blocks of color or tint, logos, and so on, can also be placed on the master pages. Grids and guidelines are generally placed on master pages. Of course, you can add extra guidelines to a document page, if you find you need them.

One interesting thing about master pages is their numbering. Even-numbered pages are always on the left and odd-numbered pages are always on the right. This is because documents of more than one page always have their first page numbered one. Front pages are always bound on the left and open on the right, at least in this country.

Applying Grids and Guides

I like to see both master pages at once when I am setting up margins, grids, and so on. To shrink your pages so you can see both of them, go to the View menu and click Fit Spread in Window. Your screen should look something like Figure 7.3. Notice that I set the measurement system to inches instead of picas. You can do this in the Preferences dialog box if, like me, you find inches easier to use.

The first thing I notice about these pages is that I don't like the margins. If you want to change the margins in your master pages, go to the Layout menu and open the Margins and Columns dialog box, shown in Figure 7.4. Here, you can enter new settings, but there's no way to preview the changes, so you have to click OK and then reopen the dialog box if you need to make further adjustments to the page. If you want to select more than one page to change, press the Shift key while you click on the pages you want to change. Shift-click allows you to select multiple items in most Macintosh applications.

If you want to create a newsletter that uses three columns per page, you can set those columns in the same dialog box.

To make it easier to place your own grid lines, you can go to the View menu and turn on Show Document Grid. If you need to reset the spacing of the

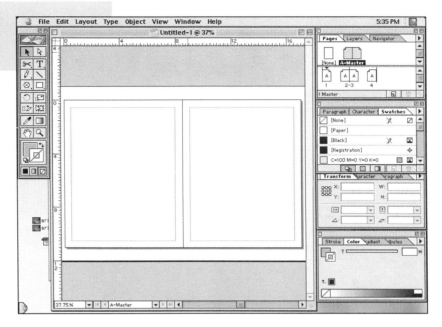

Figure 7.3 The master pages spread

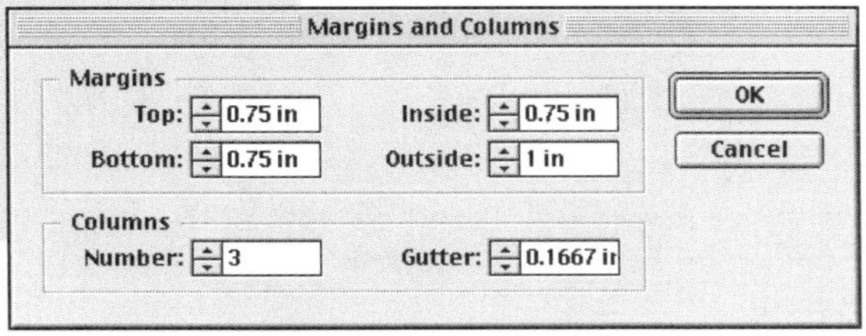

Figure 7.4 You can set margins and columns in this dialog box.

gridlines, use the Grids Preferences dialog box, which you can access from the Edit menu or by typing Command+K (see Figure 7.5).

In this example, I've set the units to one inch and the subdivision to four, which creates a quarter-inch grid on my master pages. In Figure 7.6, you can see the grid across both pages. The units are denoted by the heavier lines, and the subdivisions by lighter lines. Each inch is divided into quarter-inches vertically and horizontally.

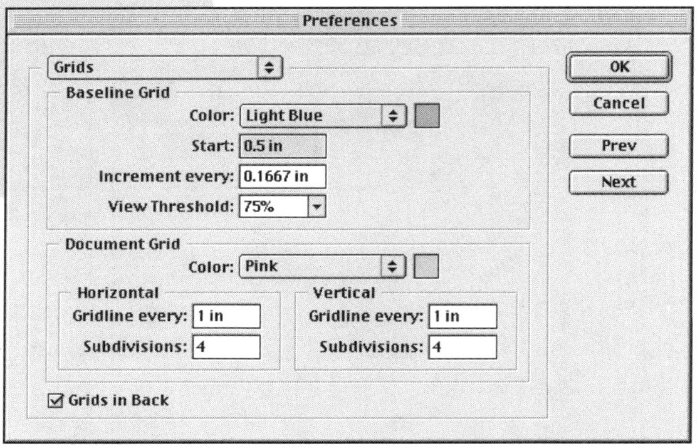

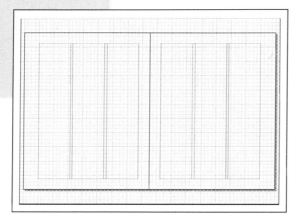

Figure 7.5
You can also change the color of the grid to make it easier to see.

Figure 7.6
If the grid gets in the way later on, you can go back to the View menu and hide it.

Numbering Pages and Sections

One of the first, and most obvious, items to put on a master page is a page number marker. This is a placeholder for the actual page numbers. It specifies both where the number will be and what it will look like. After you place the marker, document page numbers automatically appear and update as you remove, reorder, and add pages.

Your document can be up to 9,999 numbered pages long, but page numbers can go even higher. If your publication is broken into sections, you could conceivably start a section at page 9,950 and go on for another 9,999 pages with no problem. Page numbers can have as many as five digits (99,999).

You can also divide the document into sections, numbering the pages differently in each section. For example, if your publication has front matter and an appendix, you can number these sections independently, and number the text pages starting at one.

Placing a Page Number Marker

To place a page number marker, choose the appropriate master page. (If you want a page number on one page only, select that page in the document.) Place the Type tool on the page at the place where you want the page number to appear, and drag a frame large enough for the page number and any text or section number you want to display with it. Choose a font and size for the numbering, and then select Layout, Insert Page Number or type Command+Option+N. You'll see the letter name of the master page, if you've placed the marker on the master. If you've placed the marker on a document page, you'll see that page number. Figure 7.7 shows a corner of my master page with a page number marker placed.

If you want page numbers on both left and right pages, you have to place markers on both pages of the master spread. Some people put the title of the publication on each page, along with the page number. In that case, you'd need either a single, long text frame, or two separate text frames.

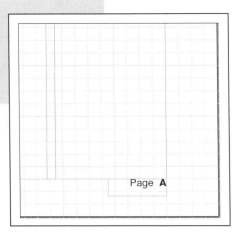

Figure 7.7
I've formatted the type flush right, with the page number in bold.

By default, page numbers start on a right-hand page, so right pages are always odd-numbered. If you need to start page numbers on a left-hand page, use the Section Options command (accessed from the Pages palette flyout menu) to change the first page number.

Dividing a Publication into Sections

Your document can have either absolute numbering, which means the numbers start on page one, or section numbering, which allows you to divide the document into sections and number each section independent of the others. Many documents are divided into sections, with an introduction or front matter as one section, the main body of the document as another, and perhaps other sections for an index, appendix, and so on. Section numbering is set as a preference. Figure 7.8 shows the General Preferences dialog box.

To create sections, first make sure that you have selected Section Numbering. Enter the number of pages needed for your document, then go to the Pages palette and select the first document page of the first section. Use the flyout menu, shown in Figure 7.9, to open the Section Options dialog box.

In the Section Options dialog box, shown in Figure 7.10, you can give the section a title or just leave the default number. Choose an appropriate numbering system for the section pages from the pop-up menu. Enter a page number to start the section and, if you wish, a section marker. Click OK when you're done. The numbers under the pages in the Pages palette will change accordingly.

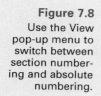

Figure 7.8
Use the View pop-up menu to switch between section numbering and absolute numbering.

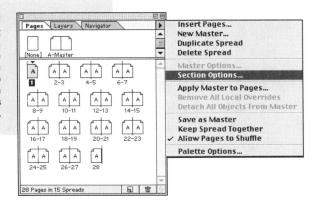

Figure 7.9
If you haven't set section numbering as a preference, you won't be able to use the Section Options command.

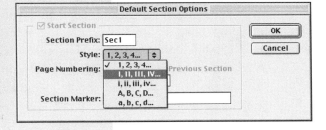

Figure 7.10
Front matter, such as introductions and tables of contents, generally uses lowercase Roman numerals.

If you do nothing else, this section numbering system will continue throughout the entire document. To divide the publication into sections, you have to define additional sections. Go to the first page of the second section, and again open the Section Options dialog box. (Because you have already defined one section, the dialog box will now be titled New Section.) Select the Start Section check box and change the page numbering system, as I have in Figure 7.11, to one that's appropriate for the new section.

Figure 7.11
First you need to check the Start Section check box.

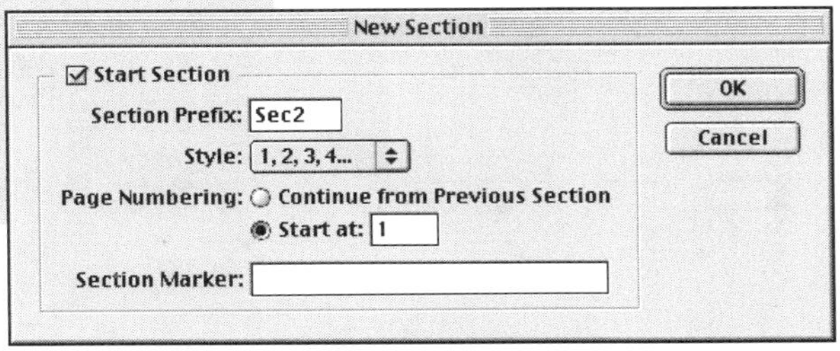

Repeat the process for as many sections as you need, choosing independent page numbering for each section or consecutive numbers.

Creating Multiple Master Pages

The concept of master pages is terrific, and they save a lot of tedious work. Nevertheless, some kinds of publications would be intensely boring, designwise, if you used the same layout for every page. Newsletters, annual reports, and brochures frequently need different looks on different pages. Perhaps you want type in two columns on some pages and three columns on others. The answer, of course, is multiple master pages.

Few things could be easier than creating additional sets of master pages. Go to the Pages palette and press Command as you click on the page icon at the bottom of the palette. A second set of master pages appears on the palette, as shown in Figure 7.12. They are labeled B-Master, so you can differentiate between the sets of master pages. Any pages in your document to which you apply the B-Master will show a B in their icons on the Pages palette, rather than an A.

Remember that you can save your master pages as stationery by using the Format pop-up menu in the Save As dialog box. Then, you can reuse them whenever a new version of the same document is needed. This is especially handy for newsletter editors, as they can build the format once and just keep adding new text and pictures for each edition.

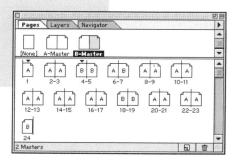

Figure 7.12
Successive additions will be called C, D, and so on.

Overriding a Master Page

Some pages only need minor changes from the master. In this case, it's silly to create a new master that's based on the first one with just one or two changes. Instead, use the original master and override the items or areas you want to be different. You can override an object or an attribute. For instance, if you want a picture where a text frame is, you can override the frame. If you simply want a different font or size in that frame, override the type attribute. All the remaining items on the page remain linked to the master page.

If you override a master object, you don't override all its attributes; changes you make to the fill, stroke, or color of the master page object carry through to the overridden frame. Changes you make to the size, position, or content of an overridden frame are not changed—that override holds.

To override an object from the master page, first be sure that the document page, and not the master page, is selected. Do not attempt to place overrides on a master page. Choose View, Display Master Items (see Figure 7.13), or type Command+Y. Select the item or frame you want to override, or press Command+Shift and use the Selection tool to select the item or frame. You'll see the outline of the frame. Press Delete to remove it. If you want to modify the item, just make the changes as you normally would.

Removing Overrides

You can also remove overrides you've placed on objects that were originally master objects. If you do this, the object reverts to its original attributes on the master page, and will be updated when you edit the master. If you change your

Figure 7.13
You can't remove master page elements if you can't see them.

mind about an override, you can remove it from one object or frame, or from a two (or more) page spread. However, you can't remove an override from an entire document. Of course, if you decide to override something for an entire document, it probably makes more sense just to change it on the master.

To remove all local overrides, use the Pages palette flyout menu and select Remove Local Overrides. If you have changed text in a frame that is overridden, you must first select the frame to revert to the master text.

Multi-Page Documents

It's uncommon for a document to have only one page, unless it's a lost dog poster or a yard sale flyer. Most of the time, you'll be working on pieces with four pages or more. Multi-page documents can be confusing. The easiest way to keep track of where you are and what you're currently working on is to keep the Pages palette active. Double-click a page or spread to go to the Pages palette. You can also jump quickly between pages by using the pop-up menu at the bottom of the screen. It shows the current page number, and if you click on the down arrow, you'll open the menu shown in Figure 7.14. Then, just click a page number to jump to it.

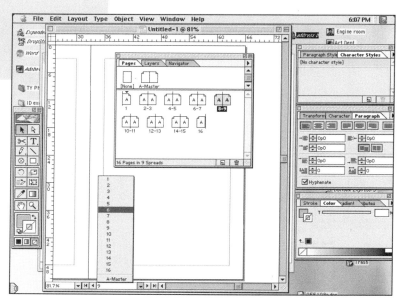

Figure 7.14
I'm jumping from page nine to page six.

Specifying Page Count

You can specify or change the number of pages in your document at any of several points in the creation process. When you open a new publication, the first item in the dialog box asks how many pages you want your document to be. Also, at any time while you're working, you can go back to the Document Setup dialog box (accessed from the File menu) and change the number of pages or the size of the pages. In Figure 7.15, I've just changed both the size and the number of pages in my publication.

Yet another method, and one that gives you the easiest control over where the pages are inserted, is to select Insert Pages from the Pages palette flyout menu. This opens the dialog box shown in Figure 7.16. Enter the number of pages to insert, and the master page, if any, to which the pages should conform. Click OK to add the specified pages.

The last method is the easiest of all, if you only want to add or subtract a couple of pages. Go to the Pages palette and click on the small Page icon located on the bottom of the palette to add a new page. New pages are added at the end of the document, unless you have selected a page on the palette. If a page is selected, the new page(s) are added following it, and the rest of the publication's pages are renumbered. Figure 7.17 shows that I am adding a new page after page 13.

Figure 7.15 To add or subtract pages, enter a new page count here.

Figure 7.16 The new page automatically becomes the active page, ready for you to use.

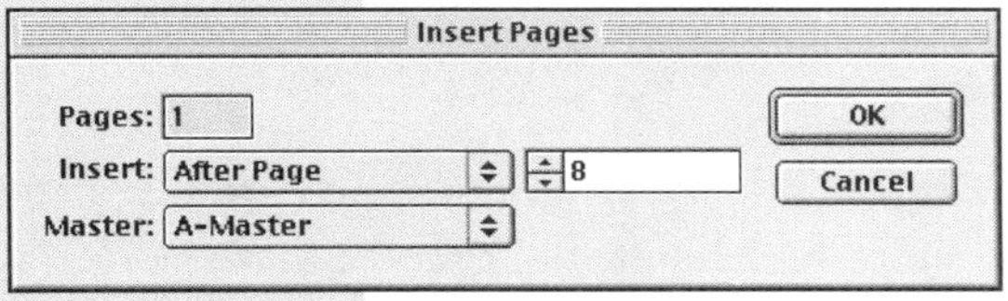

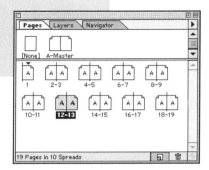

Figure 7.17
The new page is selected as the active page.

If you add or remove a single page or an odd number of pages from a document that has facing pages, you need to remove them from the end of the document, or all the pages that follow will switch sides. If you remove page three from a six-page document, it will become a five-page document, and page four, which was a left-hand page, will become page three, which is a right-hand page. Page five, which was formerly page six, the left-facing back cover of your publication, will become a right-facing page, with nothing to go on the other side. If you've planned elements for the outside edge of the page, they'll now be on the inside, unless they were placed on master pages. Master page elements update when you shift pages.

Removing Extra Pages

Removing pages is just as easy as adding them, and can be done in the same ways. You can change the page count in the Page Setup dialog box or by selecting a page or spread and dragging it to the Trash icon at the bottom of the Pages palette. When you drag a page to the Trash, InDesign displays a dialog box asking you to confirm that you meant to delete the page, to be sure your deletion is not accidental. Click OK and it's gone, or click Cancel if you change your mind.

Arranging Pages

Even if you create a nice, neat dummy and carefully plan out your pages, you might decide halfway through the process that the elements on certain pages belong elsewhere in the document. Fortunately, it's not hard to move them. To move a page, simply go to the Pages palette and drag the page icon to a new position in the document. As you drag, a vertical bar shows where the page will be inserted (see Figure 7.18). If the black bar touches a spread, the page you drag will be attached to that spread; otherwise, pages will be renumbered to allow for the reordering. If you want to move a two-page spread, I find it easier to move the right page first, and then the right page again. (The second time, the right page used to be the left page, before it got bumped over one position.) If you are moving pages that already have text placed on them, the text will reflow with the page.

In this chapter you learned about master pages, including what they are, how to add or remove objects within them, and how to apply them to document pages. You also learned about numbering pages and sections in a document, and how to add and subtract pages. Finally, you learned how to rearrange the order of the pages. In the next chapter, you'll learn about another helpful InDesign feature—layers.

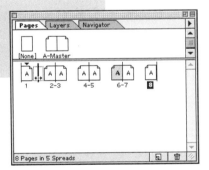

Figure 7.18
The vertical bar moves as you drag.

8
Adobe
InDesign

Working with Layers

If you have already mastered Photoshop or Illustrator, you're already familiar with layers and how they work. You can breeze through this chapter and go on to the next. Otherwise, pay close attention. Layers are incredibly useful in many situations, once you understand how to work with them.

What's a Layer?

Think of Bugs Bunny, popping out of his rabbit hole with carrot in paw. He moves while the woodland scene stays still. That's because the scenery is painted on the background, and the bunny's various parts are on different layers of transparent acetate. There's probably one layer for his body and a separate one for his head. One for each arm and leg, and probably one for his eyebrows and lower jaw, so he can talk. Each of these layers is independent of the others. You could change the legs and let him walk without moving his arms, or he could stand in one spot and gesture as he talks. Or everything could move at once, if Elmer Fudd, on *his* separate layers, was to come on the scene.

When all these layers of transparent film are stacked up and photographed, the acetate disappears and you see only the painted character parts. The order in which they're stacked determines whether Bugs' hand is in front of or behind his face. (Behind would, of course, be a mistake.) When he has to move his arm, one acetate cel is removed and another is added, with the arm in a slightly different position, and then the photographer shoots another frame of the film. Each bit of motion requires a different piece of acetate, with the arm, eyebrow, or other appropriate part in a different position.

In a graphics design program such as Photoshop or InDesign, layers serve essentially the same purpose. The layers are transparent, except for the objects you place on them. Layers let you place one thing on top of another without disturbing or changing the item underneath. Figure 8.1 shows an example of layers applied to a newsletter front page. The photo, the masthead, and the dateline are on separate layers.

In all honesty, you can probably do anything you need to do with InDesign without ever making extra layers. You can overlap frames when needed, you can fill a frame with a color and then with type, and you can pull something out from behind something else that's hiding it. Still, there will probably be situations where layers are your salvation. Think, for example, of a chain of

Figure 8.1
There are three layers in all.

restaurants. Suppose you were in charge of designing and printing the menus for two restaurants in two different cities. Each menu has the same items, but prices are higher in one city than in the other. You could make a layout and then copy it, deleting the prices and typing new ones for each city. You could also just put the prices on separate layers and show one layer while making up the printing master for Boston, and the other when you do the master for Portland. Figure 8.2 shows the menu with the Boston prices in place.

Layers are useful in many situations, not just when you have information that's different in multiple versions of the same page. Suppose you were laying out a report that had a high-resolution graphic you wanted to reduce to a tint and

Figure 8.2
The Portland prices are hidden.

use as a background for each page. You could put the graphic on the master pages, but then every time you changed pages or changed views, you'd have to sit there and wait while the graphic reloaded. Not so good, if you're in a hurry. Making the graphic a separate layer allows you to show it occasionally to see how your other elements line up against it, but not show it while you're editing the text.

Sometimes you need to work with another person on a document, passing it back and forth. If you each put your comments on a separate layer, it is easy to see who wants what changes. When you agree on the final version, you can hide the layers.

My Canadian friend uses layers on practically every bit of work she does. Living where she does, Susie has to create both French and English versions of ads, flyers, package designs, and so on. Sometimes the client wants both languages on the same piece, but more often she has to create two different pages. She does the basic layout, adds the photos, the company logo, and other non-verbal elements on the bottom layer, and then puts the French text on one layer and the English on the other. Because the two versions are seldom exactly the same length, she can make her adjustments on the text layer, instead of having to move the photo and elements for each page.

There is one thing you need to keep in mind when you work with layers. Layers cover the entire document, not one specific page. This makes no difference if your document has just one page. However, if the covers of my menu were part of the same document as the inside page, I'd be in trouble. The prices would print on the cover, spoiling the illustration and probably costing me my job.

The contents of a layer become even more critical in a longer document. If you make a layer that contains an element that will be on every page, no problem. If you need to hide it on just one page, though, you can't—it's all or nothing.

Exploring the Layers Palette

Every document starts with a default layer, called Layer 1. Layer 1 has all the elements you put on the master pages, plus any that you added to a document page. Layers, after the first one, are created and managed from the Layers palette. This important palette and its flyout menu are shown in Figure 8.3.

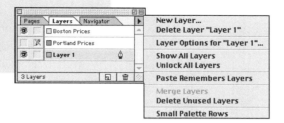

Figure 8.3
The Layers palette and its flyout menu

Take a look at the bottom of the palette. First, you have a reminder of how many layers there are in your document. Next, you have a New Layer icon. Clicking the icon is one way to create a new layer on top of any current ones. Next to that is the familiar Trash icon. If you want to delete a Layer, you can simply drag it to the trash.

Looking farther up on the palette, you can see the default layer, Layer 1. Above that is the layer called Portland Prices, and at the top of the stack, Boston Prices. I like to keep layers named when I'm working with several of them, but you can use default numbering (2, 3, and so on) if you're better than I am at remembering what you put where.

Looking again at Figure 8.3, Layer 1 and the Boston Prices layer each have an eye icon, which indicates that these two layers are currently visible. The Portland layer has no eye icon showing you that it's hidden. To toggle the layer's visibility, click the icon or the empty box where the icon will appear.

The pen point on Layer 1 indicates that Layer 1 is the active layer. You can enter text on it or add a graphics frame. The Portland layer has a square containing a pencil with a line through it, indicating that the layer is locked and you can't add anything to it. Clicking that square toggles the layer lock on and off. Inactive layers needn't be locked; it's an option. Of course, you can always unlock a layer if you need to make changes.

Each layer also has a block of color just before its name, and each color is different. This helps you keep track of what's where. Frames you create on any layer will have that layer's color as their outline. You can't see this in black and white, but the menu text on Layer 1 is in a blue frame. The Boston prices are in a green frame, and if the Portland prices were visible, they'd be in a red frame.

Creating a Layer

As I mentioned previously, there are several ways to create a new layer. The easiest method is to click the New Layer icon. Your new layer, with a default name and color, is added above the present layers. If you want to add a layer between two current layers, select the lower layer and press the Command key as you click the New Layer icon. Layers you create by clicking the New Layer icon always have the default numbers and colors. To create a customized layer on top of the existing ones, choose New Layer from the Layers palette flyout menu. This gives you the options shown in Figure 8.4.

You can also create a customized new layer by pressing the Option key as you click the New Layer icon. This opens the same dialog box shown in Figure 8.4. Pressing Command+Option as you click the icon lets you insert a customized layer between existing layers.

If you create a layer while a master page is displayed, everything you put on that layer will appear on all of the pages based on that master. Thus, if you consider the restaurant menu example, I could keep the covers and text separate by basing them on different master pages. Then, the price icons would only relate to the inside pages on the B-Master.

Naming Layers

If you have created a layer by clicking the New Layer icon, and then you decide you want to give it a real name instead of accepting the default, all you need to do is to select the layer and choose Layer Options from the Layers palette flyout menu, or double-click the selected layer. Either action opens the dialog box shown in Figure 8.4, which gives you all the same options you'd have if you created the layer using the menu.

Figure 8.4
You can name your layer, pick a color for it, and even lock it.

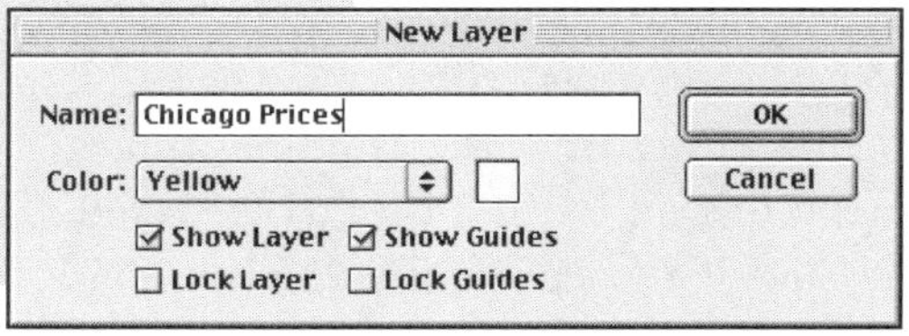

The name you assign to the layer can have as many as 32 characters. By default, InDesign applies a different color to each new layer. You needn't accept the default choice, though. The pop-up Color menu lists 27 choices, including Other. Selecting Other, or double-clicking the color sample swatch, opens the Color Picker so you can choose whatever color you like. Just remember that, for ease of use, the color needs to be visible against any background or spot colors you've already put into the document.

Take a quick look at the rest of the New Layer dialog box, and see what options are available on it. Checking the Show Layer and Lock Layer check boxes in the New Layer dialog box has exactly the same effect as clicking their respective icons on the Layers palette.

The Show Guides option lets you show or hide guides that you place on the selected layer. It's active by default, so you can drag guides wherever you need them on the layer. Guides are displayed in whatever color you chose for them in the Preferences dialog box. However, if you click on any guide you have created on a layer, the guide will temporarily change to the layer color, so you can tell which is which. If you have selected Hide Guides from the View menu or typed Command+Option+; to hide them, guides placed on a layer are also hidden.

Lock Guides obviously does just that—it locks the guides you have placed on a layer. You can't move them unless you go back to the menu and unlock them. Like the Hide Guide command, Lock Guides affects all of the guidelines in the document.

Working with Layers

Layers can be used to isolate specific objects or types of objects. You can create objects such as lines, shapes, and text or graphics frames on an active layer. You can move objects from the document page or master page to an active layer, or you can copy objects to it. However, you can't do anything to a layer unless it is active. The Pen icon in the Layers palette indicates the active layer. The layer is also shaded in the palette, to show that it's selected. You can have several layers selected at once, but only one at a time can be active. To make a layer active, click on its name. That places the Pen icon on it, showing that it is active. Only visible layers can be active.

Selecting Objects on Layers

You can select and move an object on any visible layer, but as soon as you select an object, its layer becomes the active layer. If there's a selected (active) object on a layer, you'll see a small box next to the pen on the Layers palette; Figure 8.5 shows an example. The frame with the prices is selected, and the little box is visible on the palette.

You can also select all the objects on a layer, by pressing Option as you click on the name of the layer in the Layers palette.

Placing Objects on Layers

Placing objects on layers can be accomplished by any of the usual methods. You can use the tools in the toolbox to create paths and frames, and you can use the Place command to bring in text or graphics from an outside source. Paste objects from the Clipboard or drag them from another document, and check the Paste Remembers Layers command in the Layers palette flyout menu (see Figure 8.6) to paste something from one document to the same layer of another, if the layer exists. If not, it will be placed on a new layer on top of the existing one(s).

Figure 8.5
The small box shows you that the layer is active.

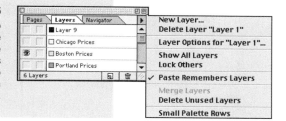

Figure 8.6 You'll need to uncheck the Paste Remembers Layers option to paste to a different layer.

Moving Objects and Layers

Remember that you're not stuck with the order in which the layers were created. You can select a layer in the Layers palette and drag it on top of or below another layer. Just don't forget that objects on a higher layer hide those directly beneath.

Not only can you move layers around, you can also move objects to a different layer, or create a new layer and then place objects on it. When you move an object to a layer that already has something on it, the new object is placed on top of the existing object, if they overlap. Thus, if the new object it is a solid object, it will hide whatever is under it. Text in frames is not considered a solid object unless there's a fill or gradient behind it, so you can place text over some other element and have the text be readable. In Figure 8.7, I've attempted to bring a background graphic into my menu. Because I brought in the graphic on a new layer, it's automatically on top of the other layers, and because it's a solid object, it hides the elements below it.

Obviously, that won't work. The graphic needs to be placed under the text. You can do this easily by clicking Layer 5 on the Layers palette and dragging it down to the bottom of the list of layers. Figure 8.8 shows the result.

Merging Layers

> Merging all the layers in a document is called *flattening*.

It's easy to get carried away and unnecessarily put each object on a different layer. The document then becomes very large and unwieldy. Saves take forever, and numerous layers eat up hard disk space as well as RAM. The answer is to merge the layers. You can merge any two or more layers into one.

To merge two layers, first click on the layer that is the target (the layer on which you want the contents of the other layer to be placed) to select it, then

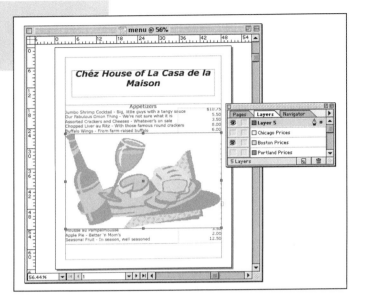

Figure 8.7
The graphic is on Layer 5.

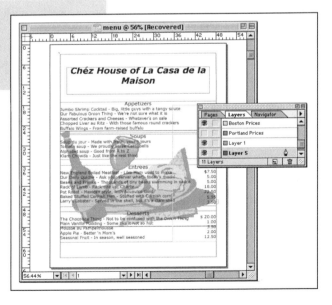

Figure 8.8
The graphic is still on Layer 5, but it's now the bottom Layer.

press the Command key and click on the layer(s) you want to merge onto the target layer. Be sure that the target layer is active, and choose Merge Layers from the Layers palette flyout menu, as shown in Figure 8.9.

Figure 8.9
The merged layers retain the name of the target layer—in this case, Portland Prices.

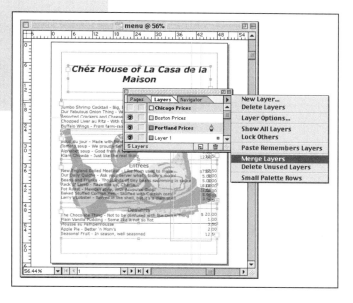

Deleting Layers

When you get "layer-happy" and create more layers than you need, merging them is one answer. Deleting unnecessary layers is another. You have already learned that you can delete a layer either by dragging it to the Trash icon on the Layers palette or to the main Trash can on your desktop. If you have several layers selected, clicking the palette's Trash can icon will delete them all.

If you have created layers and not put anything on them, there's an easy way to get rid of them. Go to the Layers palette flyout menu and select Delete Unused Layers (see Figure 8.10).

Figure 8.10
Layers 6 and 7, which are empty, will be deleted.

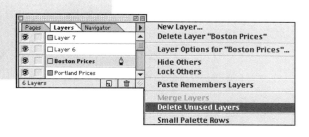

Before you delete a layer, it's a good idea to make sure that it is empty or that you really don't need whatever is on it. If you think you might need the layer object or text block, but you still want to delete the layer, copy the item to the pasteboard, where it can be stored with the document for as long as necessary.

To see what's on a layer before you delete it, turn off the layer(s) you plan to keep. Make the layer that you want to delete visible. With nothing else visible, you can see exactly what's there, and you can decide whether to keep the layer, delete it, or save the contents somewhere else.

Reducing Palette Icon Size

When you have many layers on the Layers palette, it's easy to lose track of them. You can always scroll up and down the list, but you can also shrink the display on the Layers palette so you can see all your layers at once. Open the palette's flyout menu and select Small Palette Rows. Your layer list shrinks to one that can display more layer icons, as shown in Figure 8.11.

Saving Layer Objects to an Object Library

Generally speaking, items that are important enough to be placed on a layer and used throughout your document will probably be needed for future projects, too. Items such as a newsletter masthead and banner, page headers, logos, and so on will also readily lend themselves to being reused. Such items can be stored on the document's pasteboard, but when you need them again you have to remember where you used them last, and then open that file to retrieve them. That's often more work than it's worth. However, there is a better way. You can create an Object Library and save all the reusable graphics and text frames to it. You can also save ruler guides and grids, drawn shapes, and spot color blocks. You can even have a different library for each project or client.

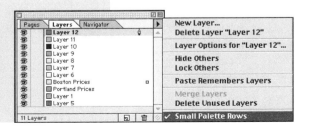

Figure 8.11
You can increase the size of the window in the Layers palette by dragging the lower-right corner.

Object libraries can be shared with your PC-using friends or co-workers, and can be networked across a server.

When you add layer items to an Object Library all attributes, including the layer level, are preserved. To start an Object Library, go to the Window menu and select Library, New. You'll be asked to give your library a name. For ease of use, give it a descriptive one, not just "Library." When you click Save, a Library palette opens on your screen, similar to the one shown in Figure 8.12.

Exploring the Library Palette

Some of the icons at the bottom of the Library palette are a bit different from those you've seen so far. Take a quick look at them. The letter "i" stands for Item information, and clicking it opens the dialog box shown in Figure 8.13.

Adding a description of the file can be useful when you have a large library. Thanks to the library search feature, which you can activate by clicking the Binoculars icon, you can use the description to help you find the file when you can't remember its name. Figure 8.14 shows the Subset dialog box, which finds subsets of items within the library.

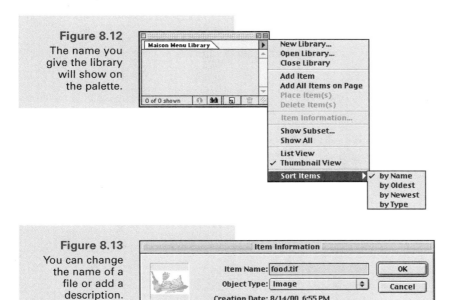

Figure 8.12
The name you give the library will show on the palette.

Figure 8.13
You can change the name of a file or add a description.

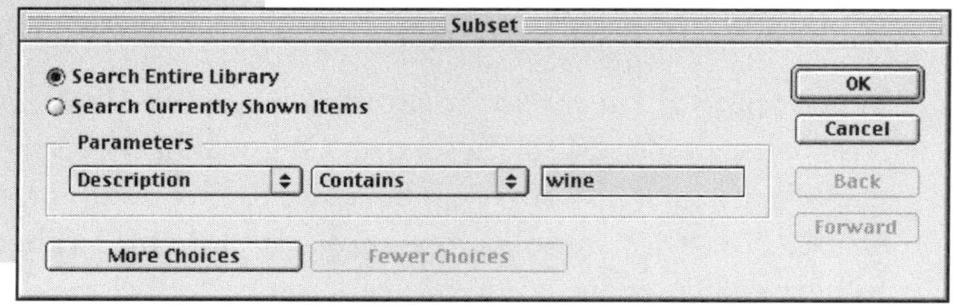

Figure 8.14
You can search by name, type, creation date, or description by clicking the More Choices button.

The New Library Item and Delete Item icons look the same as those on the Layers palette and serve the same functions. The Sort Items command at the bottom of the flyout menu (refer to Figure 8.12) lets you decide whether you want the library items sorted in alphabetical order, by age, or by type.

Adding an Item to the Object Library

To add an item to the Object Library, select it on the page and drag it to the Library palette, or select it and click the New Item button at the bottom of the palette. If you want to add all the contents of a layer to the library, choose Add All Items on Page from the flyout menu. (They'll be added as a group, not as individual items.) If you press Option as you perform any of these actions, you'll open the Item Information dialog box, so you can rename the object or add a description. You can also double click an item to display the Item Information dialog box.

To place an Object Library item in a document, drag it to the document window, or select it and choose Place Item(s) from the flyout menu.

Now you know all about Layers and the Object Library. You've seen how Layers can be helpful in some situations, and why they're not always the right answer. In the next chapter, you'll delve into working with text.

Adobe InDesign

PART IV
Text Techniques

9
Adobe InDesign

Preparing Text for Import into InDesign

In InDesign you can enter text directly onto the pages of your publication. For short bits like headlines or photo captions, that's probably how you'll choose to do it. For longer passages, however, you'll probably create documents using your word processor, and then import them into InDesign. Most of today's word processors have extensive text-formatting capabilities, sometimes so many that you'll be tempted to do most of your formatting there, which is not necessarily a good idea.

InDesign's import filters are good, but there are some kinds of formatting they ignore. Page breaks, margins, and column settings aren't imported with the text. Tab settings don't import either, so formatting a table before you import it is a waste of time. You can always turn your spreadsheet into a graphic, but if you do, you lose the ability to edit the data.

What *can* you do in your word processor to make text import easier? First, you can run a spell check and a grammar check on your stories before you import them. It's still a good idea to run the InDesign spell checker on pages before you declare them done, but it will save time if InDesign only has to check new text.

You can do basic character formatting in the word processor. Italic and bold translate perfectly, as do most foreign characters, provided the font you intend to print from contains the appropriate diacritical marks or characters. This is something you might need to check on a font-by-font basis. Some shareware fonts, in particular, might not include the foreign characters you need. How can you check? The Mac Key Caps applet, which is found in the Apple menu, shows you exactly what characters and symbols are included in a font, and where on the keyboard to find them. Figure 9.1 shows Key Caps in use. I've pressed the Option key to show the optional characters.

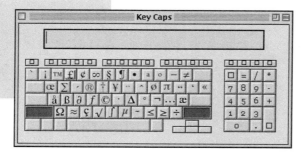

Figure 9.1
You can hold Shift or Shift+Option to see more characters.

Translating Word Processor Formats

InDesign accepts a fairly limited variety of word processor formats. The following formats can import directly into InDesign:

> RTF (*Rich Text Format*) is a Microsoft Word format developed to make file exchanges across platforms or between word processors less complicated.

- ASCII text
- Microsoft Word for Mac 4.0/5x/6.0/98(7.0)
- Rich Text Format (RTF)
- WordPerfect 6.x/7.08.0/2000 for Windows (not WordPerfect for Mac)

You can apply styles in Word and WordPerfect that will carry over and be added to the Styles list in InDesign. This method is fine for pre-formatting headlines and subheads, but InDesign can do a lot more typographically than your word processor can. InDesign was designed for page layout, and word processors were designed for writing. If you needed to tighten a screw, you wouldn't use a hammer.

No matter what kind of word processor you're using, even if it's something as basic as SimpleText, you can save your work as ASCII text. Any of the versions of Microsoft Word newer than 4.0 can be imported directly into InDesign. Word 3.0 is not supported, but you can save your document as ASCII text and import that. Similarly, BBEdit, AppleWorks (formerly ClarisWorks), Nisus Writer, and WriteNow all can save text as ASCII or RTF for use in InDesign. If you have a choice of ASCII or RTF, always choose the latter. Because ASCII text contains no formatting, you'll have to do a lot more work than you would with formatted text.

Using Import Filters

The key to importing text is to be sure that you have installed the necessary import filters. Import filters are translation modules that screen incoming text files for compatibility with InDesign. They're stored in the Filters folder, inside the Plug-Ins folder. Figure 9.2 shows the current set of filters. When new or updated import/export filters are created, they will be available for download at http://www.adobe.com.

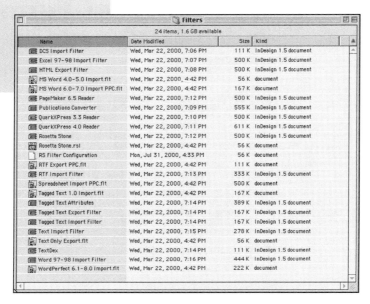

Figure 9.2
There are both import and export filters in the folder.

In addition to text, InDesign can import text from text and table editors that are included with Word, and from Microsoft Excel spreadsheets. When you use the Place command (Command+D) to bring in a file from Word, or one that's been saved as RTF in another program, you are presented with a dialog box that helps you locate the file (see Figure 9.3). The dialog box also has

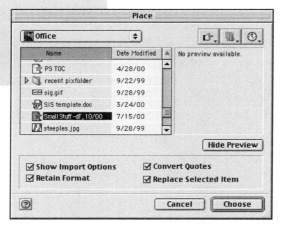

Figure 9.3
Show Import Options is the most important checkbox.

several options, which you should, under most circumstances, be sure to check. Retain Format will keep any formatting you have applied in your word processor, and Convert Quotes changes "straight quotes" or typewriter-style quotes into typographer's "curly quotes." Replace Selected Item lets you select a story or a picture and replace it with a new one in the same frame.

Show Import Options gives you more choices. You can choose from the following options:

- **Include**. Selecting this option allows InDesign to import all of the following items as part of the text (if they are included in the Word document): table of contents text, index text, hyperlink formatting, table contents, and footnotes/endnotes.

- **Condensed/Expanded Spacing To**. Selecting this option enables InDesign to interpret condensed or expanded spacing either as tracking or as the set width of characters, depending on whether you select Tracking or Horizontal Scaling.

- **User Defined Page Breaks**. Selecting this option allows you to decide how page breaks from the word-processor file will be formatted in InDesign. Choose from Page Breaks, Column Breaks, or No Break.

Figure 9.4 shows these options for Word documents. The RTF options are similar.

Figure 9.4
You can even convert Word's spacing to InDesign's tracking.

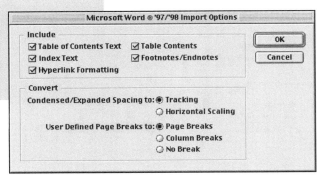

Using Add/Strip

When you get text files from a DOS or Windows user, they may not be formatted appropriately for the Mac. The document might contain a carriage return at the end of each line, too many or incorrect control characters, or the wrong kind of quotation marks and apostrophes. You can go through the text and reformat it by hand, one word at a time, or you can use the InDesign Edit, Find/Change command to change quotes from straight to curly. Either way takes time; there is a better way.

Add/Strip is a Macintosh shareware program that anyone who exchanges files across platforms should have. It cleans incoming text files of their unnecessary returns, and can also reformat your output so it can be read on DOS or UNIX-based machines. Even if you're just passing files from your own word processor to InDesign, Add/Strip can save you from having to reformat such things as quotes and apostrophes. Figure 9.5 shows the main Add/Strip dialog box.

The author of Add/Strip is Jon Wind. You can download it at http://www6.zdnet.com/cgibin/texis/swlib/mac/infomac.html?fcode=MC10921 or from most of the better shareware sites. The shareware fee is only $25, and the product will undoubtedly save you much more than that in aggravation.

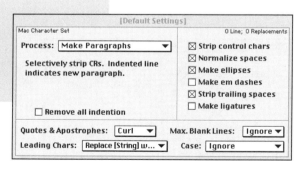

Figure 9.5
Add/Strip can remove extra white space and change just about anything.

Choosing a Format for Text Creation

The format you should use to prepare your text for import depends on what word processor you use. If you use AppleWorks, ClarisWorks, or any other fairly recent Mac word processor, use RTF to protect any formatting you've done. Figure 9.6 shows how to save as RTF in ClarisWorks. If you're using Word 4.0 or later, simply save your files as Word documents.

Importing Text

InDesign imports text styles that you've applied in Word, along with the text itself. You can create your own styles, use Word's built-in styles, or load style sheets or templates from another source. Defining a style is done in the word processor's New Style window. Microsoft Word 98's New Style dialog box is shown in Figure 9.7. If you use Word, you can access the Style dialog box from the Format menu.

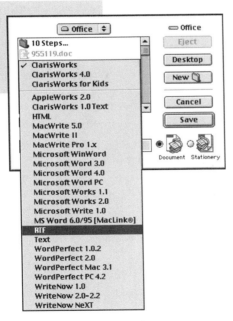

Figure 9.6
Save your work as RTF if you use anything other than Word.

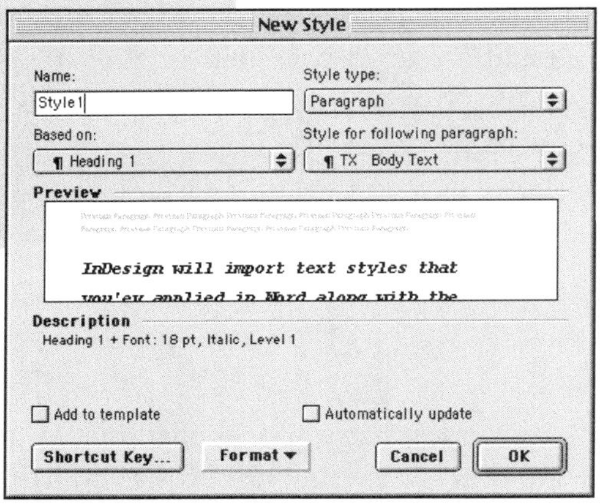

Figure 9.7
Set the parameters that define your new style, and give it a descriptive name.

Using Tagged Text

InDesign accepts tagged text, that is to say, text that has style codes applied. As an example, Prima Publishing, the publishers of this book, gives its authors a template of styles, called a *style sheet*. These are by no means the final type styles you see on the page. Instead they are placeholder styles. Authors apply them in Word, and include their tags in the file. Figure 9.8 shows what this page looks like as I'm working on it.

Figure 9.8
As you can see, the final version is very different from my working text. It has also been edited.

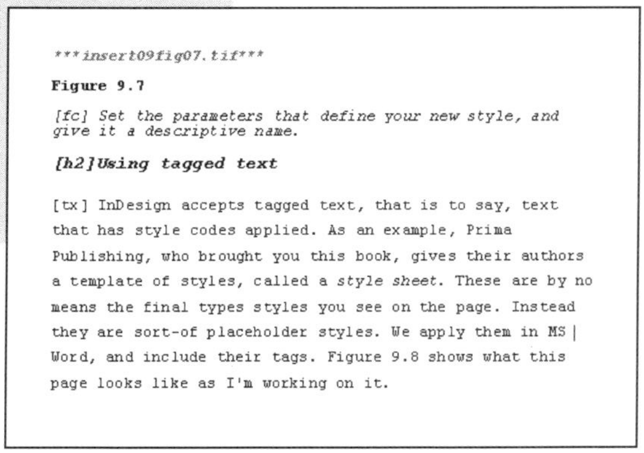

```
***insert09fig07.tif***
Figure 9.7
[fc] Set the parameters that define your new style, and
give it a descriptive name.
[h2]Using tagged text

[tx] InDesign accepts tagged text, that is to say, text
that has style codes applied. As an example, Prima
Publishing, who brought you this book, gives their authors
a template of styles, called a style sheet. These are by no
means the final types styles you see on the page. Instead
they are sort-of placeholder styles. We apply them in MS|
Word, and include their tags. Figure 9.8 shows what this
page looks like as I'm working on it.
```

The letters in brackets, for example [tx], are the style tag. Applying tags as you write takes a few seconds longer, but when the book goes into production and the chapters are imported into Prima's page layout program, the style tags are imported too. The final type styles are already entered into the page layout program, and as soon as the pages are imported, they take on the correct type font and attribute. All that's left is to paste in the figures. I can guess what the page designer has to say about this over-simplification, and of course they do more than cut and paste. Someone has to invent all those styles in the first place, and be sure the styles harmonize with each other, are easy to read, and fit the style of the book. Still, there's little doubt that working with tagged text saves them time, and makes their job a little easier.

To create tagged text, you must first create text styles in your word processor. You'll learn about creating styles in InDesign in Chapter 13, "Using Styles and Style Sheets." For now, you'll just take a quick look at the way the word processor does it. (Although I am using Word 98 for this example, other versions of Word and other word processing programs function in a similar manner.) When you create a style, you must first open the Style dialog box, shown in Figure 9.9. You'll find it under the Format menu. Don't confuse it with the Style Gallery, which lists document templates for use in Word.

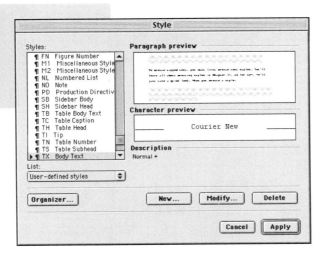

Figure 9.9
This dialog box contains a list of all the styles currently available.

Before I started writing this chapter, I copied the styles from Prima's template into Word. As you can see, all the styles have two-letter abbreviated names, as well as longer descriptive names. The two-letter codes are what you use as tags when writing. When the tagged text goes into the InDesign document, the tags are matched to the designer's styles with the same names. There's a handy reference guide to working with tagged text on the InDesign CD-ROM. Adobe InDesign Tagged Text lists each InDesign tag and explains how to use tags efficiently.

Deciding Where to Format Text

So, what's the bottom line? As you've seen, you can do a good deal of formatting in your word processor, and then import the formatted text into InDesign. But InDesign can do sophisticated formatting that's beyond the abilities of even the most recent versions of Word, and way beyond anything you could import as RTF.

You'll obviously want to do the critical formatting—kerning, and adding drop caps and other fancy typographic techniques—in InDesign. However, there's no reason not to format the basic text and headline styles with your word processor. Because you can import them, there's no time wasted, and it's generally easier to write when you can see your headlines and subheads standing out from the text.

In this chapter, you learned how to import text and how to prepare it for importing. In the next chapter, you'll work on editing the imported text.

10
Adobe InDesign

Working with Imported Text

Text is the "meat" of your publication, whether it's a catalog, a newsletter, a book, or even a Lost Dog flyer. Illustrations show what you're talking about, but it's the words that actually make up your message. Therefore, it's important that the words make sense, are spelled right, and are grammatically correct. Nothing makes a printed document or Web page look more amateurish than a spelling mistake or misused punctuation. That's why every piece of text that comes into publication, whether you wrote it yourself or got it from someone else, needs to be edited and checked for spelling errors. Naturally, you'd go through these steps in your word processor as part of preparing the story for import, and you'd assume that anyone submitting text for your publication would do the same. Don't count on it!

> **No matter whether it's fiction, poetry, a news story, or catalog body copy, just about everything you place as text on a page is either considered a *headline* or a *story*.**

Some of the best writers I know will forget to check their spelling now and then, or will make some kind of mistake as they write. And sometimes, the spell checker recognizes and accepts a word that's spelled correctly but is not the word the author meant to use. For example, "I red him the riot act." Sometimes a writer will do the editing, but then forget to save the changes. The more times you read through text before you commit it to print or screen, the more of these little mistakes you'll discover and fix.

Editing Text

The first thing you need to do before you can edit text is make sure you can read it. In a layout view, the text is often tiny, and very hard to read. You need to be able to see something as small as a period that should have been a comma, or vice versa. For this, you can use the Zoom tool. Click it on the toolbar, or simply type Z (unless your cursor is in a block of text, in which case, you can use the toolbar or the keyboard shortcut Command+=). Remember that to zoom out again, you can type Command+- or press Option while you click the Zoom tool.

If your cursor is already on or near the text to which you need to zoom, use the keyboard shortcut. The cursor acts as the central point of your zoom, bringing the text you want to see closer.

Showing Hidden Characters

If you've never poked around in your word processor or in InDesign, it might surprise you to learn that there are hidden, or non-printing, characters in your text. Things like paragraphs, spaces, tabs, and optional hyphens all have hidden characters, which are placed on the page every time you type one of them. When you're working with text that refuses to space properly or has too much space between paragraphs, it's almost certain that a hidden character is the culprit. To reveal these sneaky little marks, click Type, Show Hidden Characters (as shown in Figure 10.1), or type Command+Option+I.

Figure 10.2 shows some of these hidden characters officially called *metacharacters*. Notice the dots between words—they indicate spaces. They can help when you run across an author more at home on an old-fashioned typewriter than on a computer. Computer typography demands only one space after a

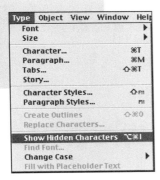

Figure 10.1
Show Hidden Characters is hidden in the Type menu.

Figure 10.2
The paragraph symbols indicate a new paragraph next.

period, while typewriter type is supposed to have two spaces, or so I learned in high school.

As you can see, InDesign's paragraph characters have nothing to do with what an English teacher would call a paragraph. They actually represent what, in the old days, were called carriage returns. The paragraph characters tell the computer to scroll down a line, even though there's no carriage to return and no bell that rings.

Getting around the Page

Whether you have a long story or several short ones to edit, the easy way to navigate between them is to ignore the document scroll bars and click in the frame or the part of a frame where you want to be. If your clicking aim is not great, navigate with the cursor keys. They're the four arrow keys shown in Figure 10.3. The left and right arrows move you along the line, one character at a time. The up and down arrows move you up or down one line at a time.

If you press the Command key while you press the right or left arrow key, you will jump one word to the right or left instead of one character. The Command key used with the up and down arrows takes you one full paragraph up or down. (By the way, all of these commands work in Microsoft Word, too.) The Home key takes you to the beginning of a line. If you press Command along with it, you'll go to the beginning of the story. If your story starts on another page, you'll jump to that page.

My Mac G3 came with the "compact" keyboard that doesn't have an End key. If you have an extended keyboard with an End key, it takes you to the end of

Figure 10.3
These are the cursor keys on my dusty keyboard.

a line, or, when pressed at the same time as the Command key, to the end of the story.

Finding and Changing Text

I had a client call recently to say that he loved the brochure I'd done for his company's new product. It was perfect in every way—except that his company had just decided to change the name of the product. How long would it take, he wondered, and how much would it cost to redo the piece with the new name? I told him I'd need about two minutes, and that I wouldn't charge him. He was astounded. Obviously, he knew nothing about desktop publishing, where a change requires only a couple of clicks. (Of course, I saved a copy of the original, just in case he decided to go back to the original name. *Always* save before you make global changes.)

InDesign's Find/Change dialog box can be accessed via the Edit menu, or by typing Command+F. It's shown in Figure 10.4.

You can find and change any word, string of words, character or punctuation mark, or text formatted in a particular way. You can do this in a selection, a single text frame, one or more stories, an entire publication, or across all of the publications open on your desktop. In the case of my name-changing client, if I'd done several pieces for him, I could have made all of the changes with one click!

Using the Find/Change Command

Start by opening the Find/Change dialog box and entering the piece of text you want to change and what you want to change it to. You can narrow your

Figure 10.4
Make changes one by one or all at once.

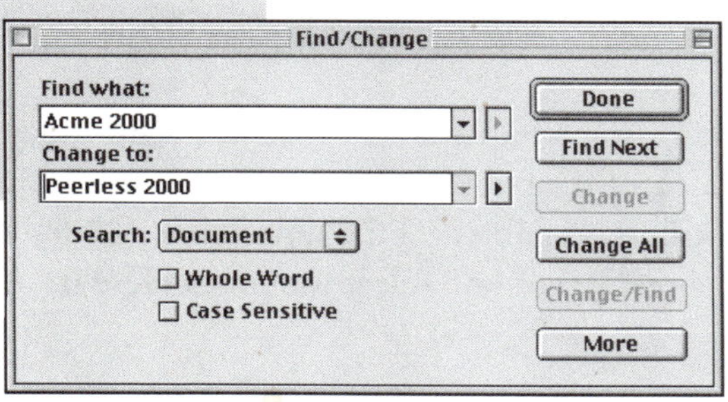

search by clicking inside a text frame to search that story, or by selecting a piece of text to search. To search several frames or stories, use the Selection tool and press the Shift key to make multiple selections.

On the Search pop-up menu, choose Document, All Documents, Story, or To End of Story. The last choice means that InDesign will only search from the section of the document where you have placed an insertion point to the end of the document. This can save time if your documents are very long. If text is selected, Selection will be an option and will automatically become the active one.

If you just want to find the text and not change it, enter the word(s) you want to find. When you click Find Next, InDesign will find the next occurrence of the word or phrase. This is helpful when you need to check a reference, such as the spelling of a name. You can search for a whole word, or for only part of it. Suppose you want to find both "company" and "companies." Enter "compan" in the dialog box, and InDesign will find either word. Sometimes, though, it's better to search for the whole word. To do so, check the Whole Word check box. In general, you should leave this option on, to prevent InDesign from making undesirable changes in the middle of words, such as asking it to change "man" to "woman," and finding it also changed "many" to "womany."

The Case Sensitive option is particularly helpful when you're looking for names that could also be words you'd use in a story, like White, Green, Page, Day, Fine. . . . You get the idea.

Searching by Metacharacter

Remember those hidden characters? You can search for tabs, paragraphs, or other special characters. There are right-pointing arrows after both the Find What and Change To text boxes. After you click in the Find What box, you can click on the upper arrow to see the list of searchable metacharacters, shown in Figure 10.5.

Suppose you have some bulleted text that you want to keep indented, but you don't like the look of the bullets. Simply choose Bullet Character from the list. Its code, ^8, will appear in the Find What box. Then, click the right arrow next to the Change To box and select Indent to Here from the menu, as shown in Figure 10.6.

CHAPTER 10 • WORKING WITH IMPORTED TEXT

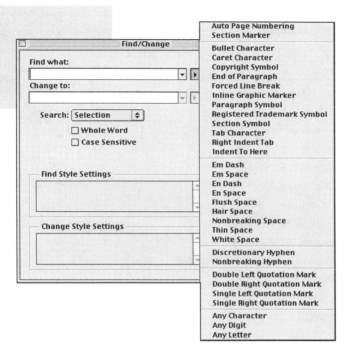

Figure 10.5
Anything you might want to change is somewhere on this list.

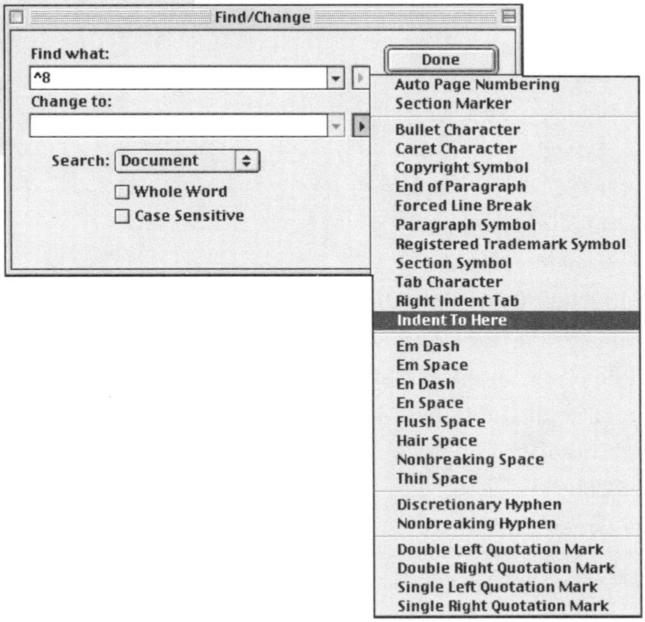

Figure 10.6
The list is the same for both finding and changing.

If you know the code for the metacharacter you want to change, you can skip the menu and just type the code in the box. Here's a list of the codes:

Item	Metacharacter
Auto Page Numbering	^#
Section Marker	^x
Bullet Character	^8
Caret Character	^^
Copyright Symbol	^2
End of Paragraph	^p
Forced Line Break	^n
*Inline Graphic Marker	^g
Paragraph Symbol	^7
Registered Trademark Symbol	^r
Section Symbol	^6
Tab Character	^t
Em Dash	^_
Em Space	^m
En Dash	^=
En Space	^>
Flush Space	^f
Hair Space	^|
Nonbreaking Space	^s
Thin Space	^<
*White Space (any space or tab)	^w
Discretionary Hyphen	^-
Nonbreaking Hyphen	^~
Double Left Quotation Mark	^{
Double Right Quotation Mark	^}
Single Left Quotation Mark	^[
Single Right Quotation Mark	^]
Any Character*	^?
Any Digit*	^9
Any Letter*	^$

* Metacharacter can only be entered in the Find What box, not in the Change box.

CHAPTER 10 • WORKING WITH IMPORTED TEXT

To start searching, click Find Next. To continue, click on Find Next, Change, Change/Find, or Change All, as appropriate. Change/Find is simply a more efficient way of telling InDesign to make the change to the word or metacharacter it has found, and then go ahead and find the next instance. Change All runs through the text and makes the change every time it finds the target. When it's finished, it tells you how many changes it made, as shown in Figure 10.7.

> **NOTE**
> Be careful, if you copy or cut and paste text into the Find What or Change To boxes, that you don't also paste hidden characters. This could throw off your search.

InDesign can remember the last dozen or so entries in the Find What or Change To boxes, except for the formatting entries described next. Use the down arrow to locate and reapply a previous change.

> **NOTE**
> InDesign can use the Any Character, Any Digit, and Any Letter metacharacters as wildcards as you search. For example, if you entered "dr^?p", you'd find both "drip" and "drop."

If you need to delete text wherever it appears, enter it in the Find What box and leave the Change To box empty. Clicking Find Next or Change All deletes the next (or all) occurrences of the designated text.

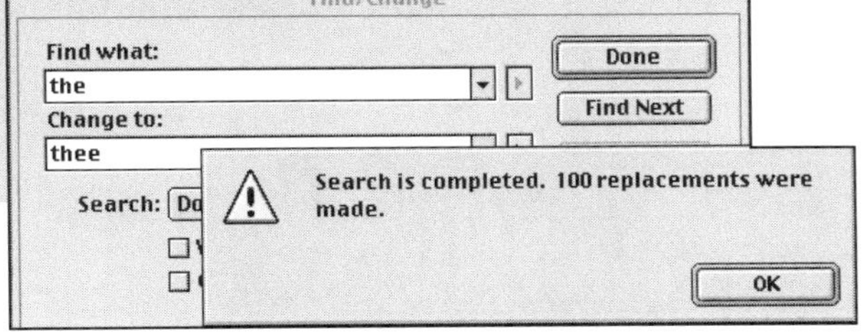

Figure 10.7
Making all these changes took about three seconds.

Finding and Changing Formatted Text

You can use the Find/Change dialog to change text formatting, including styles, indents and spacing, and even stroke and fill colors. However, you can only change text formatting in a single document at a time. You can't make changes if the search range is set for All Documents.

To change formatted text, click the More button in the Find/Change dialog box. When you do, you'll see a larger dialog box with more options, shown in Figure 10.8.

Now, click Format in the Find Style Settings section to open the Find Format Settings dialog box. It has a pop-up menu, shown in Figure 10.9, which gives you access to the various formatting options that you can change.

Each of these formatting options has its own dialog box as well. The options in the dialog boxes are familiar because they are the same options that you set when you format characters, set indents, and so on.

After you've described what it is that you're looking for, click Find to locate it, or go down to the Change Style Settings section and make the changes. Then, use the Find Next and Change All buttons to reformat the text.

Figure 10.8
The More button changes to Less button, so you can collapse the dialog box again.

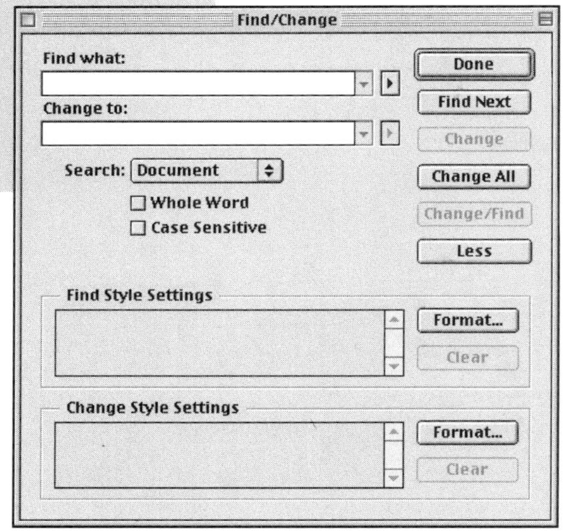

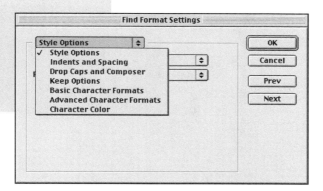

Figure 10.9
Currently hidden by the pop-up menu are the style options for Character and Paragraph styles.

> **TIP**
>
> If you get unexpected search results, check to make sure you have cleared any formatting you might have applied in a previous search.

Checking Your Spelling

Your word processor, unless it's something as primitive as Stickies or SimpleText, has a spell checker. You've already been advised, in the previous chapter, to check spelling before you bring stories into InDesign. Why should you check it again? Mistakes happen. Maybe you cut and pasted half a word. You could have typed a word twice, or failed to capitalize something that needed it. InDesign's spelling checker will catch any errors that crept in after you brought the text into your publication. As with Find/Change, you can check a selection, a story, all the stories in a single document, or all stories in all open documents.

The spelling checker can be opened from the Edit menu or by typing Command+I. Figure 10.10 shows the Check Spelling dialog box.

Set the scope of your search in the pop-up window at the bottom of the dialog box, and then click Start. When InDesign finds a misspelled word, it will appear in the dialog box, along with suggested alternates. Choose one by clicking it, and the Change button will become active. Then, click Change, and InDesign will correct the word. Figure 10.11 shows the Check Spelling dialog box with a word about to be changed.

Figure 10.10
Click Start to begin checking your publication.

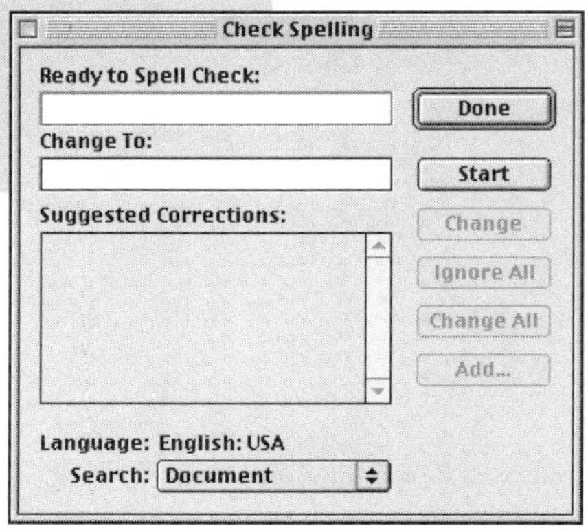

Figure 10.11
Click Change to replace the misspelled word with the chosen one.

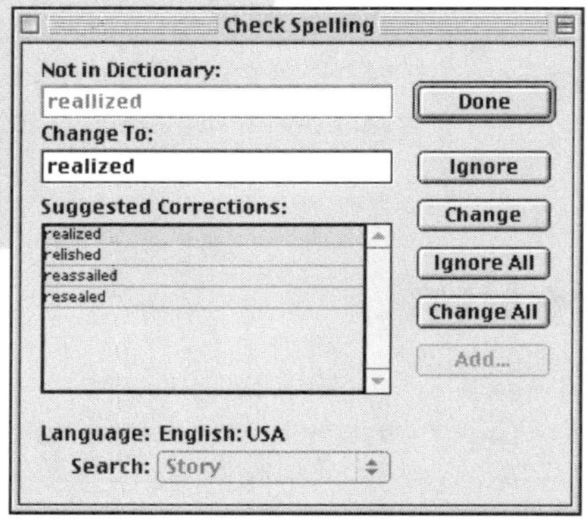

Adding Words to the Dictionary

Sometimes the spell checker will fail to recognize a word, such as a person's name or a trademark. If it's a word you'll be using frequently, instead of just clicking Ignore each time it comes up, you can add it to the dictionary.

To add a word to the dictionary from the spell checker, just click the Add button in the Check Spelling dialog box. Otherwise, select Edit Dictionary from the Edit menu. Either way, the Dictionary dialog box will open, as shown in Figure 10.12. Enter the word or words you want to add, click the Add button, and they're ready to use. Click Done when you are finished adding words.

Figure 10.12
Add proper names, trademarks, and any unusual or made-up words that you're likely to use while writing.

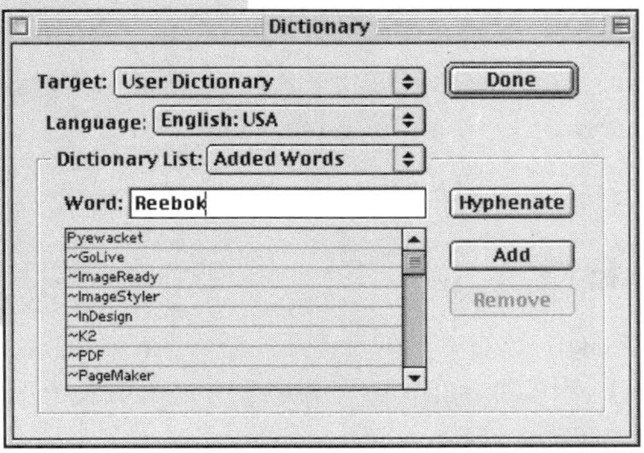

If you want to check or change the hyphenation of a word, use the Hyphenate button in the Dictionary dialog box (see Figure 10.13). A tilde (~) indicates the default hyphenation. If you want to change it, apply these rules:

- If you never want the word to be hyphenated, place a tilde in front of it.
- Type one tilde between syllables to indicate the best possible hyphenation point. If there's only one possible point, InDesign will place the tilde there.
- If there's a next-best choice, type two tildes between the syllables.
- If there's a poor, but possible, choice, type three tildes between the syllables.
- If you have no preference, accept InDesign's defaults or type the same number of tildes between the syllables.

Figure 10.13
InDesign applies its hyphenation rules to any words that you enter.

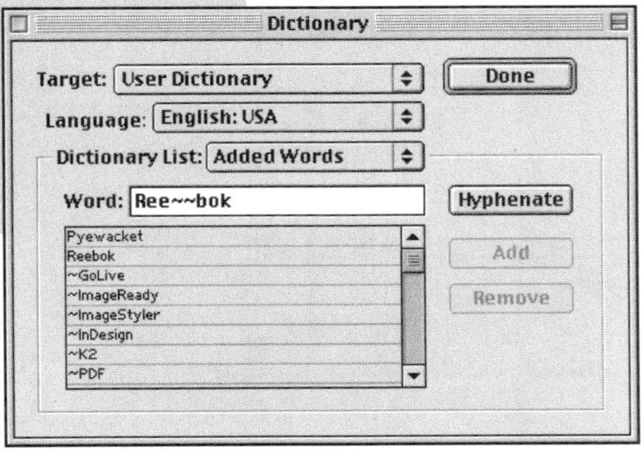

If you need to use a word that has a tilde in it in your story, such as El Niño, enter a backslash before the tilde. To put it in the dictionary, you'd type El Ni\ño. When the word is hyphenated as you want it, click Add, and then if you have no more words to enter, click Done.

Working with Tabs

Tabs allow you position text at specific locations across a line. If you have to enter a list, either with or without bullets, or if you have numbers in a column that you want to align by decimal point, tabs make the job easy. Tabs are set on the Tabs palette, which you can open either from the Text menu or by typing Shift+Command+T. Figure 10.14 shows the Tabs palette.

If you click an insertion point in the text before you open the Tabs palette, and if the top of the frame is visible, the palette will snap to the top of the frame and set its width to that of the column. Otherwise, it will snap to the top of the visible frame. If the palette gets moved, or if you want to drag it to another frame, do so, and then click the magnet icon to realign the palette with the top of the frame.

If you don't change anything on the Tabs palette, the default tabs will be set according to the unit of measurement you selected in the Preferences dialog box. For example, if you chose inches, the default tabs are set every half inch. As soon as you set a tab, you delete all the tabs to its left. If you set a second tab to the right of the first, you delete all the default tabs in between the two tabs.

Tabs may be set left, center, or right justified, and for decimals or special characters. For example, if you need to set a column of figures, you can either set the tab so they'll align at the decimal points or at the dollar signs in front of the numbers.

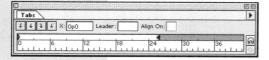

Figure 10.14
Tabs always apply to an entire paragraph.

Select a paragraph, or as many paragraphs as you want the tab to apply to, and click on one of the tab alignment buttons: left, center, right, or special. Then, click the tab ruler at the point where you want the tab, or enter a number in the X box.

To repeat a tab, select Repeat Tab from the Tab palette's flyout menu. Tabs are placed at the same intervals as the distance from the left margin to the first tab. To move a tab, click it and drag it to a new location.

To remove a single tab, click it and drag it off the ruler. To clear all tabs, select Clear from the flyout menu.

If you need to create a decimal tab, or a tab that aligns at a special character, place the decimal tab where you want it and, if it's to align to a special character such as a $, enter the character in the Align On box.

Adding Tab Leaders

A leader is a line of repeated characters, such as dots or dashes, between a tab and the text that follows it. Here's an example:

    Chapter 1..................Pg. 4

To add a leader, select a tab and then type a character or pattern of characters (as many as eight characters long) in the leader box. InDesign repeats the character string across the length of the tab.

In this chapter, you learned about InDesign's editing tools. You learned how to search and find words, and how to change them. You learned how to use the spell checker and how to add your own words to its dictionary. In the next chapter, you'll work with text in frames, threading and unthreading long stories.

11

Adobe InDesign

Flowing Text through Your Document

In the previous two chapters, you looked at preparing text for import and editing it once it's in the document. It seems like a good idea, at this point, to review how to actually import the stories and place them in your publication.

Placing Text in Frames

There are several ways to bring text into InDesign, and, of course, you can also create it there. You can import stories from your word processor, paste text in, or use the drag-and-drop method.

Typing Text in a Frame

What's important to remember is that text must be placed in a text frame. You can't just click the Type tool somewhere on a page and start typing—nothing will happen. First, you need to create a frame. Figure 11.1 shows a full column text frame.

As soon as you finish creating the frame and you release the mouse button, the type cursor jumps up to the top left of the text frame, and you can begin typing.

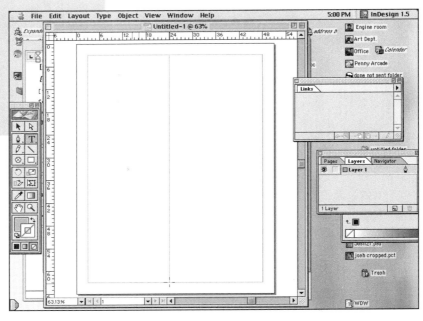

Figure 11.1
If you end up with more frame than text, you can use the Selection tool to move up the bottom of the frame.

If you've already placed a frame, you can simply select the Text tool and click inside the frame. That frame, even if it was originally intended to be a graphics frame, becomes a text frame. The cursor jumps up to the top left, just as if you'd drawn the frame with the Text tool.

Pasting Text from the Clipboard

If you've copied text from the Scrapbook or from another application onto the Clipboard, you can either paste it (Command+V) at the cursor location or use it to replace selected text. When there's no text frame selected or drawn to paste the text into, InDesign will create one in the middle of the page. In Figure 11.2, I've copied this paragraph, using Command+C, and pasted it into a new InDesign page.

The frame InDesign creates for your pasted text is always the same size (about two square inches), even if there's more text than can fit in the frame. Use the Selection tool to reposition the frame where you want it, and to resize it as needed.

If you paste text that you have copied or cut from another InDesign document, it will retain all its formatting. Text pasted from other sources will retain

Figure 11.2
Use the Selection tool to resize the frame.

foreign characters, em and en dashes, and curly quotes. If you have used a word processor that supports styles (for example, Microsoft Word), the text styles will import with the text.

Using Drag-and-Drop Text Placement

One of the advantages that the Mac has had ever since 1986 or so is the ability to multitask. You're used to it now, and you probably have lots of RAM installed, so it's reasonable to have a graphics program, a word processor, and InDesign all open at once. I generally have an Internet browser and sometimes a couple other programs going as well. One advantage to working this way is that if there's something you need to import for your InDesign work, all you have to do is to select it in the other application and drag it onto the InDesign page. In Figure 11.3, I'm dragging a headline from Word into a preselected text frame.

When you drag and drop a text selection, the formatting is lost. However, if you drag and drop the entire file, styles and most—but not all—formatting come along with it, just as if you used the Place command.

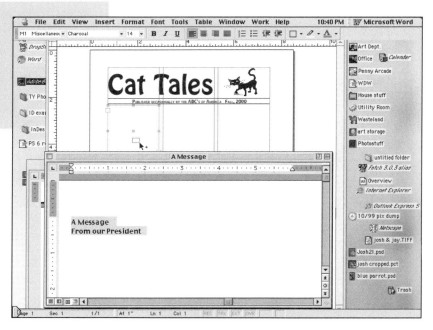

Figure 11.3
You can only use drag-and-drop if your word processor supports it—most of the newer ones do.

Placing Text Using the Place Command

If you want to be certain that all of your formatting remains intact, use the Place command instead of dragging in the text or copying it. You can access the Place dialog box from the File menu, or by typing Command+D (see Figure 11.4).

The preview window shows the first few lines of text, whether your story comes from a word processor or another InDesign document, which is a big help when you have several stories with similar names. Be sure to click the Show Import Options check box to open the Text Import Options dialog box, shown in Figure 11.5. Options are good. In the case of this particular story, which came in as e-mail from a PC user, the options to strip carriage returns and extra spaces between paragraphs are particularly useful.

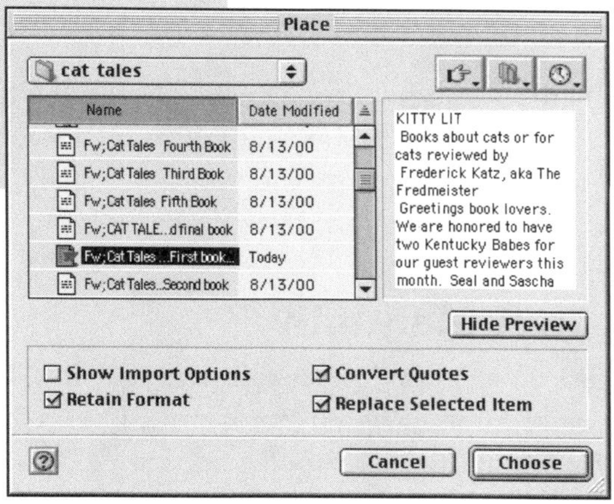

Figure 11.4
Use the scroll bar to find the desired document.

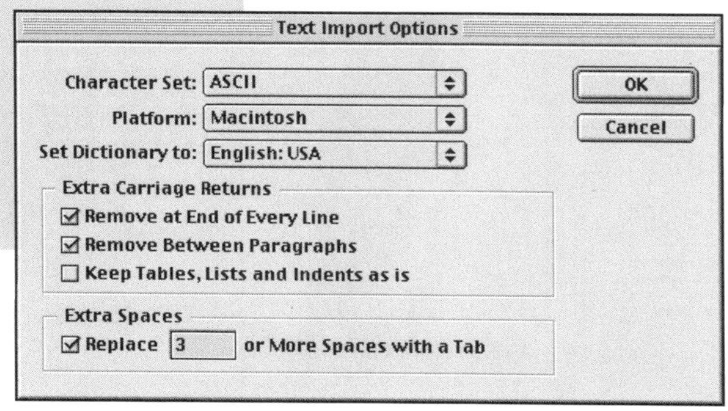

Figure 11.5
Stripping carriage returns this way is even faster than using Search and Replace.

> The remaining unset text is called *overset* text. This term dates back to the days when type was set on long sheets of paper called galleys. The designer and typesetter worked together to specify exactly how much type would fit in the designated space. Sometimes, though, somebody did the arithmetic wrong, and they ended up with more type on the galley than would fit on the page. The leftovers were called overset. In those days, it usually meant setting the type all over again. Today, you can fix it easily by adjusting leading or point size right on the screen.

You have many character set options in the Character Set pop-up menu. The two important ones for most users are ASCII and ANSI. These are both common computer language sets. You'll also see a number of foreign character sets listed. These only apply if you have the appropriate fonts installed. Otherwise, InDesign defaults to the character set of its own default language—English, if you are in the United States, Canada, or United Kingdom.

The text you import using the Place command is placed according to your current selection. If you have selected the Text tool and placed the cursor in a text frame, the text will appear there. If you have selected a frame with the Selection arrow, the text will fill it. If no text frames are selected or if there's no frame present, instead of the text, you'll see a Loaded Text icon, like the one in Figure 11.6. You can use it to create a frame for your text, or to click in an existing frame.

When you position the Loaded Text icon over a nonselected text frame, you'll see it change to text in parentheses. The text icon can also take on other forms, depending on how you have chosen to flow the text.

Flowing text is InDesign's term for actually placing the text in the frame. It's called that because you can choose how you want the text to flow from one frame to the next. You have three options: Manual, Semi-Autoflow, and Autoflow. Take a look at them one by one.

Flowing Text Manually

The Manual text flow option inserts your text only into the selected frame or into a series of linked frames, and it stops at the bottom of the frame. If there's more text to place, you'll see a red plus sign at the bottom right of the frame, in a box InDesign calls the out port. Figure 11.7 shows what this looks like. To reload the Text icon and place the rest of the text, click the out port.

Figure 11.6
The Loaded Text icon is shown enlarged.

Figure 11.7
Click the plus sign to reload the Text icon.

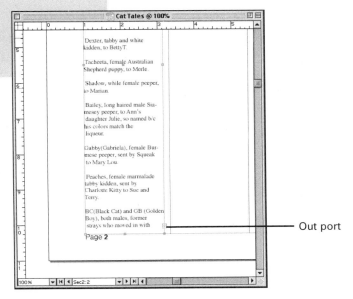

Out port

Flowing Text Semi-Automatically

To flow text semi-automatically, hold down the Option key as you make your first text placement. The text flows one column at a time, as it does with manual text flow. The difference is that instead of having to click the out port to reload the text icon, that happens automatically so you can continue placing more text in frames until you reach the end of the story, as long as you continue to press the Option key.

Flowing Text Automatically (Autoflow)

Placing text automatically is the quickest way to place text, especially if you are working with long stories. When you place text automatically, InDesign creates the necessary text frames to hold it all, and adds additional document pages, if needed. The text frames InDesign creates are fitted within the column guides you have specified. To autoflow text, press and hold the Shift key as you click the Loaded Text icon to place the first piece of text. All the rest will follow.

Threading Text Frames

Text frames can be either threaded or unthreaded. Threaded frames are invisibly connected so that text flows from one into the next. Unthreaded frames are independent. Threaded frames don't necessarily need to be on the same page of the publication, although they can be in adjacent columns or across a multi-page spread.

If you're placing a long story using the autoflow text option, all the frames InDesign creates for you will be threaded. If you add or remove text from the first frame, the last frame will shrink or grow as necessary. This is true of all threaded text, not just text that has been autoflowed.

Each text frame contains an in port and an out port. You saw the out port earlier, in Figure 11.7. The in port is a similar box at the top left of the frame. When two frames are threaded, the out port of the first and the in port of the second contain arrows, showing that the story is continued. Figure 11.8 shows the ports after the story is placed.

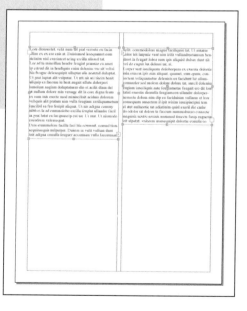

Figure 11.8
The in port and out port are empty, indicating that the entire story has been placed.

Threading Text through Frames

To thread frames, use the Selection tool to click the out port of a frame that has overset text, and then move the Loaded Text icon over the frame into which you want to thread the text. The icon changes to the Thread icon, a pair of chain links. Click inside the frame, and InDesign places the additional text and threads the frames. You can also use the Loaded Text icon to drag a new frame to fill with text. Click where you want the text to begin, and drag the frame until it reaches where you want the text to end.

If you start to thread two frames and change your mind, just click any tool in the toolbox (except the Text tool) to cancel the action.

Adding a Frame in an Existing Thread

As carefully as you plan and place your stories, sometimes the layout doesn't work, and it becomes necessary to make changes. If you decide, for example, that the text should be set in three half-page columns rather than two full-page columns, it's easy to add a third frame in the middle. To add a frame in the middle of a story, use the Selection tool to click the out port at the point in the story where you want to add a frame. In Figure 11.9, I've taken a two-

Figure 11.9
When I drew the middle frame, the text adjusted itself to fit.

column story and added a frame in the middle, so it's now three shorter columns, letting me place photos on the bottom of the page.

Unthreading a Frame

Actually, unthreading frames is so simple that you have to be careful not to do it accidentally. Double-clicking an in port or out port breaks the connection. You can also break threaded frames apart by clicking once on the in port of the frame you want to separate. You'll see the Unthread icon, a pair of outlined, rather than solid, links. Click the icon on the previous text frame, and the text flows back into that frame.

Working with Leftover Text

If you are fortunate enough to have no limit on the number of pages in your document, leftover text is no problem. You just add a page or two and fill them up. Most publications, however, don't work that way. A four-page newsletter can't become a five-page newsletter. So, you have to recompose the text in a smaller font, or with less leading. As an alternative, and if you're sure the author won't scream too loudly, you can edit the story until it fits. But some stories can't be edited without losing a great deal of their meaning. What can you do?

My solution is to store the overset text on the pasteboard while I see how I can adjust other parts of the layout to make room. Perhaps there's a photo that could be smaller, or a different block of text that could tolerate editing. Laying out a page is often a question of tweaking here and there until everything fits in some semblance of good design. When all else fails, save the story for another issue and put in something shorter. Most newspaper and newsletter editors keep files of "fillers" to fill up the blank space on a page. Figure 11.10 shows a filler used to fill out a column.

Managing Links

When you place a story or graphic from any source either by using the Place command or by dragging it in, you form a link from the original item to the InDesign version. (Copying and pasting, however, does not form a link to the

CHAPTER 11 • FLOWING TEXT THROUGH YOUR DOCUMENT

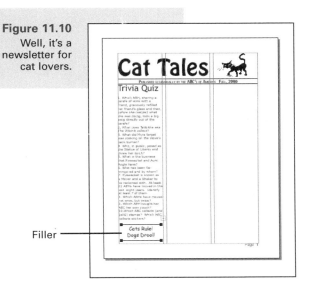

Figure 11.10
Well, it's a newsletter for cat lovers.

Filler

original.) Links are shown in the Links palette, which can be opened from the File menu or by typing Command+Shift+D. If you look at the Links palette in Figure 11.11, you can see that both graphics links and story links appear on the same list.

Why should you care about links? If you have placed a story or a picture, and you go back later and edit the original, or move it from one location of your hard disk to another, the next time you open the publication you'll get a warning like the one in Figure 11.12, telling you that the link needs to be updated.

Figure 11.11
Links to stories and graphics appear on this list.

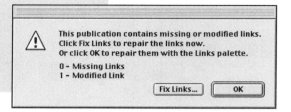

Figure 11.12
You can update the links immediately by clicking Fix Links, or later by clicking OK.

If there's a link that needs updating, it will also show in the Links palette, with a triangular yellow caution sign. To repair the link after you have opened the publication, open the Links palette and double-click the name of the link that needs to be fixed. Doing so opens a Link Information dialog box like the one in Figure 11.13, which tells you what changed, where the file is located, the file size, and other useful information. If you have edited the story both inside and outside of InDesign, you may not want to update because any changes made in the publication's version will be lost.

Click the Update button to import the changes you made in the original to the copy you placed in your publication. If you have moved the original, click the Relink button, and InDesign will scan the hard disk, locate your missing file, and reestablish the link.

There are other link tools available on the Links palette flyout menu, shown in Figure 11.14. You can go to the linked file in your publication, or locate and edit the original. You can also use this menu to sort the order in which links are listed in the palette.

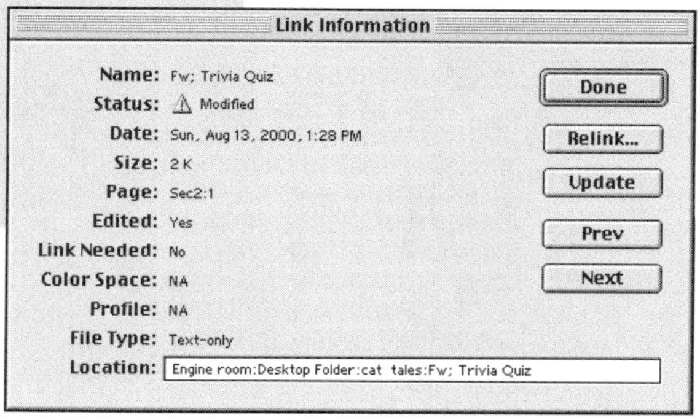

Figure 11.13
You can fix broken links as well as update changes in this dialog box.

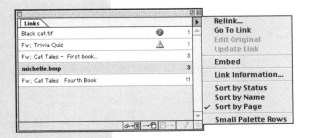

Figure 11.14
If you click Small Palette Rows, the data will be condensed to just type with no separators, which is convenient when you have many links.

In this chapter, you looked at placing text in a publication, flowing it through multiple frames, and how to thread and unthread text frames. You also took a look at link management, and you learned how to update links and how to repair a broken one. In the next chapter, you'll learn how to format all this text you've placed.

12
Adobe InDesign

Applying Character and Paragraph Formatting

Typography is basically the science of arranging and adjusting movable type to make it readable and pleasing. However, typography is even more important than that. How you format characters and paragraphs determines whether they'll be read and understood. If they aren't, your publication is only useful as a birdcage liner.

Most people won't bother to read something that's difficult to see because the type is too small or the lines are too close together. So it's up to you, as the typographer and designer, to make sure the message is clear. Without the content, the words are just ink marks on the page.

Understanding Character and Paragraph Formatting

The Character palette and the Paragraph palette are two formatting tools available in InDesign. Character formatting applies, as the name suggests, to individual characters or words. Paragraph formatting determines how blocks of text are placed, spaced, and aligned. Character formatting is the most basic tool in InDesign and has the most power to change the appearance of your type.

Formatting Characters Using the Character Palette

The first thing to remember is that you must select the text before you can apply formatting. This seems rather obvious, but many InDesign users, myself included, have wasted time trying to change a piece of text with no result, because the program simply didn't know where the change should be made.

The Character palette, which can be accessed via the Type menu, can be displayed either with or without some of its type control options. The options are toggled on and off in the flyout menu, which is shown in Figure 12.1 along with both the long and short views of the palette.

The most important parts of the palette are those that control font family and size, style, leading, kerning, and tracking. The font family is the general

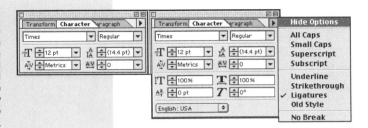

Figure 12.1
Show/Hide Options gives you access to the horizontal and vertical scale, baseline shift, and skew (false italic) commands.

classification of the type style. Font is a word that's often misused to describe the font family. A font is one size and style of type within the family. Helvetica Bold, 14-point, is a description of a font. Helvetica is the family, bold is the style, and 14-point is the size. Often, when people who aren't typographers talk about changing a font, they really mean changing a font family. If one of your clients says, "I don't like that font. Change it," be sure to find out whether he or she wants a different size and style or a different family.

You can change font and size from the Type menu. The Type menu is a good place to look if you want to determine whether a particular font has additional styles. In Figure 12.2, you can see that many of the fonts on the menu have right-pointing black arrows. These indicate submenus that list the styles available in that family.

The Type menu is also one way to access the Character and Paragraph palettes. The other, simpler way is to type Command+T for the Character palette or Command+M for the Paragraph palette.

Changing Fonts and Styles

The fonts that are currently installed on your Mac are listed in the font family pop-up menu. As you can see in Figure 12.3, I have a moderately large collection of fonts. If there are more fonts than can be displayed, you'll see a black arrow at the bottom of the list, telling you to scroll down for more. To change the font family, select a different one from the menu.

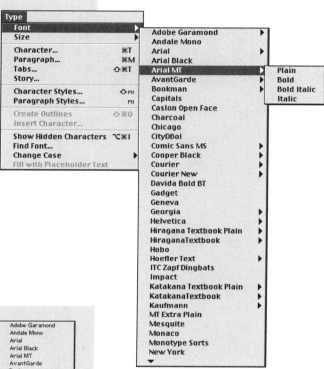

Figure 12.2
Choose a style from the Font submenu or from the Character palette.

Figure 12.3
This collection has a little bit of everything.

Choosing a Size and Style

Use the Character palette or Type menu to set a style and size from the appropriate lists. If you've selected a piece of type, it will change. If you have inserted the cursor in a text frame and it's flashing, everything you type from that point will be in the font you have just set. If you select the Type tool but have no frames active, changes you make in the Character palette become the default for all text you enter into the document from then on.

> **TIP**
>
> If you have many fonts installed, a font-handling utility such as Extensis Suitcase 9 or Adobe Type Reunion is a very helpful addition to your tools. You can group fonts according to which publication or client uses them, or you can sort by headline and body type, character type, or whatever category serves your purpose.

> Serifs are the little lines at the ends of letter strokes. When type was carved in stone, they were chisel marks.

If there are no choices in the Style drop-down menu, as shown in Figure 12.4, it simply means that the selected font didn't come with any additional styles.

If you change from one font family to another, InDesign will attempt to retain the style you have assigned. Thus, Helvetica Bold would become Times Bold. If there's no corresponding style in the font family, InDesign labels the font as missing and replaces it with the Adobe Multiple Master that comes closest, either serif or sans serif.

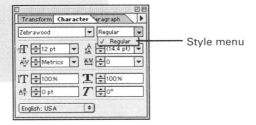

Figure 12.4
"Regular" for this font means rather heavy and wide.

Style menu

Using Other Style Options

Typefaces such as Zebrawood, which mimics the look of an old-time circus poster, wouldn't look right in italic or bold. The font designers don't supply styles they don't think will work, but that doesn't mean you have no style options. The Character palette flyout menu gives you some additional choices, shown in Figure 12.5. Small Caps looks especially good with this typeface.

InDesign has chosen not to make available shadow, outline, or reverse text unless these options are available in the font family. These styles were included with the system fonts from the very first Macintoshes, but type designers became unhappy at the design outrages perpetrated by non-artists who used outline and shadow styles on their carefully drawn type. To preserve the integrity of the fonts, Adobe doesn't make it easy for users to modify them. Nevertheless, you can. Just change the stroke and color of the text. Outline simply uses "paper" as its fill color. Reverse is white or colored type set against a dark background. If you apply a wider, darker stroke and a slightly lighter fill color, you'll have shadow text.

Superscript and subscript are primarily used for mathematical or engineering formulas (E=MC^2, $_3\sqrt{100}$), as well as for footnotes. Underline and strikethrough are seldom used, except when editing a project within a workgroup. Strikethrough places a horizontal line through the middle of characters, while underline . . . well, underlines them. Underlining was used for emphasis in the days of typewriters. It was a writer's code to the typographer, meaning "set these words in italics." Since you can now set type in italics yourself, there's no need to use underlining for emphasis.

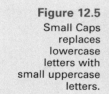

Figure 12.5
Small Caps replaces lowercase letters with small uppercase letters.

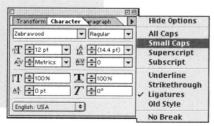

CHAPTER 12 • APPLYING CHARACTER AND PARAGRAPH FORMATTING

Ligatures and Old Style are more useful, especially if you want to earn a reputation for tasteful typography. Ligatures are special characters that combine two letters. Type designers frequently add them to a font because they look better than the two letters set separately. If you select Ligatures from the fly-out menu, InDesign will automatically apply available pairs as you place type. Figure 12.6 shows a sample of text, first without and then with ligatures applied.

Old Style refers to numerals and to the fact that in the "old days," type was set with graceful numerals that ended below the baseline. Old style numbers don't look right if the surrounding text is in uppercase letters, but with lowercase letters they are quite elegant. The notion that everything had to be on the same baseline was a by-product of the typewriter, which couldn't do anything else. When you select Old Style from the palette menu, if Old Style numerals are available in the font, InDesign will use them. Figure 12.7 shows a comparison of Old Style and regular numbers.

Figure 12.6
Notice that the "fi" combination ligature doesn't dot the i—it looks less cluttered that way.

Fifi made a fish souffle.
Fifi made a fish souffle.

Figure 12.7
This font is called Tecton Pro. Notice that the Old Style numbers, on the bottom, seem smaller than the standard numbers.

Tecton Pro:
1234567890
1234567890

Setting Leading and Tracking

Leading (which rhymes with sledding) is the amount of vertical space between two lines of type. Leading is measured in points; the amount of leading is the distance between the baseline of one line of text to the baseline of the next. The baseline is an imaginary line upon which letters like a and b sit. The lowercase letters g, j, p, q, and y all end below the baseline.

Applying Leading

You can adjust the leading yourself or let InDesign apply auto-leading, which uses a default 120% of the type size. For example, 10-point type gets 12-point leading. These numbers are expressed as "ten on twelve" and can be written 10/12, if you need to specify type for someone else to set. If auto-leading is in use, the leading amount will appear in parentheses in the palette, as shown in Figure 12.8.

If you need more or less space in a column, you can adjust the leading yourself, making it smaller or larger as needed. Use the leading pop-up menu, or just type a new number into the box.

Applying Kerning and Tracking

Tracking and kerning both adjust the spacing between letters across a line of type. Kerning adds or subtracts between specific pairs of letters, while tracking equalizes the space across a range of characters. Tracking can be done to any size type, as long as you're careful not to take out too much space.

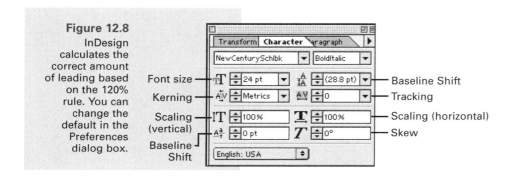

Figure 12.8
InDesign calculates the correct amount of leading based on the 120% rule. You can change the default in the Preferences dialog box.

Kerning is usually only done on headline-size type, 18 points or above. Below that size, it's not generally worth doing.

Working with Kerning

There are several ways to apply kerning. The simplest is to let InDesign do the work by applying metrics kerning, which is automatically applied by default. Font metrics is a system by which the font designer specifies the spacing between specific pairs of letters, called kern pairs. Examples of kerned pairs would include: LA, Ta, Tu, Ti, To, Wa, We, WA, Va, VA, Ya, and Yo. Metrics are included with most fonts.

If you're not happy with the look of metric kerning, or you use a font that doesn't have metrics, or you use more than one font or size on a line, you should try optical kerning. You'll find it at the top of the kerning pop-up menu, shown in Figure 12.9. Optical kerning adjusts the spacing between adjacent characters based on appearance. It tends to be "tighter" than metrics. Figure 12.10 shows some examples of unkerned, metric-kerned, and optical-kerned pairs.

If you're the kind of person who'd rather do it yourself, InDesign provides manual kerning as a third option. You can slide the letters back and forth until you're happy with the way they look. To kern type manually, insert the cursor between the two letters that you want to kern. InDesign displays the current metric or optical kerning value in parentheses in the kerning field on the

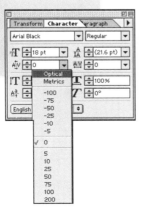

Figure 12.9
InDesign gives you several ways to kern.

Figure 12.10
There's little doubt that kerned type looks better than type that's not kerned.

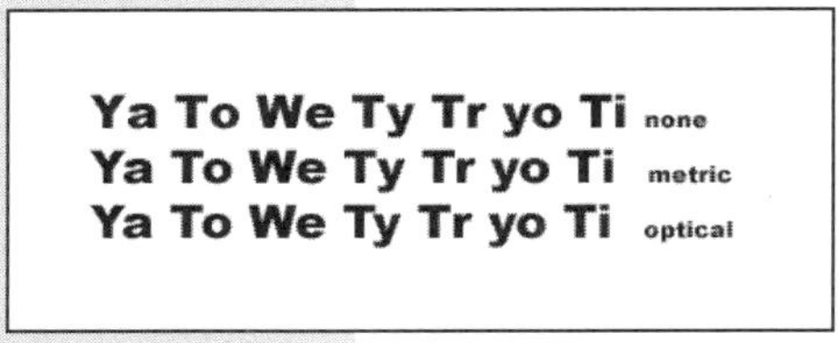

Ya To We Ty Tr yo Ti none
Ya To We Ty Tr yo Ti metric
Ya To We Ty Tr yo Ti optical

Character palette. In Figure 12.11, the pair of letters has been metrically kerned to –107. Kerning is measured in thousandths of an em.

To adjust the kerning, you can either type a new number into the box on the Character palette, or you can kern by eye. If you press Option and either the right or left arrow key, you can open or close the spacing between the letters. Each time you click the arrow, you change the spacing by .02 of an em space in the current size and font. Figure 12.12 shows the respaced letters.

Suppose you don't want the text kerned. Maybe you're laying out a table and you need the letters to be equidistant. To turn off kerning, use the kerning pop-up menu to set the kerning amount to zero.

Figure 12.11
It looks almost right, but it could be just a tiny bit closer.

To
Transform
Character
Verdana
Regular
60 pt
(72 pt)
(-107)
0
100%
100%
0 pt
0°
English: USA

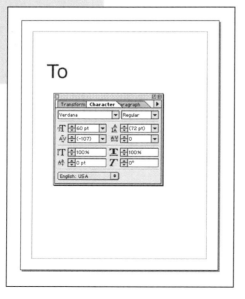

Figure 12.12
From −107 to −140 makes a visible difference.

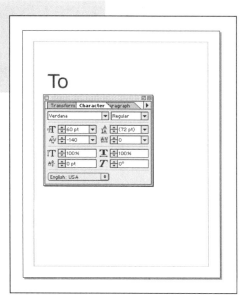

Working with Tracking

Tracking applies to the entire line of type, rather than just to pairs of characters. Tracking and manual kerning won't cancel each other out. You can adjust pairs and then apply tracking to loosen or tighten up the entire line, and the kerned pair(s) will maintain their relative positions. The default for tracking is zero, which means that the type is as set, and no tracking is applied. You can change the tracking by typing a positive or negative number in the box, or by selecting a tracking amount from the tracking pop-up menu. In Figure 12.13, I've applied both positive and negative tracking to a piece of text.

Figure 12.13
Tracking can be applied to as many words, lines, or paragraphs as you select.

Tomato no track
Tomato -25
Tomato +25

Changing Horizontal and Vertical Scaling

Scaling lets you change the height-to-width proportion of a character. This is useful if you want to create an expanded or condensed font out of a normal one. To apply scaling, enter values in the scaling boxes. In Figure 12.14, I have scaled the original type to 160% both horizontally and vertically.

Using Baseline Shift

Baseline shift moves a selected character up or down in relation to its baseline. It's useful if you are setting fractions or if you have an inline graphic that you need to adjust relative to the type around it. Apply baseline shift by entering a value in the box. Positive values raise the character above the baseline, while negative values lower it below the baseline. Figure 12.15 shows baseline shift applied to a dingbat font.

Skewing Type

The Skew effect lets you slant the characters, producing a sort of mock-italic. It's not true italics, because the proportions are distorted as the type is stretched. True italic fonts are designed with the angle in mind. However,

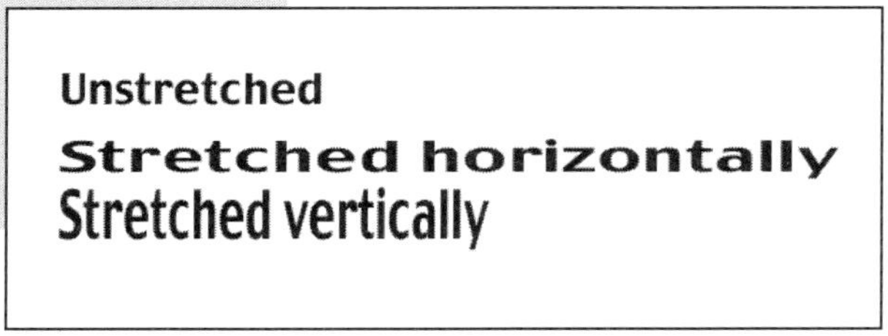

Figure 12.14
Scaling can create new fonts from existing ones.

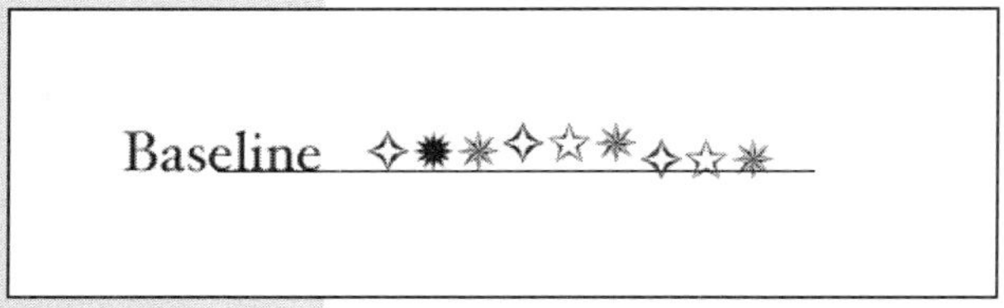

Unstretched
Stretched horizontally
Stretched vertically

Figure 12.15
This shows the dingbats in normal position, shifted up five points, and then down five points.

Baseline ✧✹✶✧☆✹✧☆✹

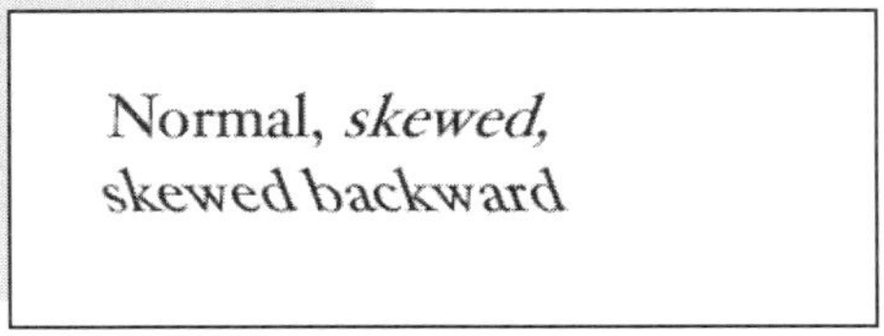

Figure 12.16
I entered –20 for the right slant and 20 for the left.

> Normal, *skewed,*
> skewed backward

skewing can be useful when you need a quick bit of slanted type. You can also apply it to lean left, slanting type backward. Entering a minus number in the box slants type to the right, while a positive number slants it to the left. Figure 12.16 shows these effects.

Formatting Paragraphs Using the Paragraph Palette

The formatting you do in the Paragraph palette affects an entire paragraph (or more if you have selected multiple paragraphs) or any range of text, such as a headline, that has a carriage return at the end. A single word can be a paragraph if it's alone on a line. To apply paragraph formatting to a single paragraph, just click it with the Type tool or select a piece of the paragraph you want to format. To set paragraph formatting for future paragraphs that you haven't yet written or imported, make sure there is no insertion point or selection, and then make your changes.

Setting Alignment

Alignment is easily the most-used paragraph formatting tool. Text is aligned with one or both edges of the text frame. When text is aligned to only one side, it's called *ragged*. If the text is aligned on the left side of the column, it's said to be ragged right. If it's aligned to the right, the ragged edge is on the left. When text is aligned to both sides of the frame, it's *justified*. InDesign gives you several options for setting justified text, depending on how you want the last line to be placed. Justified text can have the last line at the left, which makes the most sense in English, at the right, centered, or forced justified, which will justify the last line regardless of how few characters are in it.

The Paragraph palette, shown in Figure 12.17, makes choosing an alignment as easy as possible. With text selected, choose an alignment style from the icons at the top of the palette.

You can change the defaults for justification. Open the Justification dialog box shown in Figure 12.18 by selecting it from the Paragraph palette flyout menu. Adjust the spacing minimum and maximum percentages if the words look too jammed together or too far apart.

Setting Indents

Indents move text in from the edge of the frame. You can apply left and right indents. Indents may be set either from the Paragraph palette or from the Tabs palette. First line indents should always be set from the Paragraph palette rather than by tabbing or adding spaces. That way, if you later decide to change the column indent or other formatting, the indent will move in relation to the rest of the text.

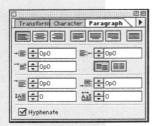

Figure 12.17
From left to right: left, center, and right "ragged," justified with last line left, center, and right, and all lines justified.

Figure 12.18
In case you're wondering, a glyph is any character in a font, including a symbol or number. Letters are letters.

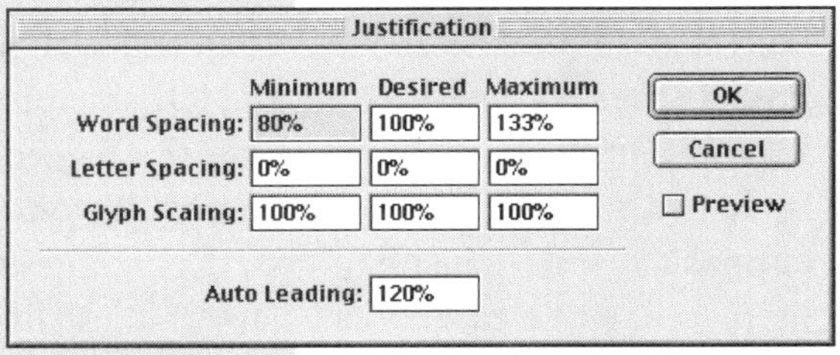

> In a *hanging indent,* the top line of a paragraph extends farther left than the rest of the paragraph.

To set an indent in the Paragraph palette, adjust the appropriate value. If you're adding a first line indent, be sure to use the first line indent box. The left and right indents will indent the entire paragraph, which can be useful when you want to isolate a block of text from the rest of the story.

To set a hanging indent, enter a negative amount for the first line indent.

Setting Paragraph Spacing

InDesign allows you to control the vertical spacing between paragraphs. It's akin to leading, but on a larger scale. You can add space before a paragraph, after it, or both, by entering the appropriate values in the boxes on the Paragraph palette. When a paragraph is at the top of the frame, InDesign will not insert space before it. If you need extra space above the first line, use the Character palette to increase the leading for just that line.

Aligning to the Baseline Grid

All publications include a grid of horizontal lines called the baseline grid. It can be shown or hidden by using the key combination Command+Option+' and it's used to help position text baselines and objects such as lines or graphics. If you lock the baselines of your text, you'll guarantee that the lines of type will be aligned across columns, which looks much neater. To lock the baseline, click the icon that shows aligned lines of text in two columns. The icon with nonaligned columns indicates that your paragraphs are not locked to the baseline grid. Click this if you don't want columns aligned to the baseline grid, or if you'd rather align columns by eye, or by using the same body text and leading across all columns.

Using Drop Caps

Drop caps are not used as often today as they were in the past. A drop cap is the initial letter, or sometimes the first word, of a chapter, which has been set lower so that the next few lines of text are indented up against it. Figure 12.19 shows some examples of drop caps.

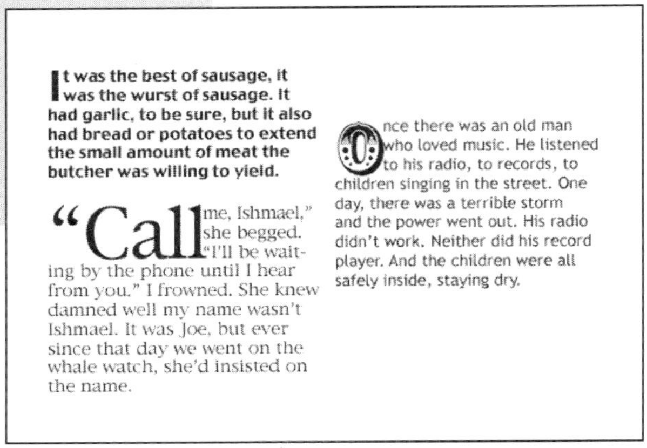

Figure 12.19
The uppercase letter (or letters) grow automatically. You don't have to change the size.

It was the best of sausage, it was the wurst of sausage. It had garlic, to be sure, but it also had bread or potatoes to extend the small amount of meat the butcher was willing to yield.

"Call me, Ishmael," she begged. "I'll be waiting by the phone until I hear from you." I frowned. She knew damned well my name wasn't Ishmael. It was Joe, but ever since that day we went on the whale watch, she'd insisted on the name.

Once there was an old man who loved music. He listened to his radio, to records, to children singing in the street. One day, there was a terrible storm and the power went out. His radio didn't work. Neither did his record player. And the children were all safely inside, staying dry.

To specify how far down the drop cap will extend, enter the number of lines in the Drop Cap Depth field in the Paragraph palette. To drop an entire word, enter the number of characters in the Drop Cap Number field. Remember that quotation marks count as a character.

After you have created the drop cap, you can go back and change its color, apply a fancy uppercase font, or even replace the letter with an inline graphic.

In this chapter, you learned about character and paragraph formatting. Some of the topics covered included applying fonts, styles, and sizes; and using kerning, tracking, and leading to space your type. You also learned about the Paragraph palette and how to set alignment, indents, and spacing. The final items discussed in this chapter were the baseline grid and drop caps. In the next chapter, you'll learn how to combine these formatting attributes into styles.

13
Adobe InDesign

Using Styles and Style Sheets

Suppose you have to produce a series of brochures. Your client wants them all to look as much alike as possible, except for the colors of the type and the paper on which they're printed. This is a pretty common request. Accomplishing this the hard way means setting up the first brochure by choosing colors, fonts, and sizes; deciding how to align the text; and even deciding how to kern pairs of letters in the title. As you saw in the previous chapter, a lot goes into formatting type. So, you finish the first brochure, and then you have to reinvent the wheel, remembering all your formatting and fonts and applying them to the second brochure. Then, you repeat the process yet again for each additional document. It's time-consuming and tedious, and if you forget one aspect of the type formatting, that brochure won't look right. Fortunately, there's a better way—you can apply styles.

A style is a collection of formatting commands that can be applied all at once to selected text, and then saved as part of a style sheet. Style sheets are kept with your InDesign document, and also as part of a template you can build for publications that use the same styles in each issue, such as a newsletter or company stationery.

InDesign also offers a way to create and save both character and paragraph styles. Styles can save time and provide a more cohesive look to your publications.

Creating Styles

It's fairly obvious that you can't apply a style until you have created it. You can load in some text and then create a style for it, or you can create the styles first and then import the text with the style applied. Unlike using the Character and Paragraph palettes, each of which handle different kinds of formatting, paragraph styles incorporate character styles as well. I find it's easier to create paragraph styles, apply them, and then add more character styles to individual paragraphs to which I have already applied the previously created paragraph styles.

As an example, I am working on a newsletter that contains several different kinds of stories. I plan to set all the book reviews in one style and the serious articles and humor in different styles. Each section will have a headline or heading of some sort, a by-line, and text. I'll create the basic styles for each story, and then modify them as necessary to add a by-line size or an italic header.

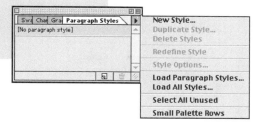

Figure 13.1
I haven't added any styles yet.

Paragraph styles and character styles are found on different palettes, but the two palettes look nearly identical. Figure 13.1 shows the Paragraph Styles palette with its flyout menu. You can open this palette from the Type menu or by pressing F11 (function key).

No Paragraph Style, which is the default entry on the list, means that no styles have been created or imported from a word processor. If you select text on your InDesign page that has had a style applied to it, the style will be highlighted on the list, so you can see exactly which style the text is. This is extremely helpful when you have a long or complicated document.

The easiest way to create styles is to bring them in from an existing InDesign publication or from your word processor, if it supports styles. Be careful: If you import a style from another document and there's a style with the same name and different attributes already in use in your InDesign publication, the new style will overwrite the old one, changing all the text in the publication that uses that style.

To bring in styles from outside your publication, choose Load Paragraph Styles from the Paragraph Styles palette flyout menu. Choose Load All Styles to import both character and paragraph styles.

Defining a Style

The simplest way to create a new style is to format a paragraph of text or a headline so it looks the way you want it to look, and then save the formatting as a style. Be sure you have applied all the character and paragraph attributes that you'll need. With the text selected, open the Paragraph Styles palette and choose New Style from the flyout menu. Figure 13.2 shows the New Paragraph Style dialog box.

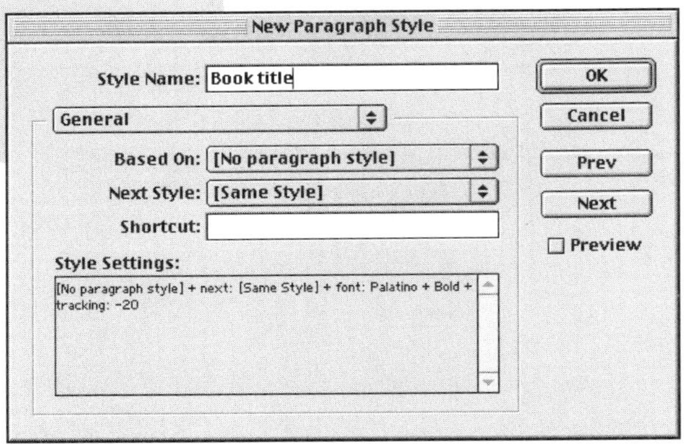

Figure 13.2
Here's where you name and edit your styles.

Enter a name for the new style, preferably one that describes its use. Headline 1, Text, and so on are not really descriptive unless you have very few styles in your publication. As you add more styles to the list, it becomes harder to differentiate between them unless their names are quite specific.

Below the Style Name box, there is a pop-up menu, shown in Figure 13.3. It gives you access to all the possible options for your style. If you want to change anything about the formatting, choose the appropriate option from this list and make your changes. For example, if you want to change the color of the text, choose Character Color. The changes will be incorporated into the style.

The Based On pop-up menu lets you choose an existing style from your palette as a basis for a new style. If, for example, you wanted to create an italic version

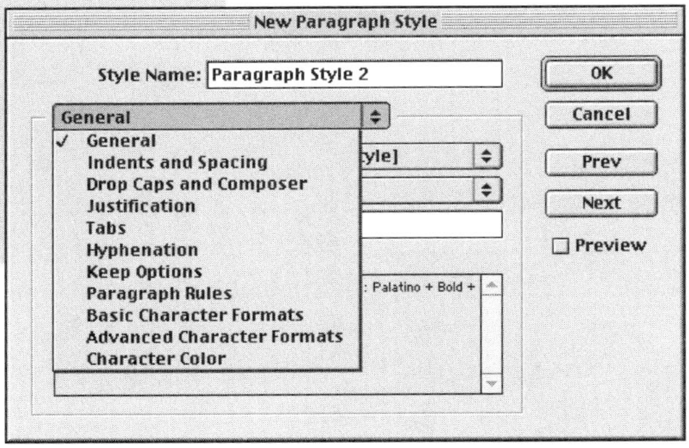

Figure 13.3
You can also use the Next and Previous buttons to cycle through the options in the pop-up menu.

of your basic body text, you would select Body Text from the pop-up menu, and then add the italic and name the style something like Body Text/Ital.

The Next Style pop-up menu has the same list of choices as the Based On pop-up menu. Use it to automatically change from one style to the next every time you start a new paragraph. Say you have a Headline style, a Byline style, and a Body Text style. You might want to start with the Headline style and make Byline the next style, and then go to the Byline style and make Body Text the next style. Then, when you apply the Headline style to some text, the text that follows will be appropriately and automatically styled for you as Byline style. If you want to add more paragraphs of body text, as you undoubtedly will, in the Body Text options, change Next style to Same style. Then, InDesign will keep applying body text to the paragraphs you place until you choose a different style or reach the end of the story.

You can create keystroke shortcuts for your styles. With the style selected, press any convenient combination of Command, Option, and Shift as you press any number on the keypad. A few combinations are reserved for system functions, like Command+Shift+3, which takes a screen shot. These combinations are not available as style shortcuts. In Figure 13.4, I've added shortcuts to my styles.

When you're completely done defining your style, click OK. If you change your mind later and want to change something about a style, you don't have to create a new one based on the old one. Just double-click on the style to open the Modify Paragraph Style Options dialog box, shown in Figure 13.5. As you can see, other than the title, it's identical to the New Paragraph Style dialog box.

There are also a couple other ways to create a style. The first way is to select the text that uses the style you want to copy, and then click the New Style icon at the bottom of the palette. This icon looks like a blank page, as do all New

Figure 13.4
Shortcuts appear on the Paragraph Styles palette, in case you forget what you assigned to a particular style.

Figure 13.5
Use the pop-up menus to make your changes.

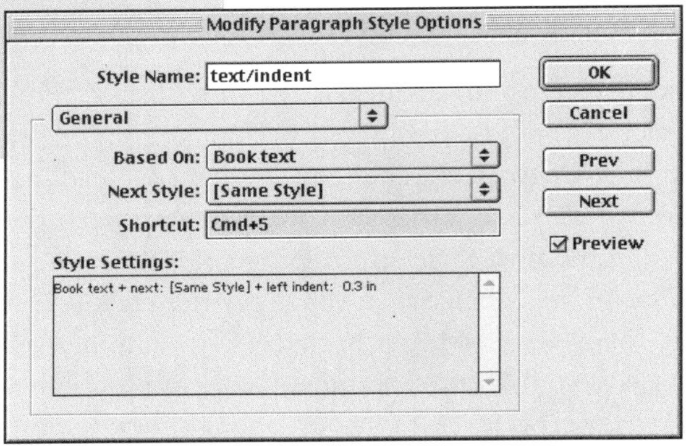

icons. Clicking the icon bypasses all the dialog boxes and creates a style based on your selected text with a default name.

The final way to style type is by using the Eyedropper tool. When you click the Eyedropper on the text from which you want to copy the formatting, the Eyedropper reverses direction and appears to be filled with ink to indicate that it is filled with the formatting you copied. When you position the eyedropper over the text you want to change, a text-insertion I-beam cursor will appear next to the Eyedropper. Drag the Eyedropper to select the text to which you want to apply the style, and it will change. As long as the Eyedropper is full, you can continue to apply the style to additional pieces of type. If you click a different tool, you'll have to refill the Eyedropper to make more changes.

You can use the Eyedropper to copy formatting from one InDesign publication to another, as long as both are open on your desktop. If you copy a paragraph style from one publication and apply it to text in another publication that has the same named style with different attributes, the differences will be applied as local overrides in the destination style.

By default, the Eyedropper copies all the attributes of a type selection. However, you can change the attributes that the Eyedropper picks up. Double-click the Eyedropper tool in the toolbox to open the Eyedropper Options dialog box shown in Figure 13.6. Choose Paragraph Settings or Character Settings in the pop-up menu, and select the attributes you want to copy or deselect those you don't want to copy. (By default, all attributes are selected.) Click OK when you're done.

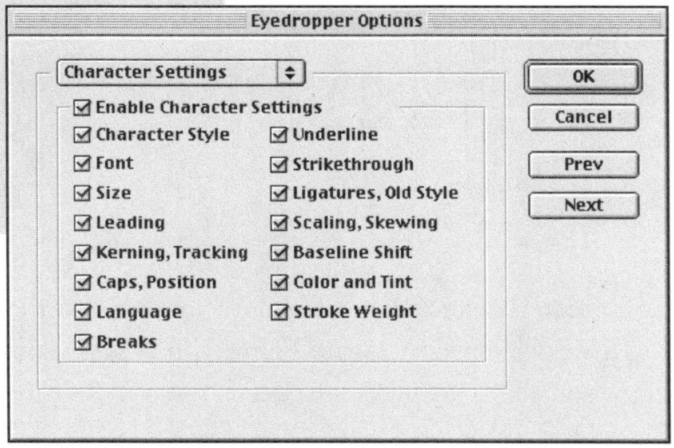

Figure 13.6
The pop-up menu also includes settings for paragraph and stroke and fill attributes.

Applying Styles

Applying styles is like applying character or paragraph formatting. You must first select the text to be styled and then click the name of the style on the Styles palette. If text is selected when you apply the style, the formatting is applied to the selected text. If no text is selected, the style formatting is applied to the text you type from that point.

If your text has any of the following formatting already applied, the styles you apply will not override these styles:

- Superscript
- Subscript
- Underline
- Strikethrough
- Language
- Baseline Shift
- Text Composer
- Special Characters

If you have more common formatting, like bold or italic text, you can protect it from being overridden. To preserve the current formatting when applying a style, press Shift+Option as you click the style to apply it to the selected text. To override all current formatting, press Option as you click the name of the

Figure 13.7
The plus sign indicates that you've added formatting on top of the style.

style. If your text has additional formatting that's not part of the style you applied you'll see a plus sign in the Paragraph Styles palette next to the name of the style when that text is selected, as shown in Figure 13.7.

Editing Styles

I change my mind a lot. After I've created a text style and applied it, I often think that I should have used a different font, or I'll discover at the end of placing a story that I have two lines left. If I reduced the point size or the leading, the lines would probably fit. When that happens, I have to change my styles. You can change the definition of a paragraph or character style at any time. When you make changes, all the text that's been formatted with that style will change. This function is a great timesaver, since you don't have to go through the document and make changes one at a time.

If you want to make a change that applies only to a specific paragraph, you can either make it as a local change to that text, or create a new style based on the one you want to change. To edit a style, double-click the name of the style you want to edit, or select it and choose Style Options from the Paragraph Styles palette flyout menu. Make the necessary changes in the resulting dialog box.

Removing Unused Styles

After you have been working on your publication for a while, you'll have created many styles. This is fine—up to a point. If there are styles that you're not using, perhaps some that you imported from other documents, they'll make your file larger and slower to open and save. You can easily delete these unwanted styles.

To delete a single style, click it on the Paragraph Styles palette and then click the trash icon at the bottom of the palette, or drag the selected style to the trash. To delete all your unused styles at once, choose Select All Unused from the Paragraph Styles palette flyout menu, and then click the trash icon at the bottom of the palette. You'll be asked to confirm the deletion.

Working with Character Styles

Since paragraph styles include character styles, why do you need character styles? Good question, and there's a good answer. Character styles let you modify bits of text within the paragraph, without disturbing the overall formatting. Instead of applying a style to a selected paragraph, you can highlight something like a book title or a Web address and apply a character style to set it apart from the rest of the text while still maintaining the rest of the formatting. For example, if the first word of the first paragraph starts with a drop cap but the following paragraphs don't, applying a character style to only that character lets you create the drop caps without having to remove them from the rest of the text.

Using character styles is just like using paragraph styles. First you create them, then you apply them. Select Character Styles from the Type menu, or type Shift+F11 to open the Character Styles palette. It looks just like the Paragraph Styles palette, so make sure you're using the correct one. Figure 13.8 shows the Character Styles palette and flyout menu, with three styles installed.

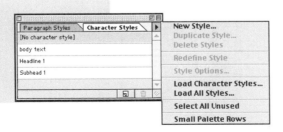

Figure 13.8
These styles were added to modify an existing block of text.

Creating Character Styles

To create a character style, first select a piece of text that you want to format. Make the changes needed, and then choose New Style from the Character Styles palette flyout menu. Enter a name that describes the style, such as URL, text-italic, or hanging indent. If this is a style you'll use often, give it a keyboard shortcut. Use any combination of Command+Option+Shift and a number from the keypad.

Removing Styles

Sometimes you apply a style to a block of text and then realize that you want to change the style, but not that block of text. In that case, you need to disassociate the text from the style, which you can do quite easily. There's a default setting on both the Paragraph and Character Styles palettes called No Style. Select the text or paragraph(s) that you want to disassociate from the applied style, then click No Paragraph Style or No Character Style on the appropriate palette. The link between the text and the style will be broken so that changes you make in the style will not apply to that text. In Figure 13.9, I am removing a style link to a headline.

Figure 13.9
Now, changes I make to the headline style won't affect this headline.

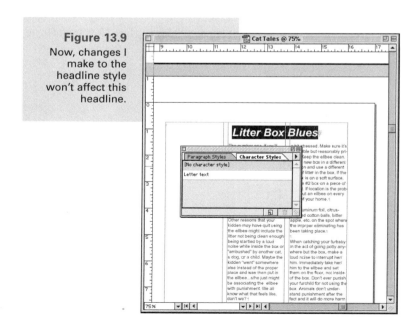

When you remove a style link, you retain the formatting that's currently applied to the selected text. If you want to remove the formatting along with the style link, press and hold the Option key while you click on No Style. This removes all local formatting.

If you have deleted a style that you've applied to some text, the formatting similarly remains unchanged, but if you click on the text, you'll see No Style in the palette.

Using a Style Sheet

Earlier in this book I talked about master pages, and how they can help you with a series of similar publications such as a monthly newsletter. You can save your master pages as a template (stationery, in Macintosh parlance) and reuse the layout every time you want to create a new issue in the series. If you create styles for the text in your publication, you can save them along with the master pages so you'll have your style sheet ready with your basic layout whenever you need to apply it.

Working with HTML Style Sheets

There's a second kind of style sheet that you'll be familiar with if you have done any work in HTML (*Hypertext Markup Language*). HTML language describes the structure of a document. A Web browser interprets HTML language and displays the page you have created. However, there's a good deal of variation between Internet Explorer and Netscape Navigator, and a user might have reprogrammed the way text displays in his or her browser. Your carefully crafted page might look great on one browser and not so great on another. Figure 13.10 shows Netscape's interpretation of basic styles.

To solve this problem, InDesign uses a World Wide Web consortium standard called Cascading Style Sheets-1 (CSS-1), which maintains your chosen styles as long as there's a standard-compliant browser. Cascading Style Sheets allow you to build on existing standard styles and change color, font, size, and so on, to make your type look the way you want.

Nevertheless, you can't expect Web browsers to support every aspect of your formatting. Some attributes don't have an equivalent in HTML language. Other attributes may be recognized correctly by HTML, but ignored by one

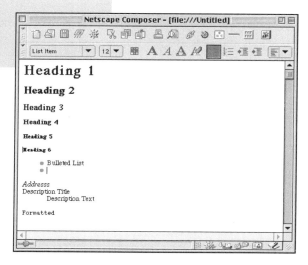

Figure 13.10
These aren't very exciting.

of the browsers. You can export the following attributes: fonts (if they're also installed on the viewer's machine), font size, leading, underline, strikethrough, alignment, indents, space before and after paragraphs, and text color. You can't export baseline shift, ligatures, Old Style attributes, tracking, kerning, paragraph rules, justification, hyphenation, no-break settings, or tab positions. However, if you convert text to a graphic, it will look the same on all browsers when you export it. To turn text into a graphic, first select the text, then choose File, Export to save the page as an EPS.

In this chapter, you learned about saving and applying styles to give your publications a uniform look. In the next chapter, you'll learn about special formatting. This includes foreign characters, dingbats, bullets and numbered lists, and hanging indents.

Adobe InDesign

PART V
Typography

14

Adobe InDesign

Working with Special Formatting

> A *dingbat* is a small decorative device. Dingbat fonts have a variety of designs and symbols. Some examples of dingbats are ✦ ✧ and ✳ ❦

Straight text usually gets the point across very well, but for more interesting pages, you sometimes need to apply some typographic tricks. You could, for example, write a list in paragraph form, but it doesn't have much impact that way. Making it a bulleted or numbered list sets it apart from the surrounding text, and adds emphasis and interest to the page. Some data is best conveyed in table form. For some applications, hanging indents are more elegant and interesting than plain block text. And there are foreign words using foreign characters or accents, other special text characters like trademark and copyright symbols, and dingbats—all of which require special formatting.

Using Hanging Indents

A hanging indent is, in effect, the opposite of a regular indent. Instead of the first line of the paragraph being set in from the margin, as in a normal indent, a hanging indent places the first line up against the left margin and indents the lines that follow. In Figure 14.1, I've created hanging indents to set off the items in a list.

Figure 14.1
Hanging indents separate paragraphs, making it easier to find the one you want.

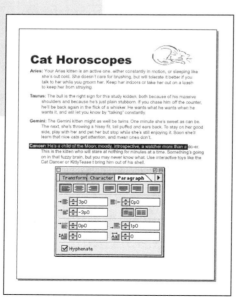

Hanging indents, aside from looking cool, are an ideal way to set off items that have a short title and a block of text, such as the horoscopes in Figure 14.1.

There are two ways to create hanging indents. The first, which is also shown in Figure 14.1, is to use the Paragraph palette. You begin by indenting all the text by some reasonable amount. In this example, I used three picas as a left indent. Then, I set the first-line indent (it's the icon below the Left indent) to the negative of the amount I indented. My indent was three, so my first line indent should be minus three. When you press Return, all the first lines of the paragraphs will shift left.

The second method for setting hanging indents is to use the Tabs palette, found under the Type menu, as seen in Figure 14.2. First, select all the text, and then drag both of the triangular markers at the left of the Tabs palette ruler to indent the block of text.

Now, drag the top triangular marker to the left until it's up against the left margin. All the first lines will shift with it, and your paragraphs will have hanging indents.

Creating Bulleted and Numbered Lists

If you're doing your writing on an up-to-date word processor such as Word or WordPerfect, it makes the most sense to format a numbered or bulleted list there rather than in InDesign, because the word processor can do it automatically. Figure 14.3 shows Word's Bullets and Numbering dialog box. You have a choice of bullet shapes, as well as the option to use a custom character as a bullet.

The bullets import to InDesign along with the text, even if you've used an unusual character like a tilde (~) or slashes (/\/\/\). As long as the same font is available in InDesign, the bullets you choose will appear in your publication.

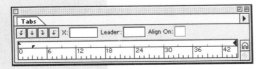

Figure 14.2
Hanging indents can also be set on the Tabs ruler.

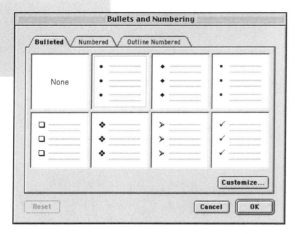

Figure 14.3
Do you prefer circles, arrows, or boxes?

Of course, you might not decide to use bullets until you have already brought the text from the word processor into InDesign. That's not a problem. You can set bullets easily, though not automatically. The advantage to doing so is that you have greater control over the placement of the bullets, as well as their font, color, and size. You can even make up a bullet style and apply it for nearly automatic formatting.

Adding Bullets

When you're creating bulleted lists in InDesign, you have several decisions to make:

◆ Will the list be indented or flush left?
◆ Do you want the text to have a hanging indent?
◆ What kind of bullets should you use?
◆ How much space should you leave between each bullet and the text?

These are all valid questions to consider. Figure 14.4 shows some possible answers.

You know how to create indents of various kinds, including hanging indents. To insert bullets, either use the standard en bullet (Option+8) or choose a more interesting one from one of the symbol fonts. In the example in Figure

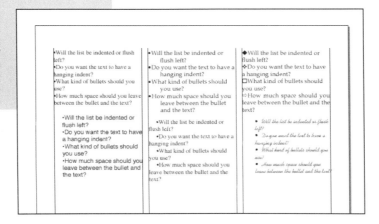

Figure 14.4
These are just some of the possibilities for formatting a bulleted list in InDesign.

14.4, I used characters from Wingdings, which is one of several dingbat fonts. (If you don't have Wingdings, you probably have Zapf Dingbats installed. It's another good symbol font.) You can use InDesign's stroke and fill features to make a custom bullet with different stroke and fill colors, or a hollow bullet with just a stroke and no fill. The possibilities are limited only by the size of the character.

To see the characters available within a font, use the Type, Insert Character command to open the Insert Character dialog box, shown in Figure 14.5. Choose a font and style from the menus at the bottom of the dialog box, and you'll see all the characters available in that font. Scroll down to see the lowercase and Option key characters. Use the large and small mountain icons to enlarge or reduce the size of the characters displayed.

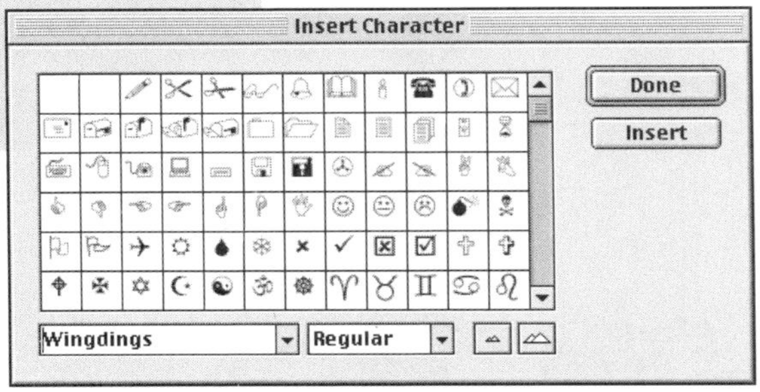

Figure 14.5
This font is Wingdings.

The best way to add a space between bullets and text is to set a tab. In Figure 14.5, I've set a tab about four spaces from the bullet. You don't want to leave any more space than this; less is okay. You just want to keep the bullet from bumping into the text, as it does in one of the examples in Figure 14.6. Be sure to select the entire list before you set the tab.

Working with Numbered Lists

Bullets are cool, but there are times when it is more effective to use a numbered list. Numbered lists can also be created in a word processor and imported into InDesign. You can still customize the numbers, just as you can with imported bullets. There are a number of ways to set numbers. You can place a period, a right parenthesis, or just a space after each number. You can make the numbers bold, set them larger than the text, use a different font, or even make them a different color.

The combination of tabs and bullets or numbers used to assemble a numbered or bulleted list can take quite a lot of time to apply. Once you've developed the look you want for bullets or numbered lists in your publication, save it as a paragraph style, so you can apply it consistently throughout the document. If

Figure 14.6
Set the tab reasonably close to the bullet, but leave a little "breathing room."

the bullets or numbers have different attributes, first save the paragraph style, and then save the character style as an override to that kind of paragraph.

Using Dingbats and Symbols

As you've just seen, dingbats can be used as bullets. They have other uses as well, depending on the particular font you have installed. You aren't limited to Zapf Dingbats or Wingdings. There are literally hundreds of dingbat fonts, and many are shareware or freeware. I did a quick search with the search engine Google and got 8,000 references. That's a lot of fonts. Figure 14.7 shows the characters from a font called Webdings.

In Figure 14.8, I've added astrological symbols from Wingdings to my horoscope page. You can also use dingbats to separate paragraphs, to mark the end of a story, or as inline graphics. As separators, dingbats should be centered on the page. For balance, use an odd number.

Only fonts accessible from the keyboard are truly dingbats, but you can also use small graphics as bullets, or for any of the other possible dingbat

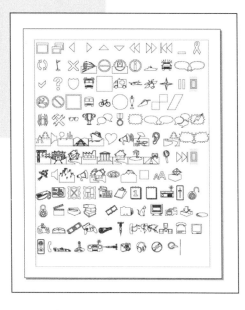

Figure 14.7
If you'd rather use solid dingbats instead of outlines, change the stroke and fill to black or another color.

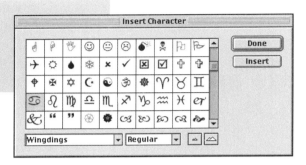

Figure 14.8
Here are some of the many dingbats in the Wingdings font.

placements. In Chapter 15, "Using Type as a Design Element," you'll learn about placing inline graphics.

If you have Macromedia Fontographer or Pyrus FontLab installed on your Mac, you can turn your logo or any other graphic into a font. My husband had to create an icon for a company for which he consults. He drew a lit match, and then brought it into Fontographer and traced it. He saved it as a character in a custom font, so now he can print it at any point size large enough to show it, and even set up a character style for it. This allows him to repeat the icon many times in a publication without having to drag in a large graphics file each time. Figure 14.9 shows the final logo in Fontographer.

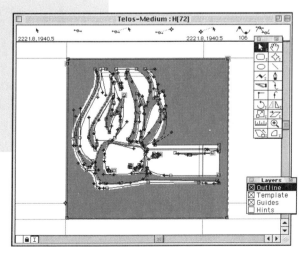

Figure 14.9
Custom characters make it easy to place icons or logos on your pages. *(Figure courtesy of Jay Rose.)*

Applying Run-In Heads

Another way to make text stand out is to use different type for the first line of a story. Many magazines start a story with a large initial cap, followed by the rest of the line or the next few words in small caps. Figure 14.10 shows an example of this technique. This is called a *run-in head* or a *lead-in*. Select the text and change it using the Character palette. Once you set up the run-in head the way you like, be sure to save it as a character style, so that you can use it throughout the publication.

Using Foreign Characters

Many foreign words have found their way into English conversation, and it's important to be able to spell them correctly. In this case, *correctly* means with the accents and special characters in place. It's not difficult; most fonts are international, and have all the required letters and accents available. To locate and apply the accents and special characters, use the Insert Character dialog box, which you can access using the Type menu. In Figure 14.11, I have opened the dialog box and scrolled down to reveal a set of foreign characters. Some of these are used in French, others in Spanish, German, and the Scandinavian languages.

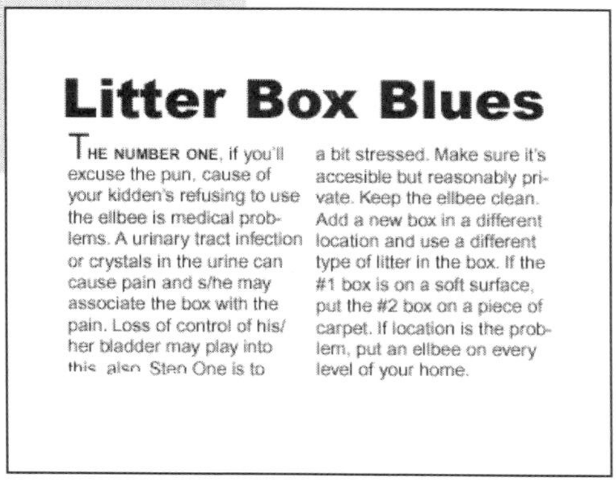

Figure 14.10
The first pair of letters may need kerning.

Litter Box Blues

THE NUMBER ONE, if you'll excuse the pun, cause of your kidden's refusing to use the ellbee is medical problems. A urinary tract infection or crystals in the urine can cause pain and s/he may associate the box with the pain. Loss of control of his/her bladder may play into this also. Step One is to a bit stressed. Make sure it's accesible but reasonably private. Keep the ellbee clean. Add a new box in a different location and use a different type of litter in the box. If the #1 box is on a soft surface, put the #2 box on a piece of carpet. If location is the problem, put an ellbee on every level of your home.

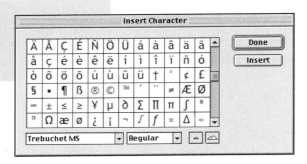

Figure 14.11
Umlauts, cedillas, and tildes ... oh my!

Actually, you can type many of these characters without using the Insert Character dialog box. There are shortcuts for adding the more common accents. Here are some that you might need:

To apply	Press these keys
Acute (´)	Option+E and then type the letter
Cedilla (ç)	Option+C; With a capital letter, Option+Shift+C
Circumflex (^)	Option+I and then type the letter
Grave (`)	Option+` and then type the letter
Tilde (~)	Option+N and then type the letter
Trema/Umlaut (¨)	Option+U and then type the letter

You can also use shortcuts for many common symbols, including:

Character	Name	Key Combination
•	En bullet	Option+8
©	Copyright	Option+G
®	Registered	Option+R
™	Trademark	Option+2
§	Section	Option+6
¶	Paragraph	Option+7
†	Dagger	Option+T

Formatting Tables

Quite often, the best way to convey certain kinds of information is to use a table. Tables are easy to read, so users can find what they want quickly, and they can dress up your pages. They're the best way to deal with numbers, particularly if you want to make the numbers and their identifiers line up in a coherent manner.

Tables can be shaded, with lines separated by rules, depending on the data and how you want it arranged. You can even place a gradient behind a table — just be sure it is not so dark that it obscures the text.

InDesign doesn't have a built-in table editor, so you might find it helpful to set up your table in your word processor and import it. You can then tweak it in InDesign. Or you can simply use tabs to separate the columns and do the formatting in InDesign. Never use spaces when creating a table. They don't import and often they don't print correctly, even in Word.

In Figure 14.12, I've formatted a simple table in InDesign, using decimal tabs to separate the descriptions from the numbers.

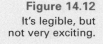

Figure 14.12
It's legible, but not very exciting.

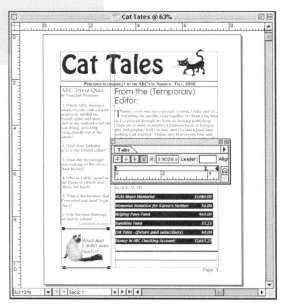

Now that I've got the table items in place, I can start to play around with formats. Simply adding lines across the table makes it easier to read. Adding a tint behind every other line makes it still easier. Figure 14.13 shows the result.

InDesign doesn't give you much flexibility for setting text in tables. Because you are limited to using tabs to lay out the table, you can't have cells of varying sizes. But you can use the different tab alignment tools to make your tables look better. For example, if you have table headings you can select them and click the Center Tab style button (it's the second button on the Tabs ruler). They'll slide neatly into the center of their fields.

The Tabs ruler has left, center, right, and decimal alignments. To use the special character alignment, choose the decimal alignment and enter a character in the Align On field. In Figure 14.14, I've set it up to align on decimal points. If you were setting up a multiplication table or a set of math problems, you could align on the times or plus sign.

Use decimal tabs to align numbers, even if the numbers don't have decimal points. By default, InDesign assumes that every number that doesn't have an internal decimal point has a period at the end. If you happen to have a table

Figure 14.13
Now this table is easier to read.

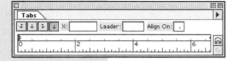

Figure 14.14
You can align to any character you enter.

that has no value for one of the cells, use a dash to indicate that there's no data. If it's within a column of numbers, the dash will align as if it were just ahead of a decimal point. In Figure 14.15, the tabs are aligned to the percent sign.

Placing Rules into Tables

You might think that the easiest way to separate table rows with lines is to simply draw them in, and then use the Align palette or the Arrange command from the Object menu to space them evenly. Well, that works—until you have to add another row to the table or change the font size, and then that system falls apart and you have to go back in and change every line by hand. Fortunately, InDesign gives you a better way to do this, with a feature called Paragraph Rules. This function will automatically place a line, in any width or style, above or below selected paragraphs. Remember, as far as InDesign is concerned, each line of your table is a paragraph, as long as it's separated by a

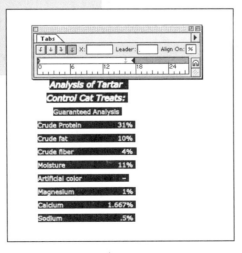

Figure 14.15
Numbers are easier to read if they're aligned.

carriage return. When you place paragraph rules, they flow with the text, so if you decide to add a row of text to the table, it will automatically come with a line before or after it. If you remove a row from the table, the corresponding line will vanish.

To apply Paragraph Rules, first select the text and then open the Paragraph palette, if it's not already open. From the flyout menu, select Paragraph Rules to open the dialog box shown in Figure 14.16.

Click the Rule On check box to activate the rules. If you don't check this box, all the options in the dialog box will be grayed out. Decide how thick you want the rules to be. One point is about right for body copy size type (up to 14 points). Beyond that, you might move up to a 1.5-point rule, or even a 2-point rule for larger text. For Rule Above, increasing the weight moves the rule upward. For Rule Below, increasing the weight pushes the rule down.

Select Overprint Stroke if the paragraph rule will be printed over another color or gray tint. This helps to avoid errors that occur with printing misregistration. Click Preview to see how your rules will look.

Choose the width of the rule. You can choose either Text or Column. Text starts at the left edge of the frame and brings the line across to the end of the line. Column runs the full width of the column from the left edge to the right. If the left edge of the frame has a column inset, the rule begins at the inset.

To set the vertical distance of the rule above or below the baseline, enter a value for Offset. Rules can be positioned accurately to within one thousandth of a point (.001).

Figure 14.16
Rules can go above or below a paragraph.

The offset for a rule above a paragraph is measured from the baseline of the top line of text to the bottom of the rule. The offset for a rule below a paragraph is measured from the baseline of the last line of text to the top of the rule. Figure 14.17 shows the difference between rules above and below the line.

You can, as an alternative to rules, place stripes behind your lines of text. Stripes are placed in the same way. Remember to make the weight of the line several points larger than the text, and to apply a light enough tint so that your text shows over it. If you set the rules above the paragraphs, use a minus offset to move them down. Figure 14.18 shows this effect.

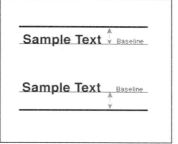

Figure 14.17
You can apply rules both above and below a line. Place one, then the other.

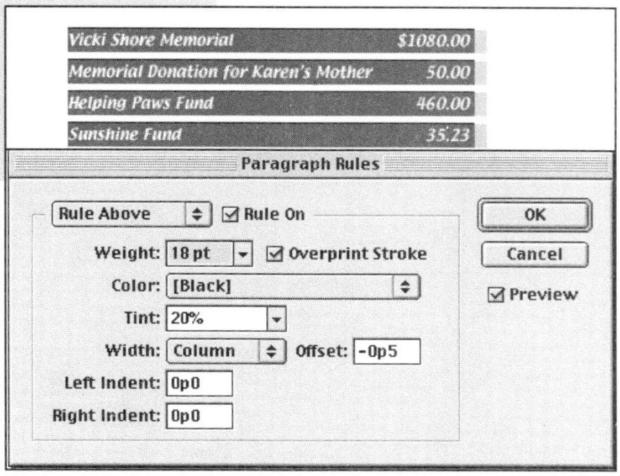

Figure 14.18
Using Preview lets you see where your lines are going.

The best reason for setting the tint this way is that if you add or delete a line, the rules (in this case the tint shading) will move with the text.

In this chapter you learned about special text characters and how to use them. You also learned about bulleted lists, numbered lists, foreign characters, and how to set up tables. In the next chapter, you'll do some typographic tricks.

15

Adobe InDesign

Using Type as a Design Element

T ype exists to convey a message; that's no surprise. What is surprising, though, is that even when the type is in a language you don't speak, it tells you something. It communicates via its style, its position on the page, and even by its font family. You wouldn't set an invitation to a tea party in the sort of bold, black type generally used for the direst headlines. Nor would you set a "War Declared" headline in script, or in a character face more appropriate for circus posters (at least, I hope you wouldn't).

Using Different Kinds of Type

You already know that there are several categories of type. Some typographers separate them into as many as eight to ten different categories. For our purposes, though, there are three kinds you need to know about: serif, sans serif, and character.

Serif Type

Garamond, Bookman, and Times are common examples of *serif* type. Each letter has little marks, or serifs, added on at the end of each stroke. Serifs date back to the time when letters were carved in stone. The serif was a simple chisel mark that ended the stroke and helped keep the stone from fracturing along that line. Figure 15.1 shows some typical serif fonts.

Sans Serif Type

Font families such as Helvetica or Bauhaus fit into the *sans serif* category, along with other fonts that don't have serifs at the ends of the strokes. In Figure 15.2, I've assembled some samples of sans serif fonts.

Figure 15.1
Just a few of the many serif faces.

> Bookman
> Caslon
> **Cooper Black**
> AdobeGaramond
> Georgia
> Palatino
> Times New Roman

Figure 15.2
Sans serif fonts have clean, modern lines.

> Arial
> **Charcoal**
> Comic Sans
> **Gadget**
> Helvetica
> VAG Rounded
> Verdana

Character Fonts

Into this broad category, I'm including decorative fonts, calligraphic and script fonts, monospaced fonts, and graphics fonts. Decorative fonts are often used for drop caps and for headlines. Choosing the right one can be tricky; there are literally thousands of fonts available. If yours is a formal publication, such as a business newsletter or corporate report, it might be wise to forego using a lot of character fonts. Also, character fonts other than delicate script should be used at a larger point size (preferably at least 18-point type), as they're nearly impossible to read at text size. Figure 15.3 shows a decorative font called Parisian at various point sizes.

Script fonts are pretty, and, some say, "feminine." To me, they can also suggest dignity and history, like fine steel engravings or the Spencerian handwriting our great-grandparents used. Some are just loose and free and fun. Figure 15.4 shows some different script fonts.

Monotype or typewriter fonts look as if they were written on a typewriter. Some have serifs, some don't. What sets these fonts apart is that each character is the same width as the others, whether it's a W or an i. Monotype fonts

Figure 15.3
See what I mean about being hard to read?

> This is Parisian at 36 points.
> This is Parisian at 24 points.
> This is Parisian at 12 points.

Figure 15.4 These are all script, but each conveys a different mood.

Alexei Copperplate
Brush Script
Dom Casual
Murray Hill
Zapf Chancery

can be used either to add the look of a typewriter to an advertisement or a poster. They also can be used when you want a partial line of type, such as a URL, to stand out from the rest of the line. Figure 15.5 shows a sampling of monospaced fonts.

Graphics fonts, or what I sometimes call fun fonts, are like pepper in soup: a little goes a long way. Graphics fonts suggest a situation or place. They're not appropriate for all uses, but if you have a project like an ad or a poster they can really make it an attention-grabber. Figure 15.6 shows a few fun fonts.

Graphics fonts can make good headlines or logos for ads, but like the character fonts, you need to use them at a large point size. You also need to choose them wisely. A font like Arriba is perfect for the headline in an ad for a Mexican or Caribbean restaurant, but it's not dignified enough for a message from the chairman of the board.

You can find fun fonts just about anywhere you look for regular fonts. You can buy font collections from many Mac software sources, including, of course, Adobe. You can also do a search for Mac shareware fonts on your favorite search engine. Google found 76,000 sites.

Figure 15.5 Some letters stretch to fill their spaces, while others shrink.

```
Andale Mono
Courier
Monaco
```

Figure 15.6
Fun fonts are fun to collect.

ALGERIAN
Arriba Arriba
Blippo
Broadway
DAVIDA
Hobo
MESQUITE
STENCIL
SHOTGUN
ZEBRAWOOD

You can easily get carried away when you start adding fonts to your collection. Each font you add has to be loaded every time you open a word processor, InDesign, or any other program that handles type. The solution to this is to invest in a font handling utility such as FontReserve or Extensis Suitcase. These utilities help you separate your fonts into groups, so you only need to load the set of fonts you intend to use. Figure 15.7 shows Suitcase in use.

Figure 15.7
I've created two suitcases. You can create and fill as many as you want.

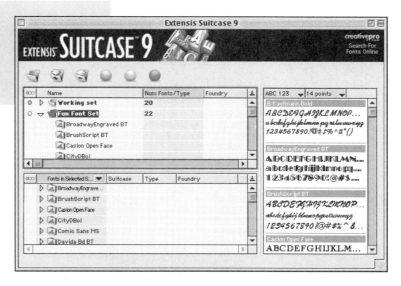

I keep all of my plain, "working" fonts in one suitcase, which is automatically installed whenever I start up the computer. Because it's not installed until after the system loads, the computer starts up more quickly, which is a definite advantage. I can turn on the other suitcase whenever I need it, and not have to load all 40-odd (some *very* odd) fonts every time I boot the Mac to check my e-mail.

Rotating Text

English-speaking people are used to reading left to right, so it's fairly unusual to want to set type some other way. Because it *is* unusual, type that's not set left to right is an attention grabber, and can be a nice design element. Rotating text and graphics is simple. InDesign has a Rotation tool in the toolbox that enables you to grab a handle on any frame and move it.

In Figure 15.8, I'm rotating a block of text. As you can see, I've also done this to other blocks on the page. Used in this way, the text has a nice casual feel, like notes tacked onto a corkboard.

Notice the Rotation box at the top left of the text box. This represents the pivot point for the rotation; the object you're rotating swivels around that

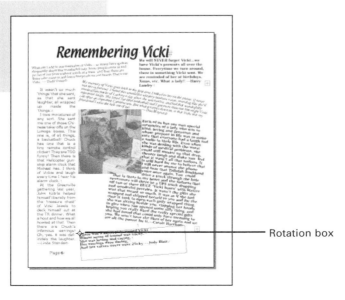

Figure 15.8
I've rotated the text only a few degrees, but you can go full circle.

point. You can drag the point before you start the rotation if you'd rather have the object rotate around its center or some other point.

You can also apply rotation numerically, if you want a precise 90- or 180-degree turn, or if you just happen to have a mathematical mind and don't want to do rotation freehand. Go to the Object menu and click Transform, Rotate, as shown in Figure 15.9.

The menu command opens the Rotate dialog box, shown in Figure 15.10. Just check the Preview check box, type your rotation amount into the angle window, and watch it happen. If the rotation is not the right amount, you can change it, using negative numbers as well as positive numbers. You can, of course, also enter the numbers on the Transform palette, but you don't get a preview.

When you're working on something that folds in half horizontally, such as a table tent sign for a restaurant, it's much easier to set both sides of the sign in the same direction and then select and rotate one side by 180 degrees (see Figure 15.11).

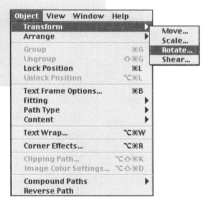

Figure 15.9
You can also move, scale, and shear using numbers.

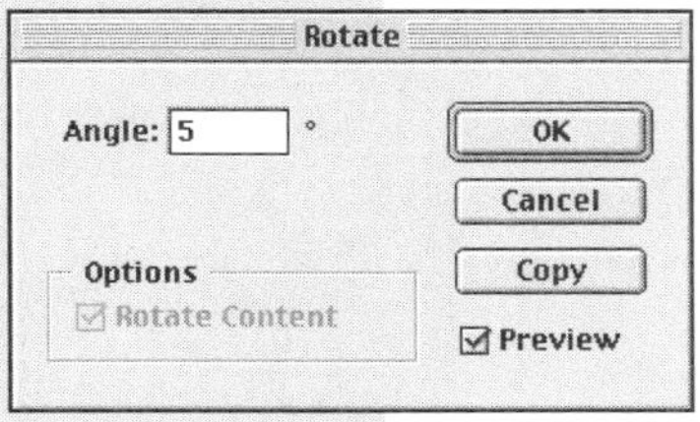

Figure 15.10
If plus five degrees raises the right corner of the frame, minus five degrees will lower it the same amount.

Figure 15.11
Group the objects on the page, then rotate 180 degrees.

Importing Headlines from Illustrator or Photoshop

When InDesign doesn't do everything you want it to with type, remember that you can create your headlines in Photoshop, Illustrator, or CorelDRAW, and then place them in your InDesign document. Figure 15.12 shows a simple logo that I created in Photoshop for a Web page. The basic font is Hobo, and I added the embossed effect and drop shadow to make the type stand out. I also decided to replace the letter L with a graphic. To bring it into an InDesign document, all I need to do is to use the Place command on the File menu, or type Command+D.

Figure 15.12
If the type has to be there anyway, you might as well have fun with it.

Transforming Text into a Path

What if you don't own Photoshop or Illustrator? Does that mean your type can't be creatively modified? Heck, no. There are many things you can do right in InDesign.

Text, as used in a vector graphics program (which technically InDesign is), is made up of a series of outlines. These are stroked and filled like any other path you might draw, and the result is solid text. InDesign, unlike some graphics programs, allows you to access the outlines to apply your own strokes and fills, thus changing the character of the text. You can apply a one-point stroke in the text color to make the letters look fatter, or you can fill the letters with white or a different color, or even a gradient. Figure 15.13 shows some simple examples.

In the Figure 15.13, the first letter is untouched. The second has a 1-point stroke and no fill. The third letter has a 1-point stroke and a medium gray fill. The fourth has a 2-point stroke and no fill. The fifth has been fattened with a 4-point stroke. The sixth has no stroke, and a medium gray fill. The second word has a 1-point stroke and a gradient fill.

You can create these type tricks using the stroke and fill boxes in the toolbox. To change the weight of a stroke, use the Stroke palette, as in Figure 15.14. I've made the stroke 10 points wide, and changed the fill to a color. The result is a new, rather funky typeface that still manages to be legible.

Figure 15.13
You can make a letter stand out by stroking the edges and applying a lighter fill.

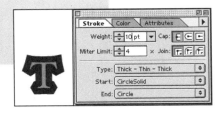

igure 15.14
Don't be afraid to experiment.

Filling text is handled using the toolbox, too. Click on the fill box and select a color or tint to apply. Use the Color palette to select your fill color or use the default setting, which is a black stroke and no fill.

If you decide to try a gradient fill, be aware that InDesign centers the gradient in the text frame. If you move the text, the gradient appears to move too. The same gradient is applied to any text on the page to which you have applied a gradient, so you can't have one letter grading one way and another grading a different way.

Using White Space

When you fill up a page with text and pictures, it can be hard to read because there are so many elements competing for your attention. It's easy to concentrate on what you're putting into a page, to the point that you ignore what you ought to leave out. The term *white space*, sometimes called *negative space*, describes the open space between design elements. It can be between words or paragraphs of text. It can be space inside or around a graphic, or between the elements of the page.

If the reader's eye is to flow from one paragraph to another, you need to give it a way to do so. That way can be through use of white space. White space is essential for providing spatial relationships between visual items, and actually guides your reader's eyes from one point to another. Readers' eyes are naturally drawn to the negative spaces. The white spaces don't have to be large—just a generous gutter between text and pictures can make a big difference, as you can see in Figure 15.15. The page on the left is jammed full of stuff. On the

Figure 15.15
You don't need a lot of space, just enough to keep things from running into each other.

right page, the same elements have just a bit of added space, and there's a noticeable difference in the "reader-friendliness" of the page.

Leading the Reader's Eyes

The way you place your stories on the page can determine whether they will be read. This is particularly important in something like a newsletter or an ad, where you want the reader to see everything there is to see. As noted previously, the reader's natural tendency is to look from top left to bottom right. If you're setting up a newsletter, the main story goes at the top, just under the banner. Balance it with a picture, and place the second most important story below the fold, again with a graphic if one is available. If not, you can use a pull quote or some other device to break up the page.

Wide margins also direct the reader's attention into the center of the page. Remember that the wider the columns, the more space is needed between them. If you have three columns of type, the gutter can be narrower than if there are only two. Allow ample leading, for the sake of legibility. Tightly spaced text "darkens" the page and makes it less attractive.

When you use a photo, try not to place it so that the subject is looking away from the page. If you have a right-facing subject, place the photo on the left. That way the subject appears to be looking at the text, not away from it. If there are no characteristics (like type) in the photo that would give away the secret, you can flip a picture horizontally to give you more flexibility in the layout. Your reader will tend to look in the same direction as the photo subject, and you want to keep the reader's eyes on the page.

Creating Coherent Documents

The main goal for your publication is to be read and understood. While it's fun to use exotic fonts and quirky layouts, don't lose sight of the goal. When you have too many gimmicks on a page, your readers won't bother with it. Limit yourself to a few interesting but legible fonts per document. Make your headlines stand out by leaving white space around them—that's better than big, black type for attracting attention.

In this final chapter on typography, you looked at ways to use type as part of your design. You learned about character fonts and how to use them, and how to rotate your text. You saw some of the tricks that can be accomplished by converting text to paths and then stroking and filling them, and you learned about importing headlines and logos from a more versatile program such as Photoshop or Illustrator. Finally, you learned about white space, and how to ensure that your document is "reader-friendly." In the next section, "Pictures on the Page," you'll delve into the mysteries of graphics.

Adobe InDesign

PART VI

Pictures on the Page

16
Adobe InDesign

Importing Graphics

While it's true that InDesign comes with some useful graphics tools such as the gradients and borders, it was never meant to be a tool for artists. For anything more than the most basic filled shapes, you really need a graphics program like Adobe Illustrator or Photoshop. I personally recommend either or both of these to anyone using InDesign, simply because the user interface is so similar that you'll already be halfway there as far as learning the program. If you're going to be working with photographs in your publication, Photoshop is almost a necessity. You can do basic picture editing and retouching in a simpler program like Adobe PhotoDeluxe or Lemke's Graphic Converter, but these applications lack the versatility of Photoshop. Today, many scanners and digital cameras ship with a copy of Photoshop LE, which is more than adequate for most of your graphics needs. Use your graphics program to create graphics, and use InDesign to add borders and basic shapes to your layout.

Preparing Graphics to Import

Assuming that you have an appropriate graphics program, what should you do to your pictures before you bring them into InDesign? Given the limitations of desktop-publishing software as opposed to graphics software, the answer is inevitable. You should do as much as you can. Once you place a picture, you might decide to scale it larger or smaller, or even to crop it. That's fine—InDesign can handle those chores perfectly well. However, it can't convert a color photo to a duotone, or change the resolution of a picture, or even touch up the contrast. It's always a good idea to do as much preparation as you can before you save the picture for placement. Your pictures will look better and communicate your ideas better if you take the time to perfect them.

Understanding Bitmaps and Vector Graphics

There are two different ways to put a picture on the screen or page. One way is to describe the picture as a collection of dots or bits, each bit carrying information about color and brightness. These dots and bits combine to make a picture called a bitmap, also sometimes called pixel-oriented or raster graphics. The other method is to describe a picture as a series of lines and curves, much like InDesign describes type. This kind of picture is called a vector graphic, or object-oriented graphic. Photoshop works primarily with bitmapped art, while Illustrator is a vector-graphics program.

Choosing a File Format

Most graphics programs can save your work in many different formats. InDesign can work with over a dozen different kinds of graphics files, so you have some choices for file saving. How you save depends mostly on what you're saving. *Line art*, which is anything that's made of lines rather than continuous tones, is best saved as an EPS, PDF, Illustrator, or PICT file. Scanned images, photos, and other continuous tone art should be saved as TIFFs, Photoshop files, or in one of the Web formats (GIF, PNG, or JPG). Figure 16.1 shows the differences between line art and continuous tone art.

InDesign imports all the following file formats for graphics:

- **BMP**. This is the Windows bitmap format.
- **EPS**. Encapsulated PostScript is a vector format preferred by professional printers and publishers. DCS (*Document Color Separations*) is a variation on this used for color separations.
- **GIF**. GIF stands for Graphics Interchange Format, and is commonly used for Web documents. It was first developed by CompuServe.
- **JPEG**. This format is also sometimes abbreviated as JPG. It's a common Web format that uses lossy compression on bitmaps to make smaller files. The name comes from the developers of JPEG standard, the Joint Photographers Expert Group.

Figure 16.1
The dog is line art; the cat is a continuous tone photo.

- **AI**. This is the native vector graphics format for Adobe Illustrator.
- **PCX**. This is PC Paintbrush format. It's a popular bitmap format from DOS, and is still used in Windows.
- **PDF**. This is Adobe's Portable Document Format. A variant of EPS, it's mainly used for any kind of document that will be viewed cross platform. Any computer can open and read a PDF file. In publishing, it's now common practice to send a PDF to your printer or service bureau.
- **PSD**. This is the native bitmapped graphics format for Adobe Photoshop.
- **PICT**. This is a Macintosh graphics format that can be either bitmapped or vector, depending on the application that created the file. PICT files are seldom used for professional work, but you might find clip art in this format.
- **PNG**. PNG stands for Portable Network Graphics. This format was introduced by Adobe for lossless compression of Web graphics, and is an alternative to the more popular GIF and JPEG formats.
- **Scitex CT**. This is a continuous tone bitmap format used by Scitex prepress systems, and some high-end printers.
- **TIFF**. TIFF stands for Tagged Image File Format. It is the most useful bitmap, and is a standard for professional publishers and graphics editors.
- **EMF**. EMF stands for Extended Windows Metafile, and is a format native to Windows. It is seldom used in professional documents.

Which one of these formats you should use depends on how you intend to publish the final product. If it's a Web page, obviously you need browser-compatible graphics formats, which are GIF, JPEG, or PNG. GIF is best used for line art or for any graphic that uses spot color rather than continuous tone. GIF is *not* a good choice for a photograph, because it's limited to 256 colors, or 216 if you only allow cross-platform color. (Macintosh and Windows PCs see colors differently, as do their users.) If you're putting photos in a Web document, JPEG is probably your best bet. Be aware, though, that repeatedly saving the same JPEG file will eventually degrade the image. This is because JPEG uses what's called a lossy compression system. Every time you save a JPEG, the program doing the saving looks at the image and decides which pixels can be averaged together. Eventually, you end up with a screen equivalent of a tenth-generation photocopy. PNG uses lossless compression, which gives it an advantage, but older browsers may not support it, which means they won't display your pages properly.

Assuming that you're printing to some variety of PostScript printer, either a home or office laser printer or a commercial printshop's imagesetter, there are several things you need to consider. InDesign can output its files as PDFs, EPS files, prepress files, or as HTML, and you need to give some consideration to the way you import your graphics. (Of course, if you're going to print to a home or office inkjet printer, there will be different things to consider.)

Working with TIFFs

> *LZW* is a compression algorithm developed by and named for Lempel, Ziv, and Welch.

If your publication will be professionally printed, TIFF is pretty much the universal graphics standard, and it's always a good choice. TIFF supports 24-bit color (16.7 million colors) in either CMYK or RGB mode, and they can be compressed, depending on how you choose to save them. Using no compression is the safest method, but most Macintosh and Windows programs also support LZW compression. Figure 16.2 shows Photoshop's TIFF Options dialog box.

Working with EPS Files

Vector graphics files can be problematic when they contain more than just lines. Your Illustrator EPS might contain lines and curves, fonts, color, and possibly even an embedded bitmap image. The different elements within the file can cause problems when you attempt to print your publication. If you use type in your vector art, you generally have the option of converting it to curves. Do so—this turns your type into vector art rather than a text file within the graphic, and makes it easier to save and print. If you choose not to convert your text to curves, be sure that your service bureau or print shop has the same fonts installed. Otherwise, the text within the graphic will print in some default font, probably Courier or Times.

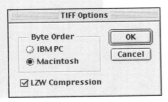

Figure 16.2
If you're passing files to a PC, it might be safer to choose no compression.

> **NOTE**
>
> There's an exception to this general rule. If your graphic has a lot of text, don't convert it to curves. You'll make the file very large, and the image might be slow to print or not print properly. Either make sure that the printer you're using has the same fonts or set the text part of the image in InDesign and wrap it around the graphics image as necessary.

Another problem that sometimes occurs with EPS graphics files is that they might not display properly on-screen, even though they print correctly. There's a reason for this. When you save a file as an EPS, it also saves a preview image as part of the header. This quickly draws a low-resolution version of your graphic when you paste it into InDesign or some other program. However, even though most graphics programs have no difficulty creating an EPS, many have trouble reading them. Taking files cross-platform between Windows and Macs will further muddy the waters. In most cases, you'll get a gray box in place of the EPS. You might also see a box that looks like a frame with an X through it. InDesign gets around this problem when it can, by creating its own preview image when you import an EPS. To save file space, if you're saving an EPS graphic in a program such as Photoshop or Illustrator, be sure to set the Preview creation options to None, as I have in Figure 16.3.

Working with PDFs

There are also some issues with PDFs. When you bring an existing PDF into InDesign, you can either open it as an InDesign document, by using the File,

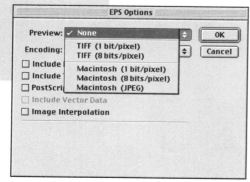

Figure 16.3
This is how you tell Photoshop not to save a header.

Open command, or you can use the Place command (Command+D) to import it. If you place a PDF that has more than one page, only the first page will be placed. This means you really can't import multi-page PDFs. Because InDesign places PDFs as graphics, you can only crop, resize, or skew them; you can't edit any text within the PDF, nor can you work with any other components of the PDF file. It's better to open the PDF as a separate InDesign document, and then move components into the document on which you're working. PDF features such as sounds, movies, hyperlinks, and so on are not imported into InDesign because the program doesn't support them.

Working with PICT Files

If you are only planning to print to an inkjet or home/office laser printer, you can use PICTs as your graphics format. PICT is the Macintosh-native format that supports either vector or bitmap art, depending on the program that created it. PICT is also the standard format for Macintosh screen captures. InDesign has no trouble working with PICTs, except that it can't make color separations from them. Because PICT is a non-PostScript format, PostScript printers cannot handle color separations except possibly at very low resolutions.

Placing Graphics Files

Let's assume for a moment that you have converted your graphics to TIFFs and are ready to import them into InDesign. Remember, TIFFs are bitmap images. Use the Place command (Command+D) or File, Place to open the Place dialog box, shown in Figure 16.4.

Be sure to select the Show Import Options check box. After you click OK, you will see the Image Import Options dialog box, shown in Figure 16.5.

Use the Image Import Options dialog box to specify a screen resolution. 72 dots per inch (dpi) is standard, but if you're not a critical viewer, 36 dpi is fine; you just want to see that there is an image there. You don't need high resolution for screen display, as long as the resolution in the actual graphics file is adequate for your printing methods. Most of the time, you can't tell the difference. In Figure 16.6, I've imported the same file twice, once with 36 dpi resolution and once with 72 dpi resolution. Seen at 100%, the lower quality image isn't that much worse.

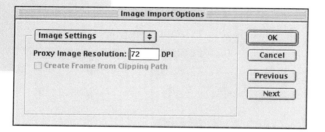

Figure 16.4
The Place dialog box handles both text and graphics.

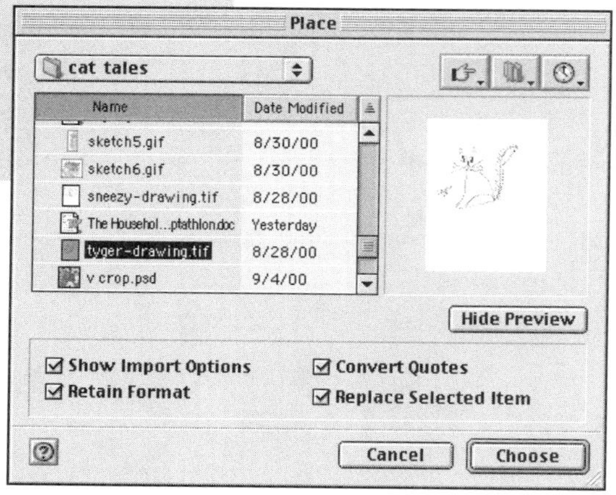

Figure 16.5
The options are the same for all types of images.

If you've been working with clipping paths in Photoshop or Illustrator, you already know how helpful they can be. When you import a graphic with a clipping path, be sure to turn on Create Frame from Clipping Path. If there's no clipping path present, the Create Frame option will be grayed out in the Image Import Options dialog box. If you have no idea what a clipping path is, don't worry. We'll cover clipping paths and their uses in Chapter 18, "Working with Special Effects."

In the Image Import Options dialog box, the color management options are on the same pop-up menu as image settings. If accurate color is important, turn on Enable Color Management. (You'll learn all about working with color management in Chapter 20, "Using Color Models and Color Modes.") Color management is a method of adjusting the colors on the monitor to match those on the printed page. It relies on a set of color profiles for the various kinds of monitors and printers. There are also default settings for use when you

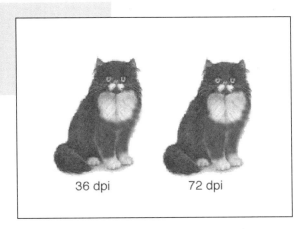

Figure 16.6
There's a slight difference, but the graphic is still useable.

don't know the printer or monitor type. Set your color profile to Use Document Default unless you already understand the use of CMS profiles. If you do, and assuming there's a profile for your output device, use it. Set Rendering Intent to Perceptual, then go ahead and place the graphic.

Working with Inline Graphics

Inline graphics are a convenient way to keep text and art together. Many word processors, including both Microsoft Word and WordPerfect, allow you to embed a graphic into your text. InDesign imports the graphic along with the text, provided you use the Paste command to place it. Graphics embedded with OLE or the Publish and Subscribe command do not import, because InDesign doesn't recognize those actions.

The graphics you import inline appear in their preview (low resolution) format. You can overcome this problem by using the inline graphics as placeholders, and replacing them with the high-resolution images just before you print. Figure 16.7 shows an inline graphic placed in Microsoft Word. When you drop the story into InDesign, the picture will be in the same relative location as it is in the Word document. If you rethread the text, the picture will stay with it, unless you choose to remove the graphic.

If you're using graphics as characters (for example, as a corporate logo or icon), the easiest way to do so is to use a program such as Macromedia's Fontographer

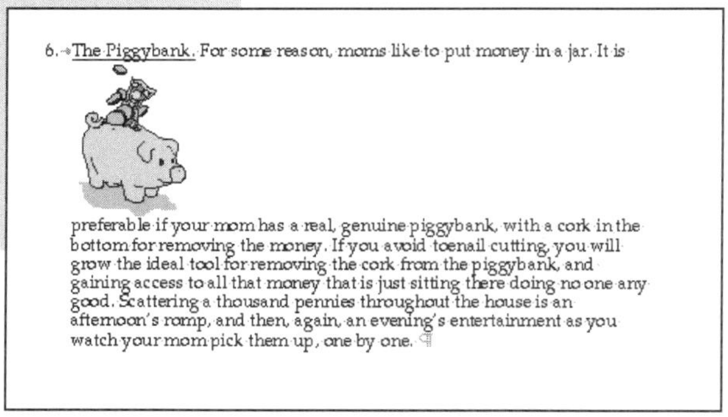

6. The Piggybank. For some reason, moms like to put money in a jar. It is preferable if your mom has a real, genuine piggybank, with a cork in the bottom for removing the money. If you avoid toenail cutting, you will grow the ideal tool for removing the cork from the piggybank, and gaining access to all that money that is just sitting there doing no one any good. Scattering a thousand pennies throughout the house is an afternoon's romp, and then, again, an evening's entertainment as you watch your mom pick them up, one by one.

Figure 16.7 Use the Insert, Picture, From File command to locate and embed your graphic.

to turn the graphic characters into a dingbat font, rather than placing a graphic each time you need one.

In this chapter you looked at ways to prepare a graphic for import. You learned about the many graphics formats that InDesign supports, and which ones are better choices for Web or print work. You learned how to apply the Place command, and finally how to add inline graphics in your word processor for import into InDesign. In the next chapter, you'll work on the changes you can make to a picture once you have imported it.

17

Adobe InDesign

Making Changes to Your Images

No matter how well you plan your graphics and how much you do to them before you import them, it's inevitable that sooner or later, you'll have to change something. Maybe the picture is too big for the space—or not quite big enough. Maybe you want to paste photos on a page at an angle, scrapbook style, or on the sides of a virtual cube. InDesign can do all of these actions with some simple mouse work.

You can also use outlines to frame your pictures. You can center a picture within its frame automatically, and you can create masking and layout effects by pasting objects into the frame.

Cropping a Picture

Every time you place a picture into an InDesign document, it is contained in a graphics frame. You might have drawn the frame first, and then placed the picture in it, or you might have allowed InDesign to create the frame as you pasted the picture. In either event, the picture is pasted starting in the upper-left corner of the frame. This often means that the picture has a good deal of white space at the right and bottom of the frame. Figure 17.1 shows a typical import. I drew a frame first, and then placed the graphic in it.

Figure 17.1
When you place a graphic, it anchors itself to the upper-left corner of the frame.

As you can see the frame is too big. There's white space to the right and at the bottom of the picture. The simplest way to crop is to grab the frame handles with the Selection tool and drag until the frame is the right size.

> **TIP**
>
> If you have trouble resizing the frame to precisely fit the picture, go to the View menu and turn off Snap to Guides, or press Command+Shift+;

If the picture has parts that you want to hide or mask out, you can do so by making the frame smaller and dragging the picture around in it as necessary (see Figure 17.2).

The frame around the image (the bounding box) shows the cropping. If you use the Direct-Selection tool, you can move the picture around inside the bounding box. If you move the picture far to one side, you'll see white space at the side of the picture. It's as if your bounding box is a cutout on the page, and you are moving a large photo under it to hide or reveal parts of the picture. In Figure 17.3, you can see the photo dragged to one side. The larger frame still indicates the full size of the photo, and the smaller frame is the bounding box

Figure 17.2
The bounding box is the actual size of the picture.

Figure 17.3
Use the Direct-Selection tool to move the picture.

> The term *clipping path* is often used in desktop publishing to describe a mask applied to, and saved with, a specific image. In your InDesign document, a clipping path is just a variation of the graphics frame.

that was used for cropping. As you slide the picture over, you can see its edge and some white space in the cropped window.

When you're moving or cropping a picture, be sure you use the correct tool and grab the correct frame. It can be tricky because the frame, the imported clipping path, if any, and the picture's bounding box are all shown as blue lines.

Centering an Image within a Frame

To center an image within its frame, or to resize a picture to fit a frame or a frame to fit a picture, you can use the commands in the Object, Fitting menu, shown in Figure 17.4.

In Figure 17.5, I've applied the commands shown in Figure 17.4 to a picture of a statue of Frederick Chopin that I placed four times on a blank page. The photo I used is slightly taller and narrower than the frame I drew for it.

The first image uses the Fit Content to Frame command. The frame is wider than the image and not as tall, so fitting the image into the box results in the image being compressed vertically and expanded horizontally.

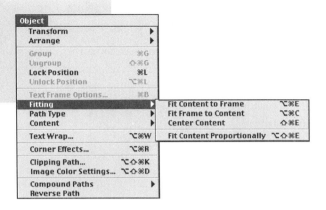

Figure 17.4
Use a menu command or one of the key command shortcuts.

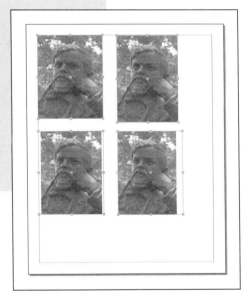

Figure 17.5
The Fitting commands applied to the same picture, clockwise from the top-left: Fit Content to Frame, Fit Frame to Content, Fit Content Proportionally, and Center Content.

The second image fits the frame to the content. As you can see, the frame changes size and shape to match the size of the photo. In this case, there is no distortion of the image, but this option might not be desirable if the picture must fit into a space with a predetermined height.

In the third example, the image is centered in the frame both horizontally and vertically. This exposes white space on both sides of the image, and trims some off the top and bottom. You could crop the white space by moving in the sides of the frame.

The fourth example uses the Fit Content Proportionally command. This retains the aspect ratio of the picture, while compressing it vertically to fit the frame. Because the photo is narrower than the box, there's white space at the side. All you would need to do to this example would be to drag in the right side of the frame to line it up with the edge of the picture.

Reshaping Frames

Tired of the same old rectangles? I am. If you don't like a four-sided frame, you can make one that's a different shape. The frame tools include both ellipse and polygon frames in addition to the rectangle. You can frame pictures as ovals or as stars if you want; Figure 17.6 shows an example.

You can also use the Direct-Selection tool, or the Pen tool and Anchor Point tools to reshape any frame. Just select the frame and drag the handles to reshape it. Because the Direct-Selection tool moves the frame independent of its contents, you can drag the handles wherever you want them. In Figure 17.7, I've reshaped the frame around Chopin in several different ways.

These shapes are much more dynamic than a simple rectangle. The trick is to fit them into a page of text without having them look out of place. Wrapping text around them helps, but be sure to leave some white space around the edges of the shape so it doesn't look crowded. (You'll learn about text wrapping in Chapter 18, "Working with Special Effects.")

Figure 17.6
Well, he was a musical star in his day.

Figure 17.7
You can create pretty much any shape you can imagine.

Resizing an Image

Cropping resizes the frame but leaves the actual image intact. Resizing an image shrinks or expands both the frame and whatever it contains. Resizing can be done in two ways: by using the Scale tool and dragging the frame until it's the right size, or by entering percentages in the Transform palette. In Figure 17.8, you can see the Transform palette and one of its pop-up menus. Be sure to set the same value for both horizontal and vertical scaling to avoid distortion.

Figure 17.8
If the menu doesn't have your choice, just enter your percentage in the box.

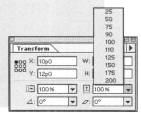

To scale an image by dragging the frame, select the Scale tool from the toolbox, or type S. When you drag the handles on the frame, the picture will change size. Drag the handle in, over the image, to make it smaller; drag the handle out to make the image larger.

If you're not sure about this scaling business, you can work on a copy of your image rather than the original. Double-click the Scale tool to open the Scale dialog box shown in Figure 17.9.

To scale a picture proportionally, click the Uniform option and enter a percentage. Numbers greater than 100% enlarge the picture, while numbers less than 100% scale it smaller. Be sure to check the Scale Content check box. If you don't, you're changing the frame without the graphic, in effect cropping the graphic. If you check the Preview check box, you'll see the immediate result of your scaling, so you can adjust the percentage up or down as needed before you commit to the transformation. If you click Copy instead of OK, you'll place a scaled duplicate of your image over the original, anchored in the upper-left corner. Drag the copy aside to access the original (see Figure 17.10).

Applying Rotation and Skew

You've already learned about text rotation, and rotating a graphic is done in the same way. You can use the Transform palette and enter an amount of rotation in degrees, as I have in Figure 17.11. You can also rotate a graphic by hand, either by selecting the Rotate tool from the toolbox or by pressing R and dragging a corner of the frame until you reach the angle you want.

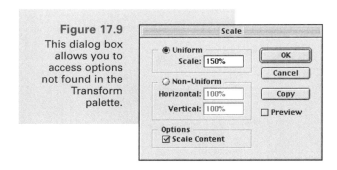

Figure 17.9
This dialog box allows you to access options not found in the Transform palette.

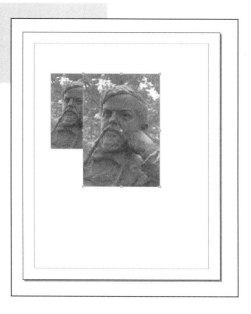

Figure 17.10
The original was hiding under the scaled copy.

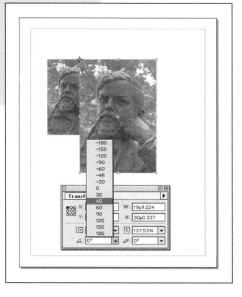

Figure 17.11
The angle pop-up menu gives you choices, or you can enter a number in the box.

As with the Scale commands, there's a Rotate dialog box that opens when you double-click the tool. As you can see in Figure 17.12, it's similar to the Scale dialog box. You can enter a number of degrees to rotate the object. Check the Rotate Content check box to transform the image and not just the frame. Check Preview to see what effect your rotation has, and click on Copy instead of OK to make a rotated copy of your image.

Don't forget that the effects of these transformations can be cumulative. If you rotate an object by 10° and then you decide you want it rotated more, so you enter 20° in the dialog box or on the Transform palette, you'll actually rotate the object by 30°. However, this won't happen if you open the Transform palette flyout menu, shown in Figure 17.13 and uncheck Transformations are Totals. (It's checked by default.)

The Transform palette flyout menu also allows you to flip an image horizontally or vertically. This is occasionally useful when you're laying out a page and want people in the photo to look to the right instead of to the left, for example. Just be careful that there are no details that will reveal your secret!

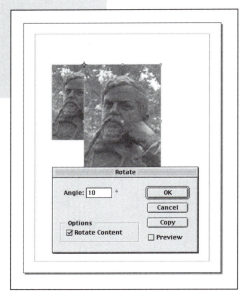

Figure 17.12
You can also reach this dialog box by selecting Object, Transform.

Figure 17.13
The flyout menu has other useful options, too.

Skewing an Image

Skewing, shearing, and slanting all mean the same thing in InDesign. They all angle your image by applying distortion to the frame and its contents. Skewing is useful for some kinds of special effects, but it's probably not something you'd use every day. You can apply skew by selecting the Shear tool from the toolbox, by entering a value in the Transform palette, or by double-clicking the Shear tool to open the Shear dialog box, shown in Figure 17.14.

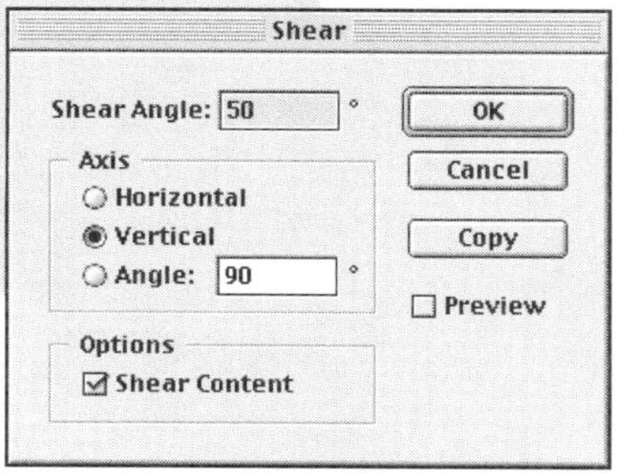

Figure 17.14
Double-click the Shear tool with the image selected to open the dialog box.

Positive skew values slant the top edge of the image toward the right and the bottom of the image to the left, while negative values move the top edge of the image left and the bottom to the right. The dialog box also allows you to specify from which axis the image will skew. Selecting Vertical keeps the sides of the frame vertical and skews the top and bottom, while choosing Horizontal retains the top of the frame and skews the image so the bottom is also horizontal. Figure 17.15 shows both options.

There aren't many uses for the Shear tool, other than for special effects. Figure 17.16 shows one possible application. This figure would look better if one of the images was darkened a bit to simulate shadow. You can't do this in InDesign, but you could always adjust one of the photos in a program such as Photoshop.

Adding Borders and Backgrounds

Borders and backgrounds can do a great deal to make otherwise undistinguished photos more interesting. If you have a picture with a light border, it may fade into the page, particularly if you are printing on colored stock. Placing a border around the picture will help separate it from its background. In

Figure 17.15
The upper example uses the Horizontal shear setting, the lower one uses Vertical shear.

Figure 17.16
Each image was sheared separately and then moved onto the cube.

Figure 17.17, I've placed the same picture twice on the page, once without a border, and once with a 3-point, single-line border.

To place a border around an image, select the frame, and use the Stroke palette to set a width and style for the border. As you can see in Figure 17.18, the palette gives you quite a few options.

Figure 17.17
The bordered picture stands out, while the plain one fades into the page.

Figure 17.18
If these frame options aren't enough, you can draw and stroke a second frame around the image, just a bit bigger.

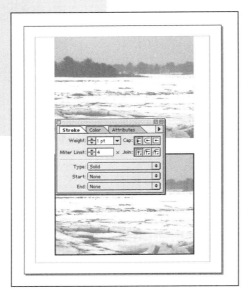

To create the picture frame effect in Figure 17.19, I started with a basic black-edged photo. I then drew a rectangular frame slightly larger than the image, filled it with a tint, and sent it behind the photo. Finally, I selected the tinted frame again and applied a thick-thin-thick border. The result is a picture that looks framed.

Figure 17.19
Experiment with different combinations of strokes until you find one you like.

If you import a grayscale or black-and-white bitmapped image, you can add a color or tint to it in InDesign. However, you can't do this to EPS or vector-based graphics. To color a picture, first select it with the Direct-Selection tool, and then open the Swatches palette and select a color. The color will be applied transparently to the frame. If there are no colors you like, use Add New Swatch to create one. To add swatches to the palette, choose New Color Swatch from the Swatches palette flyout menu, and then select the desired color (see Figure 17.20).

If you don't want to save a swatch, select an appropriate color from the Color palette. To apply a tint, rather than a full strength color, click on the Color swatch and use the Color palette to define the percentage of tint. If you select the frame first, the tint will be applied and changed as you work on it. As you can see in Figure 17.21, to choose a tint you can drag the slider, enter a percentage in the appropriate field, or click the tint ramp at the bottom of the palette.

Figure 17.20
Choose a swatch, or just choose a color from the Color palette.

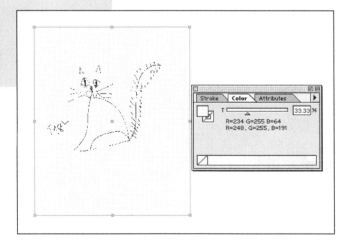

Figure 17.21
Before you can choose a tint, you need to choose a color.

> **NOTE**
>
> If you've brought in a picture and you try to color or tint it without success, check the file type. It's probably not a bitmap.

In this chapter, you looked at ways to transform the graphics you bring into InDesign. You learned about cropping and resizing images, and how to rotate and skew them. Finally, you learned about adding borders and tints to your image. In the next chapter, you'll look at the various ways to wrap text around pictures. You'll also learn about clipping paths and how to use them.

18
Adobe
InDesign

Working with Special Effects

Do you like the look of type wrapped around a graphic? How about irregularly shaped graphics or shaped text blocks? These tricks are special effects, but there's no reason you can't use them to make every publication "special." Before computers and desktop publishing, it was both difficult and expensive to wrap text around a picture. The work had to be done by hand, taking the type from the galley proof and pasting it in place one line, or sometimes even one word, at a time. Thankfully, those days are over. Desktop publishing programs such as InDesign make text wrapping easy and fast.

Text Wrapping

InDesign gives you a lot of text wrapping options—seven in all. With InDesign you can:

- Wrap text around a frame's rectangular bounding box.
- Wrap text around the frame itself.
- Jump the text from the top of the graphics frame to the bottom of it, leaving the graphic in the middle.
- Jump the text to the next column or page when it reaches the top of a graphics frame.
- Set a stand off distance between the graphic and the text.
- Place text inside the graphic's shape, rather than outside of it.
- Run text over the graphic. (Technically, this means no text wrap.)

These options are available to you through the Text Wrap palette, shown in Figure 18.1. You can open this palette by choosing it from the Object menu or by pressing Command+Option+W. Use the icons and options on this palette to determine how text flows around an object.

Wrapping Text around a Frame

It's simple to wrap text around a frame. To do so, you need a block of text and a graphic. (You also could apply this feature to a second block of text that you want to use as a pull quote.) Place the graphic on top of the text at the place where you want it. Then, with the graphic selected, open the Text Wrap palette. Click the icon that shows text wrapped around all sides of a graphic. The text automatically wraps around the graphic, as shown in Figure 18.2.

CHAPTER 18 • WORKING WITH SPECIAL EFFECTS

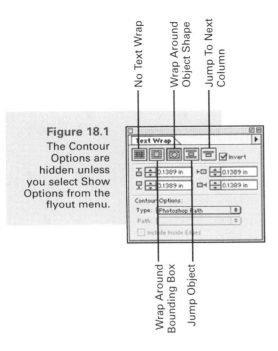

Figure 18.1
The Contour Options are hidden unless you select Show Options from the flyout menu.

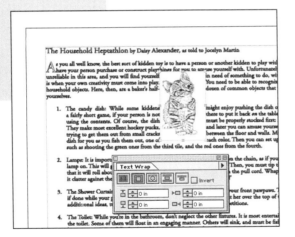

Figure 18.2
I've temporarily hidden the text wrap options. We don't need them yet.

If you would rather have the graphic touching the margin on one side and wrapped on two or three sides, use the same wrap option, but place your graphic at the edge of the text frame. Figure 18.3 shows what this would look like. If you've already applied a text wrap, the text will wrap in the same way no matter where you drag the graphic.

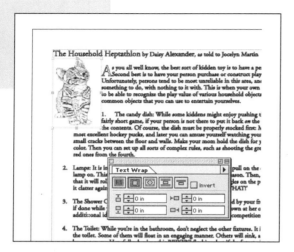

Figure 18.3
Wrapping the text this way makes a more effective layout.

Wrapping Text around a Bounding Box

You might have noticed in Figure 18.3 that the offset fields contained zeros. Offset refers, in this case, to the distance between the bounding box and the frame. There was no offset, so the bounding box and the frame were the same. In Figure 18.4, I've added an offset to each of the four sides of the graphic and I've selected the icon for wrapping text around a bounding box. The offset, in this case, adds a bit of margin between the text and the picture.

The neat thing about wrapping around a bounding box is that you can reshape the bounding box. There's no good reason why your graphics have to be

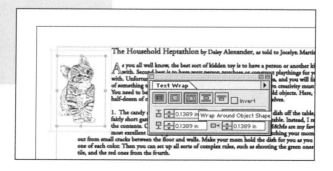

Figure 18.4
The amounts I entered are in fractions of an inch.

rectangles. You can drag the bounding box into any shape you want and add points with the Add Anchor Point tool (the pen with the plus sign) to make the box flex around curves or corners. In Figure 18.5, I've reshaped the bounding box around my kitten graphic.

Now I can place the kitten in the middle of the text, and let the text fit itself around the picture. Figure 18.6 shows the results of reshaping the bounding box and wrapping text around it.

Figure 18.5
Be sure to select the Add Anchor Point tool and not the regular Pen tool.

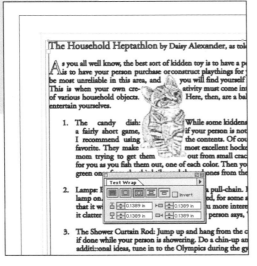

Figure 18.6
It's best to work on this at 100% or greater magnification, so you can see exactly what you're doing.

> **TIP**
>
> Text wraps often look better if they're applied to justified text. Try it both ways and see which you prefer.

Setting Text to Jump a Graphic

If you have set text in a column, you can use the text jump option to place a picture in the column and have the text automatically jump from the top to the bottom of the picture. The text remains threaded, so changes you make will reflow the text without moving the graphic. When you apply this option text only will flow above and below a graphic, even if the graphic isn't the full width of the frame. Figure 18.7 shows an example of "jumping" text.

Setting Text to Jump to the Next Column

This text wrap option, unlike the previous ones, isn't technically a wrap. Your text will flow to the top of the graphic and then jump to the next column. This option can be useful with larger pictures, or with charts and graphs that you want to keep associated with the text to which they apply. In Figure 18.8, I've applied Text Jump to the large photo.

Figure 18.7
If you remove some text above the picture, the rest of the text will move up to fill in the space.

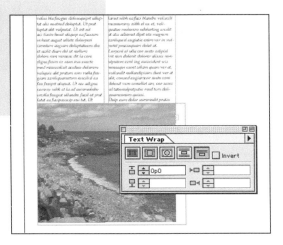

Figure 18.8
Any changes you make to the text in first column will also affect the text in the second column.

Using No Text Wrap

Aside from its obvious use as the default setting when you don't want text and graphics to affect each other, the No Text Wrap option enables you to run text over a picture or over a block of color or tint. As long as the type is dark enough and the graphics object is light enough, you can end up with an interesting effect. As you can see in Figure 18.9, I've drawn a simple shape and added a light gray tint to the object, and then placed the page of text on top. Tints, of course, are created with the Color palette.

To move your graphic behind the text, select Object, Arrange, Send Backward or type Command+[. If you have trouble placing your graphic where you want it, don't forget that you can press the Command key while you click to select an object that's behind another. This lets you slide the graphic around under the text until it's in just the right spot.

Applying Inverted Wraps

This trick is similar to placing text inside a drawn shape, but instead of limiting your options to whatever you can create with the Shape tool, you can import a drawing or photo from some other source and fill it with text. Use the Wrap Around Object Shape option. First, wrap the text around the object,

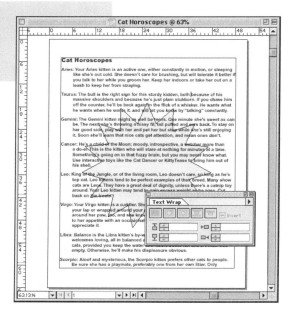

Figure 18.9
This is only a seven-percent tint.

taking care to make the bounding box as much like the shape as possible. Use the Pen tool to add anchor points to the box as needed, and use the Direct-Selection tool to drag the box to follow the shape of the object. Then, click the Invert check box on the Text Wrap palette. The text flows inside, rather than outside, the bounding box. If your graphic is dark, as mine is in Figure 18.10, you will probably need to reverse the type, using white letters on black instead of the usual black text.

Solving Text Wrap Problems

If you have problems applying a text wrap, there could be several reasons why. The text frame could be set to ignore text wrapping. To find out, and to change the setting if that's the problem, select Object, Text Frame Options. Figure 18.11 shows the Text Frame Options dialog box. (You can also access the dialog box by using the shortcut Command+B.) The Ignore Text Wrap check box is in the lower-left corner. Make sure it's not checked.

If the object you are trying to wrap text around is part of a grouped set of objects, the text will attempt to run around the entire group of objects rather

Figure 18.10
First, wrap the text around the object, then invert to wrap the object around the text.

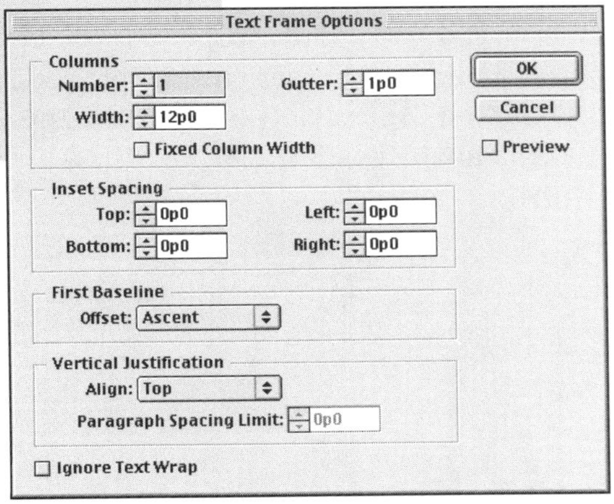

Figure 18.11
The Text Frame Options dialog box

than just the one you intended. This is the case when a text wrap doesn't conform to the bounding box as it should. The solution is quite simple. First, select the group, and open the Text Wrap palette. Then, click the No Text Wrap icon to remove the wrap you applied. Ungroup the objects and select the one around which you want text to wrap. You can also leave the objects grouped and use the Direct-Selection tool to select just the graphic around which you want to wrap text.

If the text refuses to wrap, it's possible that you have inadvertently placed the wrapping object on a master page. Text can't wrap around another object unless both are on the same page. You can override the master item by clicking it while you press Command+Shift. You might need to drag the text out of the way so you can select the object. This should allow the text to wrap.

Working with Clipping Paths

A clipping path is basically a mask that hides part of an object. In InDesign, it's a kind of graphics frame that is not as large as the graphic it contains, thereby clipping some of the image. You can create a clipping path in a graphics program such as Photoshop and bring it into InDesign, along with the graphic with which it's associated. You can do this to place an object or graphic into InDesign with a transparent background; placing the graphic this way avoids the usual white rectangle that comes with imported graphics that don't have clipping paths. If you want to do a text wrap around the object, or just place it on a colored background without the object's background interfering, creating a clipping path in your graphics program can save you a lot of work. Figure 18.12 shows an example of a graphic imported without a clipping path, and then imported with one.

Figure 18.12
The clipping path masks the background on the dish graphic, which allows it to merge into the page rather than be isolated from it.

Saving a Path as a Clipping Path

If you're using Adobe Photoshop as your graphics program, follow these steps to save a path as a clipping path. (If you are using some other graphics program, consult its help screen or manual for information on clipping paths.)

1. In Photoshop, draw and save a path around the object, or convert an existing selection into a path. In Figure 18.13, I've drawn a path, and saved it as Path 1.
2. Choose Clipping Path from Photoshop's Paths palette menu to open the Clipping Path dialog box (see Figure 18.14). For Path, choose the path you want to save, and then click OK.
3. Save the image with its path in TIFF format in Photoshop, and export it to Adobe InDesign.

Simple, huh? When you bring the clipped image into InDesign, all you'll see is the unmasked (unclipped) part.

> **NOTE**
> You can also save clipping paths as EPS or PSD files.

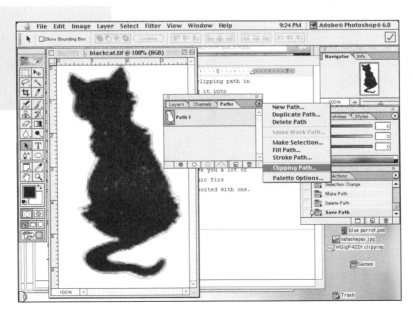

Figure 18.13
Path 1 is the default name. You can name a path anything you choose.

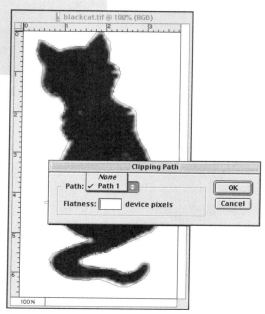

Figure 18.14
Saving turns the path into a clipping path.

If you've forgotten to create a clipping path in your graphics program, or you decide after you've placed an unclipped graphic that you don't want the background, you can still apply a clipping path. You can do this by hand, using the Pen tool, or automatically.

Creating Automatic Clipping Paths

After you've placed an object onto a page and discovered that its background interferes with other objects on the page, or you've decided that you want to run type closely around it, you can let InDesign create the necessary clipping path for you. This works best with white and light-colored backgrounds. If your graphic has a dark background, you'll have to draw the clipping path by hand. To create a clipping path in InDesign, choose Clipping Path from the Object menu, or press Command+Option+Shift+K to open the Clipping Path dialog box, shown in Figure 18.15.

Set the clipping path type to Detect Edges. Threshold determines the darkest pixel value that InDesign looks for in defining edges. (Edges are detected by evaluating the difference in value between adjacent pixels.) Raising the threshold

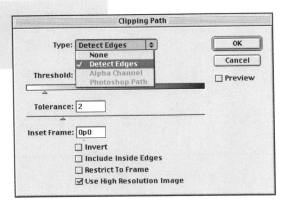

Figure 18.15
The Clipping Path dialog box

makes more pixels transparent, but don't overdo it. If the threshold is set too high, light values that you want to retain could become invisible. Because my picture is fairly light, I've kept the threshold relatively low, as shown in Figure 18.16. If you check the Preview check box, you can see the path you're drawing, so you can increase or decrease the threshold as necessary.

Set the Tolerance field to indicate how close a pixel's value must be to the threshold for it to be hidden. In general, a low tolerance means a more precise path while a higher one produces a looser, smoother path. However, a low tolerance means also that the path has many more anchor points, so it will require more memory and possibly be harder to print. Figure 18.17 shows the differences. The lemon on the left was set for a low tolerance; the one on the right was set for a high tolerance.

Figure 18.16
Set the threshold by dragging the slider or typing a number into the Threshold field.

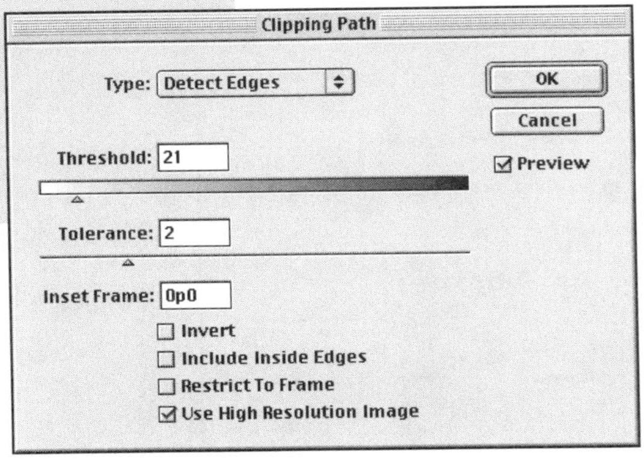

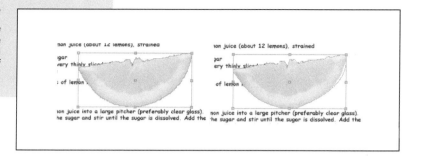

Figure 18.17
You can see the difference especially well on the bottom of the image.

Inset Frame shrinks the shape of the clipping path uniformly, making it fit tightly against the object. However, if you type a negative amount into the box, you expand the frame uniformly by that amount. This enables you to precisely offset the clipping path from the object. In Figure 18.18, I've applied an inset of ×0p8 (8 points), just enough to keep the type from touching the lemon.

Figure 18.19 shows the final result, with the text wrap applied.

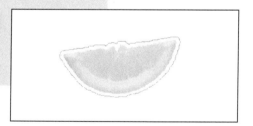

Figure 18.18
The path is moved out from the lemon edges by 8 points.

Figure 18.19
This also makes great lemonade!

> **NOTE**
>
> You can also use the Clipping Path dialog box to create clipping paths from Alpha Channels or multiple paths saved with a Photoshop graphic. Alpha Channels are a way to save masks created in Photoshop or similar programs.

In this chapter, you looked at some of the many special effects that you can apply typographically. You learned about the various kinds of text wraps and text jumps, and how to apply them. You learned how to import clipping paths and how to create them in InDesign. In the next chapter, you'll explore the mysteries of the pen tools.

19
Adobe
InDesign

Creating Original Graphics

First of all, you need to understand that InDesign is *not* a graphics program. It was never intended to be a substitute for Illustrator, Photoshop, Freehand, or whatever your favorite drawing or painting program is. However, it does have some useful tools that will allow you to whip up a simple illustration or an interestingly shaped text frame without having to open a new application. You can control the shape, outline (if any), and fill of the objects you draw. The drawing tools and techniques are the same in InDesign as they are in Illustrator or Photoshop. You have a freehand Pen tool, tools to add and delete anchor points, a tool to convert direction points, and a scissors to make a closed shape open. There is also a set of shape tools.

Drawing Closed Shapes

InDesign's shape tools make it easy to draw simple shapes, based on rectangles, ellipses, and polygons. Shapes are closed paths if they are created with a shape tool. What this means is that the path, or outline around the shape, returns to the point at which it started. You can also draw a freeform shape with the Pen tool that's a closed path with no end points. You simply have to end up at the same place where you began to draw. Figure 19.1 shows a selection of closed shapes.

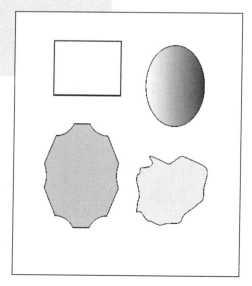

Figure 19.1
Closed shapes can be filled or empty.

Drawing Open Shapes

Open shapes are lines. They can enclose and describe a space. A straight line is considered to be an open shape. (Forget what you learned in geometry class....) In an open shape, the path doesn't reconnect to itself. Open shapes, like closed shapes, can be filled or left empty. Figure 19.2 shows some examples of open shapes.

Filling a shape

You can use a solid fill, a color tint fill, or a gradient fill with your shape. You can also stroke the edges, remembering that a path with neither stroke nor fill applied to it won't print. Paths are invisible unless they are stroked. You can, however, fill a path without stroking it. In that case, the fill defines the edge of the shape.

Drawing Freeform Shapes with the Pen Tools

First, go ahead and review the pen tools. Figure 19.3 shows the pen tools expanded.

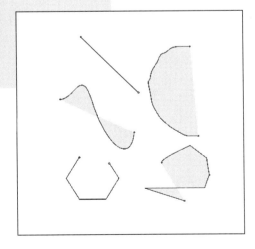

Figure 19.2
It's an open shape if the path doesn't join itself.

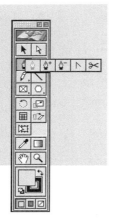

Figure 19.3
From left to right, the Pen tool, the Add Anchor Point tool, the Subtract Anchor Point tool, the Convert Point tool, and finally the Scissors tool

The Pen tool is the basic drawing tool. It can draw straight lines and Bézier curves. To draw a straight line with the Pen tool, select the tool and click somewhere on the page. That point is one end of the line. Move the mouse (*without* holding the mouse button down) to where you want the line to end, and click again. A line connects the two points. These points are called corner points. If you clicked again to add another line, they'd meet at a corner (see Figure 19.4).

Clicking and dragging produces curved lines. Click to set the start of a line, then click to end it, dragging the mouse while you make that second click. This action makes the line curve as you drag. You've created what's called a smooth point, because additional segments of line that you draw from this point will join in a smooth curve, rather than at a corner. You've also created a set of handles that stick out on either side of the point. In Figure 19.5, I'm dragging the lower handle to make the curve bulge upward.

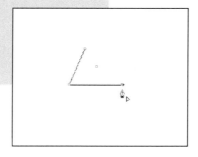

Figure 19.4
Clicking places points, and two points create a line.

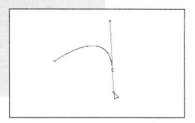

Figure 19.5
If you dragged the other handle, the curve would be down instead of up.

You can keep drawing more smooth points to add to this line. Each segment, if you drag its end point, will join smoothly with the line already drawn. Figure 19.6 shows a shape made of smooth points and curves. I've left some handles showing.

Sometimes you want two curves to join at an angle, rather than smoothly. To do this, you use what's called a sharp point. Follow these steps to make a pair of curves with a sharp point.

1. First, create a curve, as I did previously.
2. Click the end point of the first curve, and then press Option as you click and drag to make the high point of the next curve.
3. Move the cursor to where you want the line to end, and then click and drag in the opposite direction from the line you already dragged.

See Figure 19.7 for an example of the steps used to create a pair of curves with a sharp point.

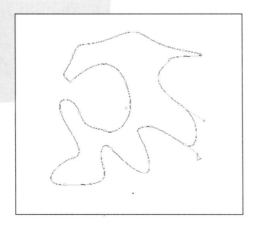

Figure 19.6
Clicking any handle lets you drag and reshape that part of the curve.

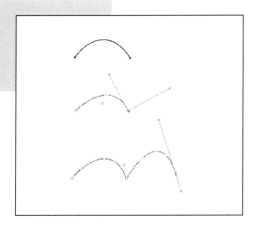

Figure 19.7
This could be a seagull, or the top of a heart, or. . . .

Using Anchor Points

Corner points, smooth points, and sharp points all come under the general heading of anchor points. Anchor points anchor parts of a path. Each line segment has two anchor points, one at the start and one at the end. The anchor points at the end of a closed path are called endpoints. When you look at a path with several anchor points, you'll notice that the last one you placed is a solid box, while the previous ones are hollow. The solid box indicates that the point is selected. To select a different point, click it with the Selection tool.

If you use the Add Anchor Point and Delete Anchor Point tools, you can adjust your path quite precisely. Select the correct tool and click the path where you want a new point, or click a point that you want removed. Use the Direct-Selection tool to move an anchor point, which will, of course, move the line with it.

NOTE
Anchor points and path handles appear on the screen in light blue, indicating that they do not print.

You can also move an anchor point while you're working on its path by holding down the Command key and then clicking and dragging the part you want to move. This temporarily changes the Path tool to a Selection tool.

The Convert Direction Point tool allows you to change a corner point into a smooth point and vice versa. Just click the point you want to change, and the point changes, leaving handles to help you adjust the line position. When you change a point, the path from it to the previous path appears to flatten. You can reshape it with the handles, as shown in Figure 19.8. I used the Convert Direction Point tool to change a sharp point to a smooth point.

Using the Scissors Tool

As you might expect, the scissors tool cuts off pieces of paths. Use it to turn a closed path into an open path, to edit out parts of a shape, or to split an empty text frame. If you want to remove part of a path, you need to apply the scissors in two places. Otherwise, with only one click, you've opened the path but not removed any of it. In Figure 19.9, I've cut up a path.

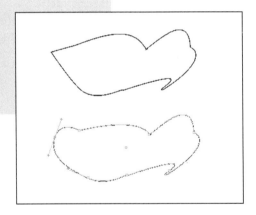

Figure 19.8
Once you convert the point, you can use the handles to reshape the path.

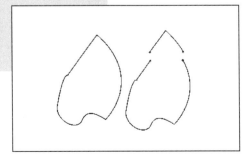

Figure 19.9
Before and after using the scissors.

Cutting a path is like cutting a ribbon, in that if you want to remove a piece after it's cut, you must drag it out of the way or delete it. If you leave the cut piece in place, you may not realize that you've cut it. In Figure 19.10, I made one cut on the path and used the Selection tool to drag it aside. Because I didn't change the lower anchor point, the line pivots on that point, rather than moving aside.

Working with Compound Paths

Compound paths are combinations of straight and curved paths. Generally, when you need to draw a complicated shape, you'll be using both kinds. If you just remember that dragging makes a smooth point, and clicking without dragging makes a corner point, you should have no problem.

If you have two open paths that you need to connect, position the Pen tool over one of the endpoints that you want to connect. If you see a small diagonal slash next to the pen point, it's correctly positioned. Click on the endpoint, and then position the pen point over the other end point. The small icon next to the pen point will change to a hollow block, showing that you're adding a point; click on it. The line will be drawn when you release the mouse button. Figure 19.11 shows the steps.

Figure 19.10
Making a single cut in a path

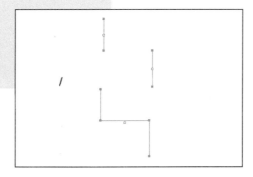

Figure 19.11
I drew a path between the two existing paths to connect them.

There's another kind of compound path that you might find useful. It's actually a combination of several paths, and you can use it to place a transparent area inside a shape. You can also group several separate paths into a compound path so that you can apply a gradient across all of them. To group paths for a compound path, select them with the Selection tool and choose Object, Compound Paths, Make, as shown in Figure 19.12. You can also use the keyboard shortcut Command+8, but be sure the shapes are selected with the Selection tool; otherwise, the command is unavailable.

In Figure 19.13A, I've drawn three shapes and filled each one with a gradient. As three separate paths, each contains its own gradient. In Figure 19.13B, I've turned these shapes into a compound path and applied the same gradient. The result is quite different. It's as if the one gradient filled the page and the shapes were windows revealing parts of it. Simply grouping the shapes wouldn't do this; they must be compound if they are to share a gradient.

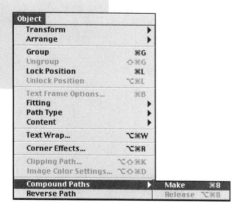

Figure 19.12
Using this menu command unites any selected set of paths.

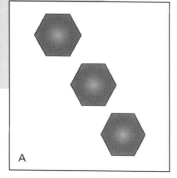
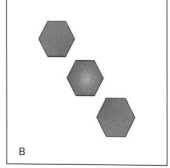

Figure 19.13
If I'd grouped the three shapes, the result would be the same as A, not B.

In Figure 19.14, I've used both compound and simple paths, and several different gradients. The circle is a simple shape, filled with a radial gradient. The sailboat is three paths merged into a compound path, with a linear gradient applied. The strip of ocean is a simple zigzag path, duplicated and moved down slightly. I closed the ends of the thick line formed by the two paths, and filled them with a different linear gradient.

There's one other neat trick you can do with paths. You can use them as text frames. When I created the graphic in Figure 19.15, I started with two ovals, made them into a compound path, and then edited away most of the upper one, leaving only the curve that covered the lower one. I used this as a

Figure 19.14
This isn't great art, but it would do for a logo or as art behind some text.

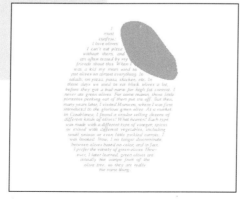

Figure 19.15
This doesn't show up as well in black and white . . .

container to place a block of text about olives, colored the print olive green, and added a freeform pimento as a finishing touch.

If you've created a compound path, and then you decide it shouldn't have been one, select the path and go back to Object, Compound Path, and select Release or press Command+Option+8 to separate the path into its component paths.

Applying Stroke and Fill

A path that hasn't had either stroke or fill applied to it is invisible. It's there, but there's no way to see it. You can use the Stroke palette to apply a variety of different strokes—for different folks and different publications. Figure 19.16 shows the Stroke palette, and an effect I created by stroking a circle with a very heavy dashed line.

In Figure 19.17, I've applied some of the other stroke variations to some shapes. The triple loop was created by first drawing a long oval and then using the Pen tool to place additional points so it could be dragged across itself.

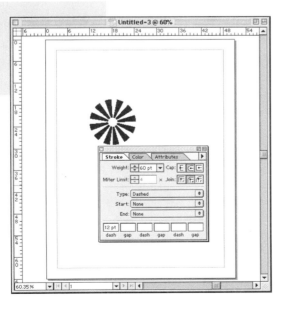

Figure 19.16
You can experiment with different line weights.

Figure 19.17
The snowflake effect is simply a 30-point dashed line over a multi-pointed star.

So, that's the scoop on graphics. In this chapter you learned some tricks for creating graphics within InDesign. You learned how to work with the pen tools and how to create compound and complex shapes. In the next chapter, you'll begin to learn about color and how it works in a computer.

Adobe InDesign

PART VII

Working with Color

20

Adobe InDesign

Using Color Models and Color Modes

Color is everywhere. I am fortunate enough to live near the ocean, where I see an endless variety of shades of blue in the water and sky. My friend who lives on the prairie rhapsodizes about fields of golden wheat and all the shades of green that spring brings her. If you drive down the Strip in Las Vegas or stand in Times Square, you'll see colors that don't exist in nature. If you make a point of noticing colors, you'll begin to see the subtle variations that make our world so interesting, and so beautiful. Capturing these colors on paper or on the screen is sometimes difficult, even for those who understand color theory. For those who don't, it's impossible.

Even if all your publications are limited to black and white, understanding how color works will help you manage your grayscale photos. If you work, even a little, with color, you really have to know about color modes and models and how they affect what you see on the screen and in print. Before you get started, let me suggest that you read this chapter with InDesign or another graphics program open on your screen. You'll understand more if you can see what I'm discussing.

Working with Color Models

The first thing you need to know is that InDesign addresses color in terms of modes and models. Models are methods of defining color, while modes are methods of working with color based on the models.

> In InDesign, a *ramp* is a gradient that gives you access to the available colors or tints. It's located at the bottom of the Color palette, and you can choose a color or tint by clicking on it.

Color models define the different ways that color can be displayed on a screen or printed on paper. InDesign uses three color models:

- ◆ **RGB**. Red, Green, Blue
- ◆ **CMYK**. Cyan, Magenta, Yellow, Black
- ◆ **LAB**. Standards based on analysis of hue, chroma, and brightness

When you open the InDesign Color palette, you won't see any colors. The grayscale ramp is selected by default. You can use the flyout menu, shown in Figure 20.1, to select a color model when you're not working in black and white.

However, before you move on to color, take a look at the grayscale palette. The palette has the familiar stroke and fill icons in the upper-left corner, and a ramp that shades from white to black, with a slashed square at the left to let

Figure 20.1
Press F6 or use the Window menu to open the Color palette, then use the flyout menu to select a color model.

you choose "no color," and pure black and pure white squares at the right to allow you to choose black or white. The tint slider reproduces the ramp below, but with a triangle you can slide back and forth to select the color. Moving the slider or typing a number into the box gives you a shade of gray, or a tint of a color you have previously selected.

The RGB Model

> *Value* is the relative strength of the color. Because the RGB model mixes colors of light to achieve white light, the full strength of all three primaries is 255 (white). When you combine all three primaries at a value of 137 (half of 255), you get medium gray.

If you look at a performer spot lit on a stage, you can often see the overlapping circles of the three RGB primaries: red, green, and blue. Where all three colors overlap you get a pure white light—a color which can't be duplicated with a single light bulb. When you apply strong filters to the three lights, you end up with white.

The RGB model, which computer monitors and TV screens use for their displays, assigns values on a scale of 0 to 255 for each of the three RGB primaries. As an example, pure green has a red value of 0, a blue value of 0, and a green value of 255. Pure white places the values of all three RGB primaries at 255. Pure black sets the values of the RGB primaries to 0.

Figure 20.2 shows the RGB version of the Color palette, with pure green selected. You can select a color by clicking the RGB spectrum at the bottom of the palette, by clicking or moving the sliders, or by entering values in the R, G, and B windows.

Because RGB color is what your monitor shows, it's generally a good choice for your "working" color model, particularly if your publication is going on the Web. If you're printing to a home or office inkjet printer, it's still a good choice, as inkjet printers make the adjustment from RGB to CMYK automatically.

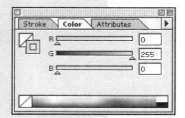

Figure 20.2
The Color palette also has the black, white, and "no color" squares at the ends of the spectrum.

The CMYK Model

The CMYK model, which is used for most commercial printing, defines colors according to their percentages of cyan, magenta, yellow, and black. These are the four colors of printing inks, both in your home inkjet printer and in the fancy, high-resolution color laser printers and printing presses that service bureaus and commercial printers use. (However, service bureaus and commercial printers usually call it *process color*.) A six-color inkjet printer, like the Epson 750, adds light cyan and light magenta. Figure 20.3 shows the CMYK version of the Color palette.

As noted previously, most inkjet printers handle the conversion from RGB to CMYK very easily. You don't need to convert colors yourself, or make a point of working in CMYK, unless your document has full color art and is going to a commercial printer.

However, for accurate color reproduction, you might want to check your RGB art in CMYK mode in Photoshop or a similar graphics program, just to make sure that it's not "out of gamut." Here, *gamut* refers to the range of colors that can be printed or displayed. Some colors, especially some of the very bright ones, are impossible to duplicate with CMYK inks. Thus, they are out of

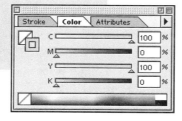

Figure 20.3
CMYK has four sliders instead of three.

gamut. Your eye has a much wider gamut, and can distinguish more colors than the RGB screen on the computer can display. The screen has a wider gamut than the printing press, and that's where colors can go wrong.

When you are working with CMYK color, InDesign will warn you if a color is out of gamut by displaying a warning icon (see Figure 20.4). It's a small triangle with an exclamation point inside. Next to it, InDesign places a small box with the closest color available in the CMYK gamut. Click the box to select that color instead of your original color.

The LAB Color Model

The L*a*b color model is based on the model proposed by the *Commission Internationale d'Eclairage* (CIE). The model was proposed in 1931 as an international standard for color measurement. In 1976, it was refined and named CIE L*a*b. It defines a color gamut that is broader than any of the other models. This system is often represented as a two-dimensional graphic, which more or less corresponds to the shape of a sail (see Figure 20.5).

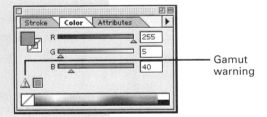

Figure 20.4
Attempting to print an out of gamut color will generally give you a washed out version of the color.

Gamut warning

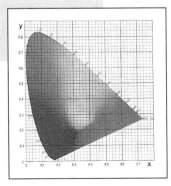

Figure 20.5
The LAB color "wheel"

LAB color is defined as Luminance plus two components (A and B), which go respectively from green to red, and from blue to yellow. The red components of a color are tallied along the x-axis (horizontal) of the coordinate plane and the green components are tallied along the y-axis (vertical). In this way, every color can be assigned a particular point on the coordinate plane. Colors on the left tend toward gray, which means that their spectral purity is decreased.

InDesign displays the LAB spectrum in a different way; instead of displaying the "sail," it displays the spectrum along a ramp, the same way it displays RGB and CMYK colors. Figure 20.6 shows the LAB palette. The dark colors fall in the center and the light colors are on the ends.

InDesign uses the CIE LAB model, because its gamut is so broad, to convert from one color model to another. LAB color is designed to be device-independent, meaning that colors defined in this model appear and print the same, regardless of whether you are seeing them on paper or onscreen.

Working with Color Modes

The difference between the modes and the models is simple. Models are methods of defining color, and modes are methods of working with color based on the models. When you create a color in an InDesign document, you can choose RGB, CMYK, or LAB mode as your working mode. Which one should you choose? The answer depends on your final product. If your pages will be printed in process color (CMYK), obviously you need to work in CMYK mode so you're not specifying colors that the printing process can't reproduce.

If your pages are only going on the Web, it's best to work in RGB. Because RGB is the way you see color on your screen, it's the most accurate. However,

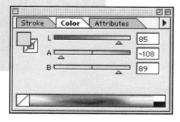

Figure 20.6
The LAB version of the Color palette

if you're working on something that will be used both on the Web and in print, use LAB. Its wide gamut covers both Web and print colors.

If you switch color modes while you are working and color management is turned off, InDesign will convert the colors to the most mathematically accurate equivalent. If color management is active, it will convert colors using the source profiles for the monitor and printer you are using.

Using Color Management Systems

Color management, or *CMS*, is a sort of fancy way of saying "what you see is what you get." When you use CMS, InDesign tracks the colors in the source image, the colors your monitor displays, and the colors your printer can print. If you choose a color that's not compatible with the monitor or with the printing method, CMS automatically finds the closest useable equivalent and converts the document color.

To turn on color management, select Edit, Color Settings, Document Color Settings, as shown in Figure 20.7. This opens the Document Color Settings dialog box, shown in Figure 20.8. This dialog box enables color management and sets defaults for your document. Don't worry, it's not as complicated as it looks. For now, just make sure the Enable Color Management box is checked, and close the dialog box. We'll come back to the pop-up menus later in the chapter.

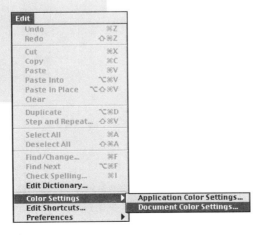

Figure 20.7
Set the document color first, and then the application color parameters.

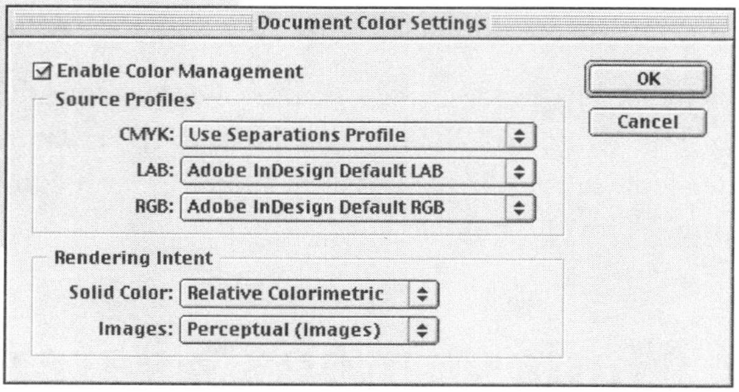

Figure 20.8
To manage color in your document, click the Enable Color Management check box.

Now, go back to the Edit menu and choose Color Settings, Application Color Settings to open the Application Color Settings dialog box, shown in Figure 20.9. Because you're working on a Mac, your options in the Engine pop-up menu are Adobe CMS, Apple ColorSync, and Heidelberg CMM. Windows machines have Adobe CMS and some other Windows-specific options. Choose a CMS that is compatible with your printer. If your work is going to a commercial printer, ask whether they use Heidelberg CMM. If not, choose Adobe CMS or Apple ColorSync. These work equally well.

The method by which CMS does its color calibration involves looking at three different color profiles: the monitor, composite (essentially, the printer), and separations. Separations is really only used if you are making color separations for CMYK printing.

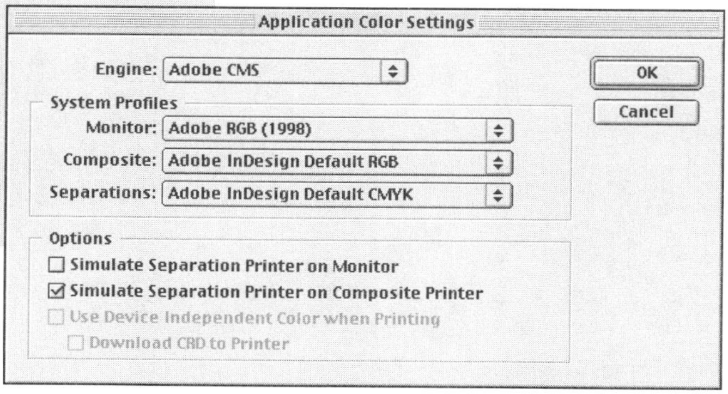

> *Color separations* are the four separate colored printing plates used in CMYK process printing. InDesign can do the color separations for you, or you can let the service bureau or print shop do them.

Figure 20.9
Adobe CMS is a good choice for working with Adobe applications such as InDesign and Photoshop.

Understanding Color Profiles

Color profiles, also known as ICC profiles, specify the gamut for each device with which you work. For example, your monitor has a color profile specific to its model and brand. Printer color profiles vary according to the paper you are printing on as well as the printer you are using. Separation profiles match the device doing the separations, usually a very high-end prepress proofing system. Scanner profiles describe the way in which the scanner interprets colors. ICC profiles for common devices are supplied with InDesign and with the Mac as part of the ColorSync system.

First, set the monitor profile by selecting your monitor from the Monitor pop-up menu in the Application Color Settings dialog box. If your monitor isn't on the list, or if you don't know exactly what kind of monitor you have, choose either Adobe RGB or Apple RGB if you are using Apple ColorSync as your document's default. You can also choose one of the generic EBU or P22 monitor settings. If you choose to go this route, be sure to choose the one with a gamma of 1.8, because that's what the Macintosh screen uses.

> *Gamma* refers to the midpoint of the monitor's brightness setting. 1.8 is the Mac standard, while 2.2 is the Windows standard. That's why Mac screens look a little bluer than Windows screens.

Next, choose your printer from the Composite pop-up menu. If you're working in process color, this will be a proofing printer, which will give you a composite rather than color separations. If your printer isn't on the list, go with the Adobe InDesign default RGB or CMYK. Finally, choose the device that generates your color separations from the Separations pop-up menu.

These settings will be your defaults for all your InDesign publications. You can override these settings (for a single document) by using the Document Color Settings box to select a different monitor, printer, or separation method.

You also have some options available for the way InDesign handles color on the screen and when printing. If you want to see an onscreen approximation of what your separations will look like when printed, check the Simulate Separation Printer on Monitor check box. This option can give you, at best, a rough idea of what your separations will look like; at worst, it will be nothing like what prints. My advice? Don't bother. The same could be said for the Simulate Separation Printer on Composite Printer option, except that it's always a good idea to check your separations this way. The result won't be wonderfully accurate, but it should come closer. Be careful—these files may print very slowly.

Device Independent Color only works when you're printing to a PostScript printer, and then it simply tells InDesign to ignore the CMS settings. Don't use it without first checking with your service bureau.

Getting Consistent Color

Several factors come into play when you talk about color. First, there's the monitor. What bit depth is it displaying? For color calibration you need to set a minimum of 16-bit color depth (thousands of colors); 24-bit color is even better. Use your Mac's Monitors and Sound Control Panel to check and reset your bit depth. Figure 20.10 shows the best (millions) setting.

If you decide to use Apple ColorSync instead of Adobe CMS, use the Monitors and Sound Control Panel to access the ColorSync profiles seen in Figure 20.11.

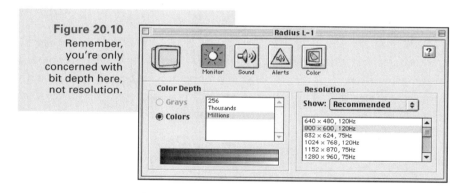

Figure 20.10
Remember, you're only concerned with bit depth here, not resolution.

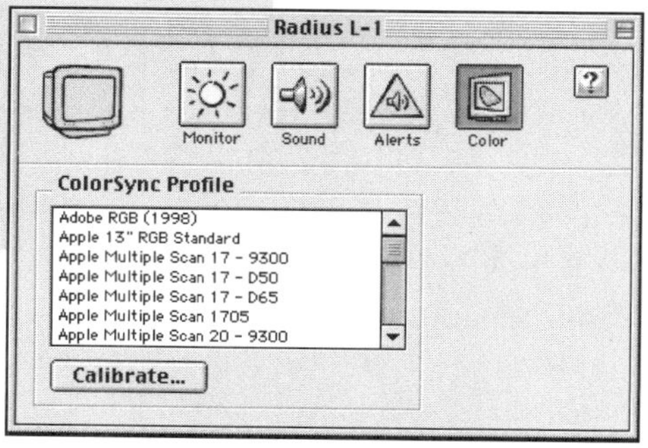

Figure 20.11
Scroll through the list until you find your monitor.

If there's no ColorSync or Adobe profile for your monitor, you can easily create one. You can either use the Adobe Gamma Control Panel that installed with InDesign or the Apple ColorSync Control Panel. Either one will walk you through the steps for calibrating your monitor and developing a profile for it. The profiles are compatible, so it really doesn't matter which one you decide to use. You can access the ColorSync calibration system by opening the Monitors and Sound Control Panel and then the Color panel, shown in Figure 20.11. If you click the Calibrate button, you'll open a window that leads you through the calibration process. Figure 20.12 shows one of several calibration exercises. The Adobe Gamma Control Panel is found on the Apple menu.

Don't try to calibrate a monitor until it has been running for 30 minutes or more. It takes a while for the monitor to warm up and stabilize. Also, monitors deteriorate over time. It's a good idea to check your monitor calibration every month or so. If it becomes impossible to calibrate the monitor, replace it.

Obtaining CMS Profiles

Calibrating the monitor is just one step toward getting accurate color. You also need profiles of your other color devices, such as scanners and printers. The ICC profiles supplied by the makers of monitors, printers, and other color devices are produced by testing several units of each device and averaging them. These profiles don't allow for individual differences in machines, and they don't give you absolute accuracy.

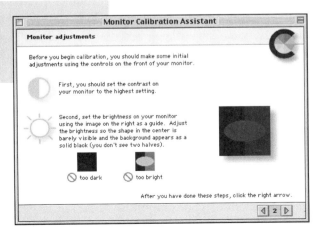

Figure 20.12
This is the first step in calibration.

The only way to get absolutely accurate ICC profiles is to buy the necessary profiling hardware and software, and create your own profile for each piece of equipment and, in the case of printers, for each type of stock on which you will print. It's expensive and time consuming, but very precise.

Considering the Working Environment

Viewing conditions influence color accuracy, both on your monitor and on paper. Colors look different under different lighting conditions. Indirect, even lighting is best for reducing glare. D-50 (5000 degrees Kelvin) is the ideal type of lighting for accurate color. Fluorescent lights can add a yellowish cast to images; I prefer the "full-spectrum" fluorescents sold for growing plants. Keep the shades drawn to avoid "contaminating" your work area with sunlight. Remember, colored walls, colored carpets, and colored draperies can all add a color cast to the room light. Stick with neutral colors in your workspace. Colored desktop patterns can also affect what you see onscreen. Here again, neutral gray is best, though it's not as much fun as an interesting pattern.

Color Management for Prepress

When you are using process color and a commercial print shop, the business of color management becomes a lot more critical. Your best bet is to consult with the service bureau or print shop before you start a project. Find out what CMS system they use and get a copy of the relevant ICC profiles, if possible.

Also, when you import graphics from other sources into InDesign, be sure that you bring in embedded profiles with them. When you use the Place command (Command+D), you open a dialog box that has a check box for Show Import Options—be sure to check this box. When you click OK, you'll see the Image Import Options dialog box, shown in Figure 20.13. (You may have to select Color Settings from the pop-up menu.)

First, check the Enable Color Management check box. You'll see two pop-up menus: Profile and Rendering Intent. If your document has an embedded profile, use it. If not, selecting Use Document Default from the Profile pop-up menu should give you good results. That pop-up menu also lists all of the installed ICC profiles, but unless you know, for example, that a particular scanner on the list generated your graphic, it's best not to get too specific.

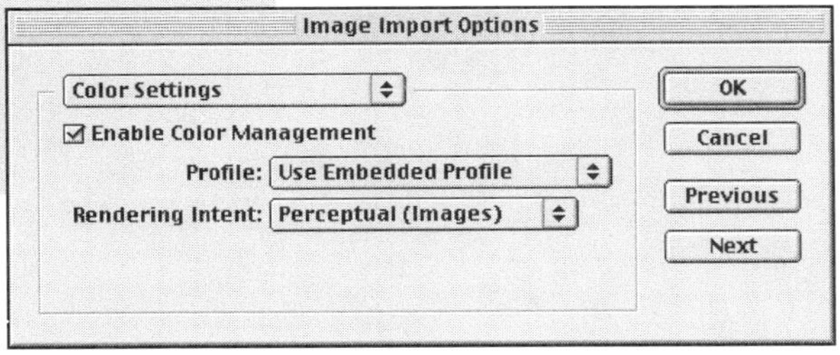

Figure 20.13
The Image Import Options dialog box

For Rendering Intent, use Perceptual (Images) if your graphic is a scanned or digital photo. The other options aren't appropriate unless your picture primarily contains areas of flat color.

This chapter has been about the theory of color. You learned how InDesign's color models and color modes work, and you saw how the Color palette works. Finally, you learned about color calibration. You learned how to calibrate your monitor and how to use ICC profiles for your input and output devices. In the next chapter, you'll put color theory into practice as you apply color to your publications.

21
Adobe InDesign
Applying Color

Color can add a lot of style to your publication. It doesn't have to be four-color process printing—just a single spot color can brighten up your page, whether it's colored text, a block of accent color, or a tinted photo.

Colors can be either process or spot. Process colors are made from layers of cyan, magenta, yellow, and black, while spot colors are printed by single-colored inks specifically matched to those colors. You can combine spot and process color, if necessary. You might do this if there's a particular logo color or product color that's out of gamut for process printing. Applying a spot color is more accurate—and more expensive—than printing a CMYK version of it. However, for products that are identified by color as much as by name, it's almost mandatory. Ask yourself how you'd respond to an orange or pink can of Coke. Probably not very well. You'd most likely assume it had been on the shelf forever or that it was some sort of counterfeit product. The average human eye is remarkably adept at recognizing and remembering colors. Even if the Coke can were just a couple of shades off, you would know there was something wrong.

Spot colors require a separate printing plate for each color, unlike process color, which uses four plates to print a full-color page. If you plan to use four or more spot colors, it might be cheaper to use process color instead. Metallic inks are printed as spot color; the reflective powder that makes them appear shiny can't be applied as part of the CMYK Process. Similarly, when varnish is applied to colored inks so they'll stand out, it's applied by a spot color plate.

One thing that you need to be aware of in importing colored photos or full-color art is that InDesign has no color correction tools. If you don't want to spend the money for Photoshop, look for Lemke's Graphic Converter. It's an excellent shareware program for working with art and photos. Graphic Converter has the needed color adjustment tools, and can also translate from virtually any graphic format to any other. You can download it from http://www.lemkesoft.de. Please don't forget to register; this software is worth much more than its cost.

Understanding Spot Colors

You need to choose a spot color ink carefully, keeping in mind the paper on which it will be printed as well as the ink color. You also need to be sure that the ink you choose is from a color-matching system that your print shop uses.

Before you start the job, ask the print shop whether they use Pantone, Trumatch, or some other system, and then be sure to choose your colors from that swatch library.

The swatch libraries listed in InDesign include:

- **DIC (Dainippon Ink and Chemical)**. This is a spot color system used mainly in Japan. There are 1,280 colors in the DIC system.
- **Focoltone**. This is a CMYK-based spot-color system popular in Europe, but not common in the United States. The Focoltone set includes 763 colors.
- **Pantone**. This is the most popular system in American print shops, with several thousand colors. InDesign supplies three sets of Pantone swatches—for coated paper, for uncoated paper, and a CMYK-based set that can be used as spot color or translated accurately into CMYK.
- **Toyo**. This is another primarily Japanese spot color system, with over 1,000 colors.
- **Trumatch**. This is a CMYK-based set of over 2,000 spot colors which, like Pantone's CMYK spot colors, can be accurately separated into CMYK. The Trumatch Color Finder, available from graphic arts supply stores, displays 40 tints and shades of each hue. The set also includes four-color grays, using different hues.
- **System colors**. These are available on both Mac and Windows systems. They are the 256 (8-bit) "native colors" that each system uses to display information onscreen. Use them for material that will be viewed onscreen instead of on paper.
- **Web colors.** These are 216 "safe" colors that will look the same on a Windows screen as on a Mac screen. Because Mac and Windows users can rarely agree on anything, it's a pleasant surprise that all but 40 of the system colors are shared.

Defining Colors

CMYK colors are "defined" by the percentages of each of those four colors. If you look at the numbers on the CMYK palette in Figure 21.1, you can see that the percentages don't necessarily add up to 100%. That's because you're looking at the relative amounts of each ink needed to make up the color.

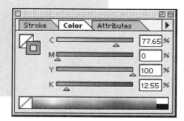

Figure 21.1
If you could see this in color, you'd see a sort of pea soup green.

Process colors are printed as small dots of color, not as flat areas. Your eye blends the dots to see the colors they represent, and the percentages refer to the density of dots of cyan, magenta, yellow, and black that must be on the paper for your eye to see that color.

> **NOTE**
>
> If you are at all familiar with the work of pointillist painter M. Georges Seurat, he used the same concept. Seurat's experiments with color led him to paint in small dots of color, which are arranged in such combinations that they seem to vibrate. Individual colors interact with those around them and fuse in the eye of the viewer. The concept is not unlike the dots or pixels in a computer image or those of process color printing. If you magnify any computer image or colored page sufficiently, you will see individual colors that, when set together, produce an image. Seurat was interested in the way colors worked together to create a particular tone. Figure 21.2 shows a detail from one of Seurat's works.

Figure 21.2
Even in black and white, you can see the differences in the dots.

When you need to reproduce colored photos or continuous tone artwork, CMYK is the only way to do it. Pictures that you import from a graphics program have their color information attached to the image. If your art is vector graphics, save your work and apply it in InDesign as EPS files. If you are importing a photograph or bitmapped art, work with it in the TIFF format. InDesign is very friendly toward both TIFF and EPS, and these are the de facto standards for the printing industry.

A few things can occasionally go wrong when you import EPS files. If your drawing program doesn't use standard color-definition methods, you may find yourself with EPS drawings that print in black rather than in color. You could also find your spot colors separated into CMYK, even though you set them up in the graphics program as spot.

Defining Spot Colors

Spot colors are defined in a different way than process colors. Each spot color uses a different ink. InDesign ships with fourteen different libraries of spot colors, each with anywhere from one hundred to several hundred different colors. The library list is shown in Figure 21.3. Some of these libraries are used primarily in Japan or Europe. Pantone is probably the best known and most complete of the color libraries. This library comes with different sets of color for coated and uncoated papers. You can also get swatch books for all Pantone inks. The swatch book displays the printed color plus several percentages of tint of that color. It's a handy way to see in advance what your colors will look like on the page, and is helpful when a client wants to choose a color to match the product. You can haul around a collection of swatch books much more easily than a computer, and you will see more correct color than can be displayed on the monitor.

When you select a set of spot colors from this menu, it opens as swatches on a palette, through which you can scroll. If you're trying to compare colors, you can have several swatch palettes open at one time. In Figure 21.4, I've opened several spot color libraries, and dragged them apart so that I can find the closest color to the one I want to use.

The icons to the right of the color name in the palette indicate that it's a spot color based on the CMYK color model. Actually, that's a moot point. If you are printing them as spot colors, your print shop will make a plate and use the ink color you have specified. If you decide to have your spot colors printed as process

Figure 21.3
Click a set of colors to open its palette.

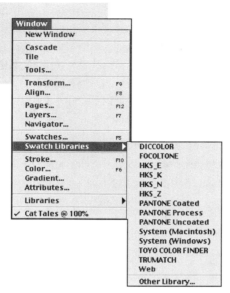

Figure 21.4
In the Pantone system, the CVC part of the color name defines it as being intended for coated papers; CVU colors are used with uncoated paper.

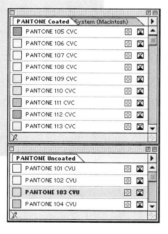

colors, they'll be separated along with everything else. If you hold the mouse over a color name in the palette, InDesign will show you its CMYK equivalents.

There are more color libraries than the ones InDesign supplies. You may encounter Pantone Hexachrome or ANPA (a standard set by the American Newspaper Publishers Association). If you have a swatch book for one of these color libraries and your print shop wants to use it, just pick any close color from one of the other libraries and be sure to specify the Hex or ANPA color number that the printer should use. What you get won't necessarily look like what's on your screen, but it should be fairly close.

Working with Tints

Tints are paler versions of a color. Tinting is a cheap way to make your publication look more colorful than it is. You can use a single spot color at different percentages of tint and have it look like several colors instead of just one. Tints of spot colors are printed from the same plate as the solid area. The difference is that the individual dots of ink are smaller. This is true whether you are printing a tint of a spot color or a process color. Tints of process colors have smaller clusters of CMYK, but use the same inks.

You can create a tint using the Color palette. First, open the appropriate swatch library and select a color. Double-click it to add it to the Swatches palette. When you select a swatch from the Swatches palette (not the library), the Color palette will switch to a tint display, like the one you see in Figure 21.5.

The tint percentage is shown in the box. To change it, you can click the tint ramp, use the slider, or type a percentage into the box. After you've found the perfect tint, you can (and should) save it to the Swatches palette, by clicking the New Swatch icon at the bottom of the Swatches palette. The tint appears as a swatch with its tint percentage and the name of the base color, as shown in Figure 21.6.

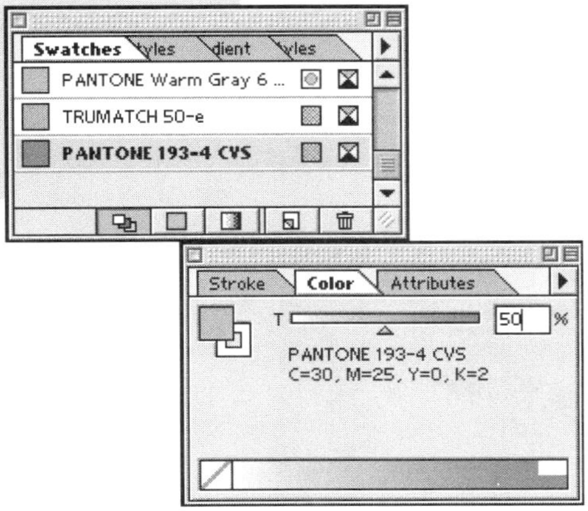

Figure 21.5
Notice the tint ramp at the bottom of the window.

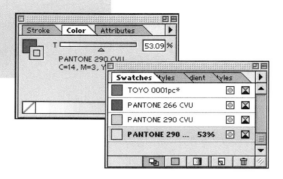

Figure 21.6
You can add more tints of the same base color.

You can edit a tint swatch by double-clicking it and changing the tint percentage. Doing this will automatically update all frames that use that tint. You can also change the base color, which will change any tints based on that color. Another way to edit a swatch is to open the New Tint Swatch or Swatch Options dialog box. The New Tint Swatch dialog box is shown in Figure 21.7. Except for the title, the Swatch Options box is identical. Use the Swatch Options dialog box to change an existing tint, or the New Tint Swatch dialog box to create a new tint. Both dialog boxes are accessed via the Swatches palette flyout menu. If you don't want to add a new swatch, use Swatch Options to adjust the color or tint of your swatch.

If you use several tints of one base color, your publication will look as if it has several colors instead of just one spot color. This can work out nicely, as long as you use the color and tints carefully and don't overdo them so they become distracting. In Figure 21.8, I've created a distinctive stripe for a page accent,

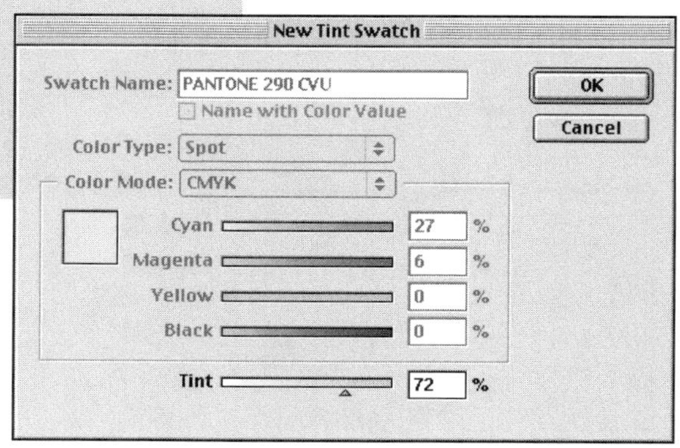

Figure 21.7
Move the sliders or enter values in the boxes to change the tint.

Figure 21.8
I overlapped lines of different stroke weights to make this multi-toned design.

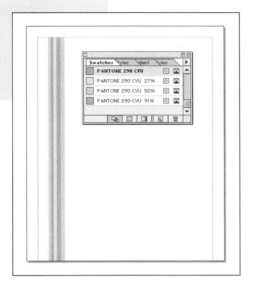

using three tints of a single Pantone color. This accent prints for the cost of a single color.

Tints (even tints of gray) are great for putting a drop shadow behind a picture. Choose a medium shade and either draw a frame slightly overlapping two sides of your picture, or run a wide stroke along the two sides. Figures 21.9 and 21.10 show the different effects.

Figure 21.9
This example uses two 12-point strokes to simulate a shadow.

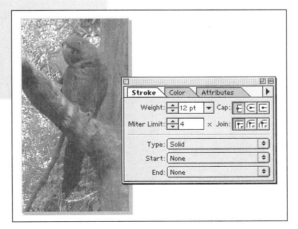

Figure 21.10
The gradient is applied at an angle, so there is a dark corner.

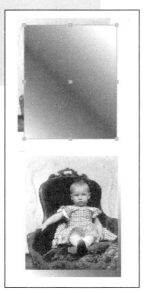
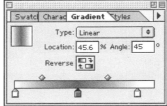

For Figure 21.10, I first drew a rectangle overlapping the frame. Then, I filled it with a gradient applied at an angle. This is shown in the upper photo. For the finished version, I simply used Object, Arrange, Send Backward to place the shadow behind the photo.

In Figure 21.11, I took the same photo and cropped it to an oval by setting it in an oval frame smaller than the photo. Then I set an oval frame behind it, applied a radial gradient, and experimented until I achieved the picture frame effect that I wanted.

Figure 21.11
Drag the sliders until you have the kind of gradient you want.

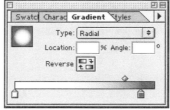

Using Color Blocks with Text

Tints or spot color blocks can be used as accents on an otherwise unremarkable page of text, or they can be used to highlight a page number or title. In Figure 21.12, I've applied a block of a medium blue tint, with the numbers reversed out of it.

To do this, you need to first create the text page, then the color block. Use a shape tool to draw a block and fill it with the spot color you want to use. Apply No Text Wrap to the block, and then place a second frame over it to hold the type. Set the Type Color to Paper on the Swatches palette, and enter your type.

Obviously, InDesign doesn't include all the tools one might hope for, in terms of type design. Don't forget that you can go as wild as you want in a program such as CorelDRAW, Illustrator, or Photoshop, and bring in your text as a graphic. Figure 21.13 shows an example of what Photoshop 6 can do.

You can find some fairly fancy type effects in Microsoft Word, too, but unfortunately, they don't transfer to InDesign unless you do it with a screen shot. The resolution won't be good enough for print, but should work fine on a Web page. In Figure 21.14, I've set some type in Word using the WordArt tool. If

Figure 21.12
The color block makes the page numbers easy to find, and provides a nice, strong design element.

Figure 21.13
The Type tool in Photoshop 6 lets you bend type in many preset patterns.

Figure 21.14
This type's a little bit ragged, but adequate for a Web page.

you create the text large and scale it down in InDesign, you'll have somewhat better results.

Reversing Text

One of my favorite tricks with type is to convert it to a graphic. Then, I can either fill the letters with white or a color so they can be reversed out of a picture, or I can convert the letters to outlines and use them as a mask. In this case, the image appears inside the letters. To do this, you must first import the graphic you want to use as background or fill. Then, you set the text, making sure that you have chosen the right font, size, kerning, and other attributes. Once the type is converted, you can't go back and edit it.

To reverse type, follow these steps:

1. Place the graphic on the page.
2. Place a text frame over it and enter the type.
3. Kern it, and adjust it as needed.
4. Change the fill to "paper" or to a color that will stand out against the art.
5. Finally, press Command+Shift+O to turn the type into outlines. This may take several seconds, depending on the speed of your Mac.

Figure 21.15 shows the result, with white type against a colorful background.

Filling Text with a Graphic

Cutting out letters from a graphic is equally easy. Set your type and convert it to outlines as described in the previous section. Draw a frame over it and send the frame behind the type. Use Command+D or File, Place to locate the graphic and import it into the letters. In Figure 21.16, I've filled the text with flowers.

Figure 21.15
The lettering is in white here, but you can use any color that will show up over the art.

Figure 21.16
You can treat the text as you would any graphic—rotating, skewing, and scaling it to fit the available space.

Don't forget that all the letters inside the text frame will be treated as a single graphic when you convert them. If you want to convert a single letter, such as for a fancy capital, convert it in its own frame so it will be independent.

In this chapter you looked at spot and process colors. You learned the difference between them, how to apply them, and some neat tricks for using them. You also learned about working with tints and swatch libraries. In the next chapter, we go to press!

Adobe InDesign

PART VIII

Putting It in Print

22
Adobe InDesign

Outputting to Your Own Printer

Now comes the fun part—printing your pages. It's also the most important step, because your work isn't considered a publication unless it's published. Your newsletter, poster, annual report, or Great American Novel can be printed on a home or office laser printer, posted on the Web, or commercially printed. In any case, it's a good idea to print proofs of your pages before you start the actual printing job, because many things can go wrong. Fonts can be missing, and pictures might not come out as you intended. Graphics might have moved or been renamed since you placed them. Because InDesign depends on maintaining links to your imported text and graphics, lost links might not print at all, or they might print in low resolution. The point is, you really have to check out everything, whether your job is being printed across the country or across the room.

By the way, you might think you know all about using your own printer and be tempted to skip this chapter. I'd urge you not to do so—InDesign has a few quirks you need to know about in order to get accurate results.

Getting Ready to Print a Proof

Before you can print, you must make sure that your printer is correctly set up with the proper printer drivers and PostScript Printer Description files (PPDs). To check this, go to the Chooser and select the printer on which you intend to proof. (If the printer isn't connected and turned on, you won't see it listed in the Chooser.) Adobe InDesign comes with its own PostScript printer driver. If it was installed with the rest of the software, you'll see it in the Chooser. Figure 22.1 shows my Chooser, with the AdobePS driver selected.

You should also verify that the Adobe driver is the correct version, as you may have older ones installed from other Adobe applications. To find out the version number, go to the Extensions folder in your System Folder, and locate the AdobePS extension. Select it and press Command+I to open the Info dialog box, shown in Figure 22.2. The correct version number should be 8.6 or higher. Make sure you're looking at the Adobe driver. There's also an Apple LaserWriter version 8.6 that installs with the operating system.

If you don't have version 8.6 or 8.7 of the printer driver, go back to your InDesign CD-ROM and install it, or go to http://www.adobe.com/products/printerdrivers/main.html and download the latest version.

CHAPTER 22 • OUTPUTTING TO YOUR OWN PRINTER

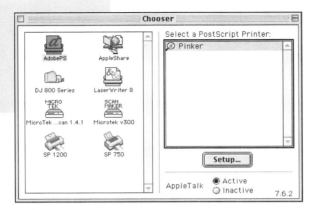

Figure 22.1
The LaserWriter 8 driver doesn't work reliably with InDesign. You need to use the Adobe driver.

It's fine to have several different printer drivers installed. The Chooser lets you access them so you can choose the right one for each application. InDesign is designed to work with the Adobe driver, while your word processor might be happier with the LaserWriter driver. Get into the habit of checking to make sure the correct driver is selected before you print.

Figure 22.2
Remember, it's A for Adobe on the printer driver icon.

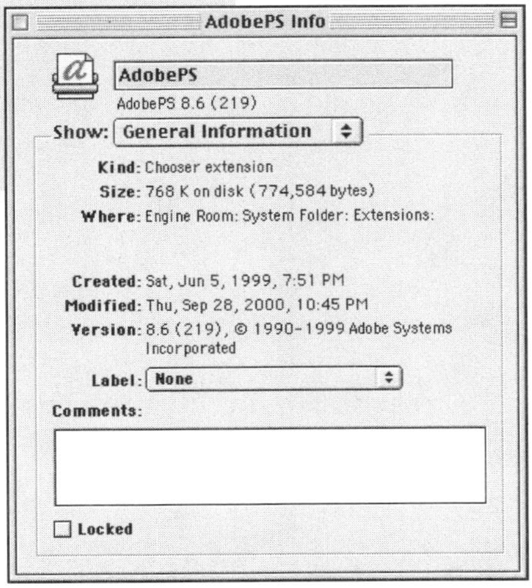

Printing to an Inkjet Printer

Well, the bottom line is, you can't—without help. InDesign doesn't work with non-PostScript drivers, such as you'd use with an Epson, Hewlett-Packard, or other brand of inkjet printer. But all is not lost—you can use Adobe PressReady to enable many non-PostScript printers to simulate a PostScript Level 3 printer. As of this writing, PressReady supports the following printers:

- Canon

    BJC-8500

- Epson

    Stylus Color 800

    Stylus Photo 870 *

    Stylus Color 850

    Stylus Photo 1200 *

    Stylus Color 900 *

    Stylus Photo 1270 *

    Stylus Color 1520

    Stylus Pro 5000 *

    Stylus Color 3000 *

- Hewlett-Packard

    DeskJet 895C

    DeskJet 930C *

    DeskJet 950C *

    DeskJet 970C *

    DeskJet 1120

    DeskJet 1220C *

    DeskJet 1220C/PS (PressReady is bundled with this printer.)

    DesignJet ColorPro GA (PressReady is bundled with this printer.)

    2000C

Drivers for the printers with asterisks on the list can be downloaded from http://www.adobe.com/products/pressready/printers.html after you have installed PressReady. You can buy PressReady online at http://www.adobe.com or through software dealers. It retails for $249.00 US.

If you're using PressReady, follow the printing instructions that come with it. If you don't want to invest in more software, there's another way you can get around this problem. You can convert your document to a PDF, and then print it to the inkjet. You'll learn more about PDFs in Chapter 23, "Working with Service Bureaus," because they are also a good way to send files to the service bureau for printing.

Setting up Pages

Assuming that you are printing to a PostScript printer and you have the Adobe printer driver enabled, the next step is to set up the pages for printing. Open the Page Setup dialog box by choosing Page Setup from the File menu, or by pressing Command+Shift+P. This opens the dialog box shown in Figure 22.3.

The first thing to check is that your printer is selected in the Printer pop-up menu. If you have more than one PostScript printer, they'll all be listed here. The second pop-up menu should be set to Page Attributes. In the Paper pop-up menu, set the paper size you plan to use. Set the orientation of your pages by clicking on the appropriate icon. If your pages need to be reduced or magnified, set the percentage in the Scale box.

Don't enable Booklet unless you are printing a booklet with two pages per printed sheet. Booklet sorts out the pages into the correct order so they can be folded and stapled in the center to make a half-letter size booklet (or half of whatever size page you are using).

> A *service bureau* is a kind of print shop that also does photo scanning, makes color separations, and outputs to a variety of imagesetters or high-quality proof printers. Most also do collating, copying, and trimming and binding. Kinko's is a nationwide chain of service bureaus.

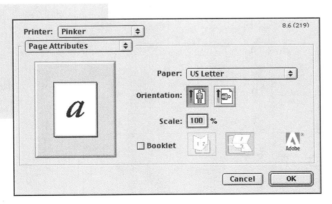

Figure 22.3
If you have the correct driver enabled, you'll see the Adobe logo on the right side of the box.

You can ignore the Watermark option that shares the Page Attributes pop-up menu. It's an undocumented feature. Nowhere in the Adobe manual or Online Help is there a mention of how to load a watermark. If you intend to use one, place it on a master page instead.

PostScript Options, which also shares that pop-up menu, is more important. It has two sets of options, which you can see in Figure 22.4. The first is for visual effects, and allows you to flip the page horizontally or vertically, which you can use if you are printing to film. You can also invert the image to make a negative, in which white prints as black and black as white.

The Image & Text options determine how InDesign will handle any adjustments to the text or graphics. Generally speaking, the only item you need to check is Unlimited Downloadable Fonts. Substitute Fonts replaces Mac system fonts with comparable PostScript fonts, changing Geneva to Helvetica, New York to Times, and so on. It's really not necessary if you've used only PostScript fonts. Smooth Text and Smooth Graphics should be ignored; they help if you are using a very old, low resolution printer, but Adobe no longer supports these anyway. (I can only assume this option is a legacy from earlier Adobe drivers.) Precision Bitmap Alignment forces pixels to print at their original locations. This can do more harm than good, forcing a high-resolution printer to create moiré patterns, or to misprint a graphic. Ignore this option, too.

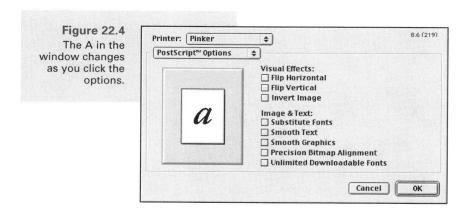

Figure 22.4
The A in the window changes as you click the options.

Running a Preflight Check

Pilots won't fly their planes until they've done a preflight check to make sure all systems work, and that everything that needs to be loaded is in place. Doing a similar preflight check on your publication will keep you from crashing and burning when you try to print. Because InDesign documents can get very complex, with multiple fonts, linked graphics and text, and process and/or spot colors, the preflight is tremendously important.

Fortunately, preflighting isn't difficult. InDesign comes with a built in preflight tool. You'll find it under the File menu, or you can open it by pressing Command+Shift+Option+F. When you do, InDesign will immediately check your publication and open a dialog box with a summary of the missing fonts and graphics. You might wonder how fonts or graphics could get lost. It's really very simple and quite common. After you have placed a picture into your document, you might rename the file, or drag it from one folder to another. That breaks the link, and all InDesign has left to show is the low-resolution version, which won't print very well. When you first open a page in InDesign, you get a warning if links are broken or fonts missing. However, if you start juggling files around after you have opened the document, InDesign won't know it without the preflight check. Fonts get lost if they're in a closed suitcase. If you work on a network with others, fonts and graphics are even more apt to go south.

Understanding the Preflight Summary

Figure 22.5 shows the Preflight dialog box for a publication with several problems. It opens with a summary of the faults found. The pop-up menu at the top also gives you access to windows for Fonts, Links and Images, Colors and Inks, and Print Settings. If your document has hidden layers, you can use the check box at the bottom of the window to scan them as well. If there are no hidden layers, the box remains grayed out.

Working with Preflight Fonts

The warning signs are there to call attention to difficulties, in this case with links and fonts. I've used 29 fonts which, for aesthetic reasons, is probably too many anyway. Two are missing and one is incomplete, meaning that I have the

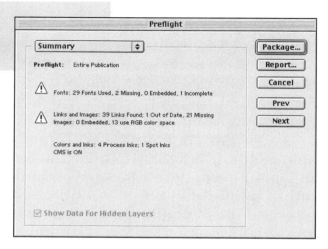

Figure 22.5
This page has many problems.

screen font but not the printer font. To find out more specifically what's going on, you can choose Fonts from the top pop-up menu. You'll then see a dialog box like the one in Figure 22.6, listing the fonts and whether they are Adobe PostScript, TrueType, or bitmapped screen fonts. TrueType fonts will print correctly on your home laser printer, but high-end imagesetters at service bureaus often can't handle them. If your work will be printed commercially, replace TrueType fonts with equivalent PostScript fonts, or use a program such as Macromedia's Fontographer to translate the fonts from TrueType to PostScript.

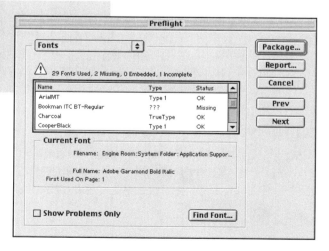

Figure 22.6
Scroll down the list until you find the problem font.

The dialog box also tells you where the font is first used. You can install the missing font, or you can go to the part of the document that uses it and change the type to a different font. If you choose not to reinstall a missing font, be sure to remove it from the fonts list so you're not tempted to use it again. Use Sherlock to find fonts that are somewhere on your hard drive but not in the correct folder. After you locate the font you need, drag it to the System Folder, then quit and restart InDesign.

Working with Preflight Links

The Links and Images window, shown in Figure 22.7, shows you whether any graphics files are missing or have been modified and not updated in InDesign. Use the Relink button to locate and relink the missing graphics one by one, or use Repair All to have InDesign prompt you to find and fix each broken link.

The list shows the type of file, the page it is on, its status, and whether there's an imbedded ICC profile for the image. It also shows whether it's an RGB file. You needn't correct this if you're printing at home; most printers handle RGB images quite well. If your document is going to a commercial printer, it's better to go back to the program that created the image and save it as a CMYK file, rather than trusting the printer to do the conversion. If you do it yourself, you have some control over the result.

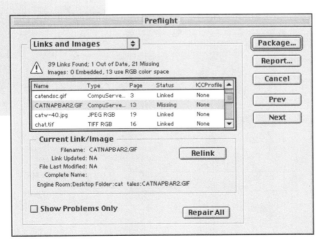

Figure 22.7
Click an image file to see more details, such as where it is and when it was updated.

Working with Preflight Colors and Inks

The Colors and Inks window, shown in Figure 22.8, shows you what process and spot colors have been used in the document, based on what InDesign finds on the Swatches palette. If for some reason you have removed the cyan, magenta, and yellow swatches from the palette, the dialog box won't show them, even though your publication may have lots of colored pictures. Don't worry about it; the color separations will print just as well.

Working with Preflight Print Settings

The final window is Print Settings, shown in Figure 22.9. It reviews and lists all the settings you have made in the Page Setup and Print dialog boxes. After you have checked the settings, save the report by clicking the Report button and send this text file to your service bureau or commercial printer when you send your files. If you're printing at home or in the office, you needn't save the report unless there are settings you think you might want to change after seeing a proof print. The Package button prepares the files for transfer to a service bureau. (We'll cover this option in the next chapter.)

Figure 22.8
My document uses four process colors and one spot color.

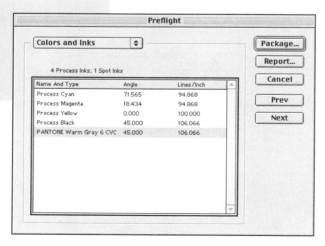

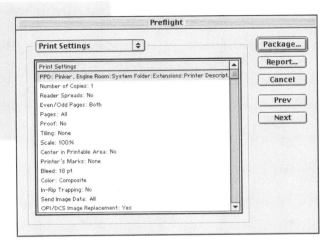

Figure 22.9
All the decisions you made in the Page Setup box are listed here, along with any current Print dialog box settings.

Almost Ready to Print

Well, you're in the home stretch, but you're note quite ready to click the Print button. First, you have to check the settings in the Print dialog box (see Figure 22.10). It will take some time to get through them all, as the pop-up menu covers 12 windows in addition to the one you see here. Use the pop-up menu to open the remaining windows when you're ready. This window is pretty straightforward, if you have ever printed anything on a Mac.

Figure 22.10
The General settings are similar to those in any other Macintosh application.

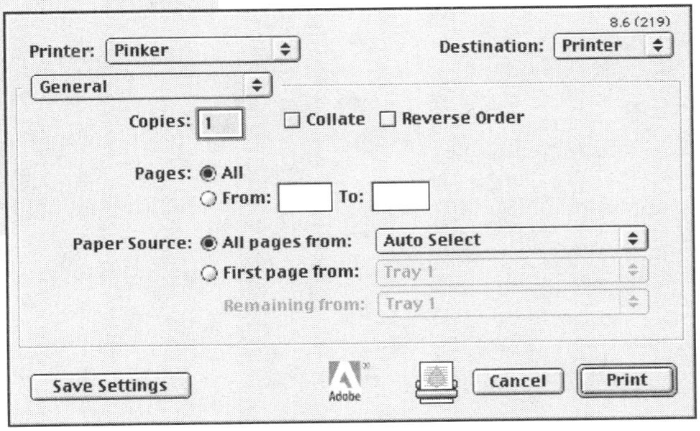

Set the number of copies you need (just one if you're printing a proof), and which pages to print. Tell the printer what paper source to use, if yours has more than one tray. If you are printing multiple copies, the Collate feature is convenient, but it slows printing time, especially on long documents. InDesign has to send all the pages to the printer multiple times unless the printer has enough RAM to hold them all. If it does, your pages will be stacked in order as they come out of the tray.

The Advanced Page Controls window, shown in Figure 22.11, reflects the page range settings you made under the General controls, but lets you fine-tune them by allowing you to print some pages, skip some, and then print some more.

The Color window (see Figure 22.12) lets you manage color printing. Here you can choose whether to print a composite or color separations, and whether

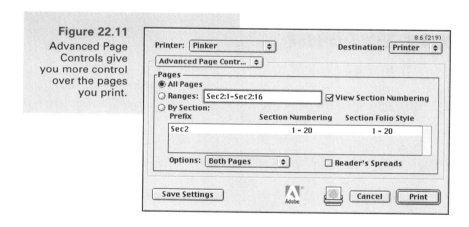

Figure 22.11
Advanced Page Controls give you more control over the pages you print.

Figure 22.12
The Color window lets you choose which colors to print.

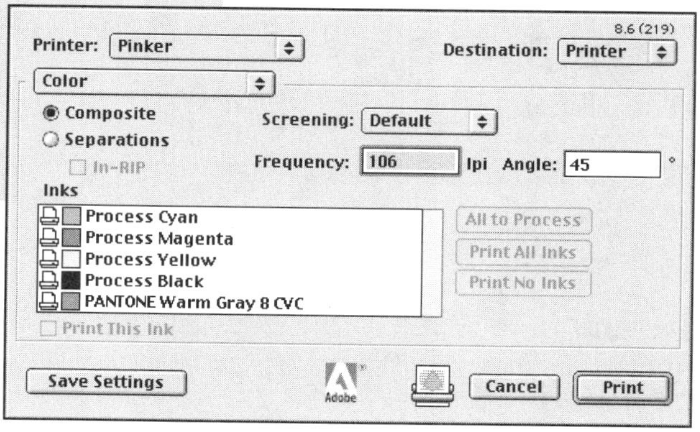

to have InDesign do the separations or to send them to Adobe In-RIP (included with many Level 3 PostScript printers). If you are doing separations, you have some additional options. You can have InDesign translate the spot colors into process colors, and you can choose which colors to print.

The Scale and Fit window, shown in Figure 22.13, lets you print documents that are otherwise too large for the paper. You can scale a page either up or down, or you can tile large pages so they'll print on multiple pages, which you can then join. Choose Auto from the Tiling pop-up menu to let InDesign decide where to break up the page, or select Manual to tile it yourself. To scale a page, just enter the percentage by which to increase or decrease in the boxes. Ordinarily, you wouldn't do this unless you wanted to check fine print or fit large pages onto smaller ones for proofing.

The title of the Graphics window is somewhat misleading. As you can see in Figure 22.14, it gives you control over fonts as well as graphics in your document. Unless you're in a hurry, leave All as the default pop-up for Send Image Data. Choosing to print your graphics at 72 dpi is only reasonable when you already know they'll print properly, and you're checking something else on the same page. Proof Print strips out all the graphics and replaces them with outlines of the frames with Xs through them. Again, don't use it unless you have already checked the graphics.

OPI/DCS is used when you've had a service bureau make high-resolution scans of your art or photos. It tells InDesign to replace the low resolution image you used in the layout with the high resolution version.

Figure 22.13
Click the Center Page in Imageable Area check box to center the document on the page.

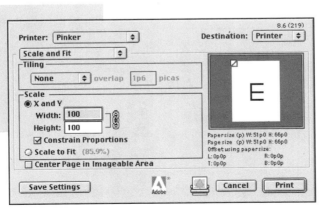

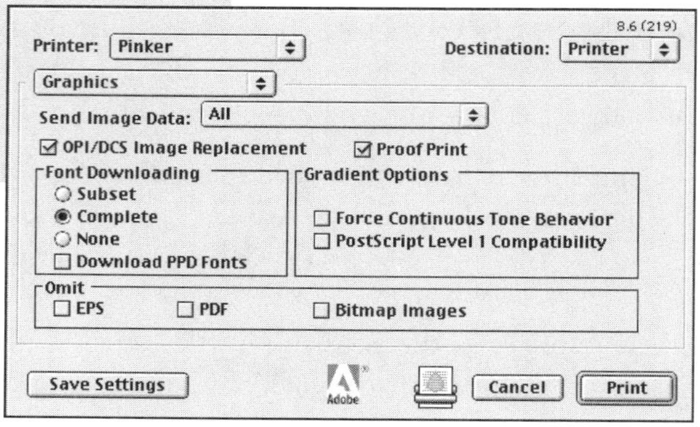

Figure 22.14
You can also use this window to ignore specific types of art.

When you're printing to a home or office printer, set Font Downloading to Subset. This sends the font information to the printer as it's needed. Choose Complete if your printer has a lot of memory, or if your document has very few fonts. Choose None if you know that all the fonts you used are built into the printer's memory or stored on a hard drive attached to the printer.

The Page Marks window does exactly what it says it does—it places registration, crop, and other kinds of printer's marks on your page. It's shown in Figure 22.15. Click All Printer's Marks or choose only the ones you need. Crop marks show where the page should be trimmed, if your final output is smaller than the paper on which you are printing. Page information is the file name and page number. (You've probably already put this on a master page, and you can ignore it here.) Registration marks are necessary for color separations. Color bars print samples of CMYK so the print shop can see whether

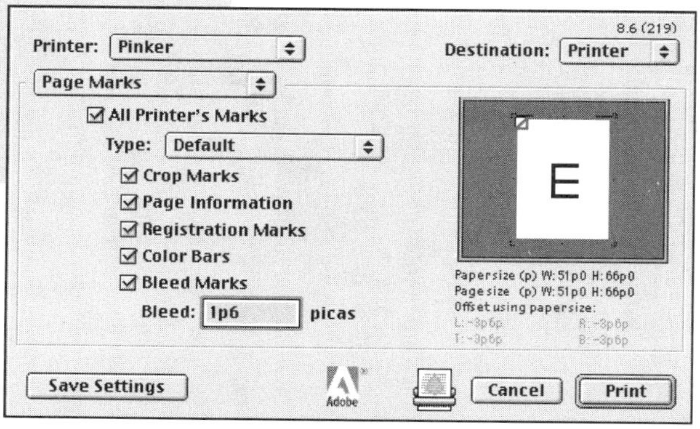

Figure 22.15
Some printers will have only the default Type option.

the ink is properly saturated. Bleed marks show where the bleed extends if you have an image that bleeds off the page.

The Edit Trapping Inks window is best ignored, unless you are working closely with a service bureau. The default settings are usually fine, and changing them without knowing exactly what you're doing can really mess up things.

PostScript Settings control the way PostScript files are generated. You can choose either PostScript Job, which sends the pages to the printer, or EPS with or without a header (see Figure 22.16). The latter option converts your entire document to an EPS file, for transmission to a commercial printer or service bureau. You can also set the level of PostScript the EPS employs, and which fonts are included in the file. Choose Binary for the data format to make a smaller file, or choose ASCII if you want to be able to edit the file (and you understand the PostScript language enough to do so).

The Error Handling window simply determines how InDesign informs you that there is a PostScript error. The Layout window, shown in Figure 22.17, lets you add a border to your pages and print multiple pages on one sheet.

The Cover Page window lets you specify a different paper source for a cover sheet, and whether the cover prints before or after the rest of the document. Use this if you are printing a report with a cover on cover stock. The Background Printing window should be familiar to Mac users. It allows your pages to print in the background while you play Solitaire, surf the Web, or do some other computer task. It's slower, but it lets you be more productive. You can also use this window to set the computer to print while you're having lunch, after hours, or whenever it's convenient.

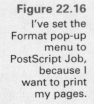

Figure 22.16
I've set the Format pop-up menu to PostScript Job, because I want to print my pages.

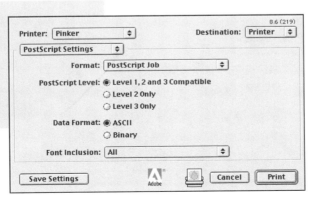

Figure 22.17
You can print up to 16 pages per sheet or 36 sheets tiling to a single page.

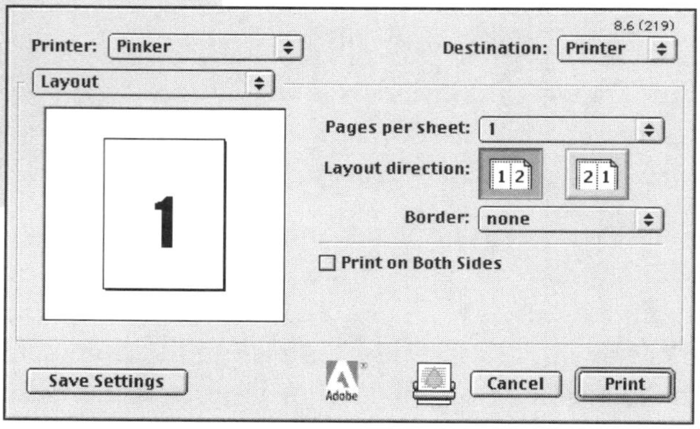

Printer Specific Options will vary depending on your printer. The options for my GCC Elite 1212 laser printer are shown in Figure 22.18. Yours might be similar, or you might have even more options. Fortunately, they are all self-explanatory.

Now, at last, the moment you have been waiting for . . . click the Print button. The data is sent to your printer, and soon you have pages in your hand—your pages, your publication. Congratulations, you did it.

This chapter discussed printing to a local (home or office) printer and looked at all the steps from preflight to page setup to the final output. In the next chapter, you'll learn about service bureaus. You'll learn how to package your files and how to work with commercial print houses. You'll also look at sharing documents within a work group, and you'll learn to resolve cross-platform issues.

Figure 22.18
Your printer might have different options.

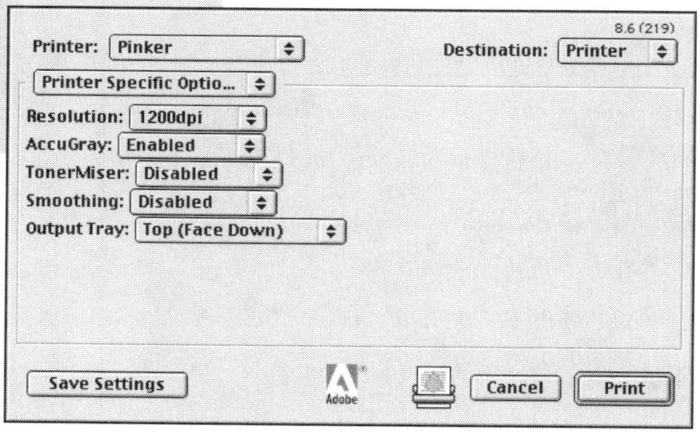

23

Adobe InDesign

Working with Service Bureaus

Working with a service bureau can make your job much easier—or much harder—depending on how you approach it. They're the experts; a service bureau has the equipment and know-how to handle almost any job that's thrown at them. Whether they choose to spend time making your page look good or just run it through the press, however, is up to you. If you hand them a document that is ready to go, they'll be much friendlier, and you will save time and money. If you give them a disorganized disk full of random files, with graphics missing and needed fonts that can't be found, you'll pay extra for them to sort out the job.

Preparing Files for the Service Bureau

Communication is the key to success here, as it is in most endeavors. Visit the service bureau before you start the job, and find out what they can do and can't do. Some can print on very large sheets of paper and cut the pages apart. Others prefer to print on small sheets on a "work and turn" basis, where many copies of one side of a page are printed and then the bundle of paper is turned over to print the second side. Find out which color matching system they use, if your publication has spot color. Ask about media formats. Do they want a CD-ROM, a Zip disk, or a Jaz disk? Do they want the media sent via e-mail or uploaded to a Web site or FTP site?

Find out whether they want the files you are going to send saved as InDesign, EPS, PostScript, or PDF files. There are advantages and disadvantages to each. Saving in the InDesign format creates a document file that can only be opened by InDesign. However, document files, even if all the graphics are included, are smaller than output files, so it takes less time to upload them. They can also be changed, and this is both good and bad: Bad, because document preferences such as text flow could be lost, making the page print incorrectly; good in that, if you have made mistakes in setting up the pages, the service bureau can go in and correct them. EPS and PDF files can't be altered or edited. If you're sure of yourself and your document, send a PDF or EPS. Otherwise, send the document files.

Two things you can do that will always help the service bureau are to preflight your documents and send both the report file and a proof copy of your pages. That way, if questions arise, they have a better chance of knowing what you intended.

There are also a few special circumstances that need to be addressed ahead of time. First, will any of your pages bleed? (I know, only if you stick a pin in them....) A bleed is the technical term for having the picture right up against the edge of the page, with no margin. What this means to you is that you have to extend the image beyond the crop marks, so that if the press is slightly off, the paper shifts, or the trim isn't quite precise, you still have a bleed and not a thin white line. Most printers ask for about an eighth of an inch bleed, but check with your service bureau. They might need more, and they seldom need less.

Second, are you planning to print to a standard size paper, or are your pages oversize? Be sure to tell the service bureau if you are printing to a larger than standard size of paper, so they can adjust their imagesetter accordingly.

Color Trapping

Have you ever seen a colored page that has a thin white line between colors that were obviously meant to touch each other? That's called misregistration, and trapping is the way to prevent it. It would be nice if all color separations could be printed in perfect register, but that's unlikely to happen, so you can compensate for it by making one of the inks overlap the other a little bit. The overlap is called overprinting, and it is usually done by expanding the lighter ink into the darker one.

Because trapping depends on knowing the spreading qualities of specific inks and papers, it's generally a mistake to do it yourself. Talk to your service bureau about it. They may be able to suggest ways to minimize the difficulties, or to avoid them altogether by using process colors that don't need trapping, or by doing the trapping in another program such as the graphics program that created the art.

> **TIP**
>
> If process colors that meet share a colored ink, you don't need to trap. For example, if you have a green ball on a blue table, both colors have a lot of cyan in them. The cyan will print as a single area containing both the ball and the table, thus avoiding any registration gaps. You can often plan a document's color scheme to avoid the need for trapping.

Making a Document Package

At this point, go back to the Preflight dialog box, shown in Figure 23.1. Open it by choosing File, Preflight or by pressing Command+Shift+Option+F.

You've done the preflight, corrected the problems, and printed a report for the service bureau. Now, you can package your job. Packaging makes life easier for your service bureau or print shop, and also for you. If you package your job, your service bureau won't call you at the last minute to say there's a file missing. Packaging creates a folder and places in it a copy of everything needed to print your publication.

When you click the Package button, you'll open the Printing Instructions dialog box (see Figure 23.2). This form tells the service bureau contact information, special instructions, and whatever else you think they need to know. It's saved in the package as instructions.txt, unless you choose to rename it something like "Read Me First."

Be sure you've entered your information correctly. A typo in your phone number could really slow down the process if the service bureau needs to ask a last-minute question. When you're done, click Continue, and the Create Package Folder dialog box will open. It's similar to the familiar Save dialog box, except this one saves the package. It's shown in Figure 23.3. Be sure to check the Fonts and Linked Graphics check boxes; otherwise, your publication will use default fonts and gray boxes.

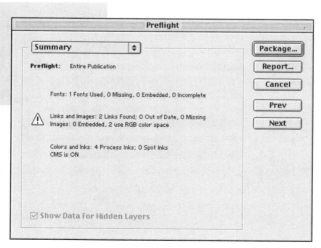

Figure 23.1
You probably remember this dialog box from the previous chapter.

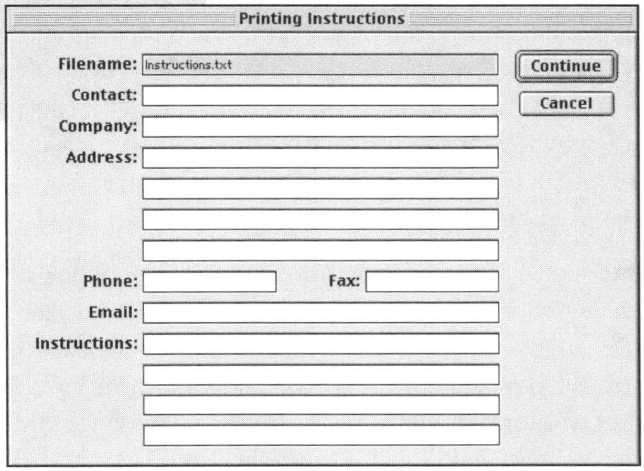

Figure 23.2
Type your data in the boxes.

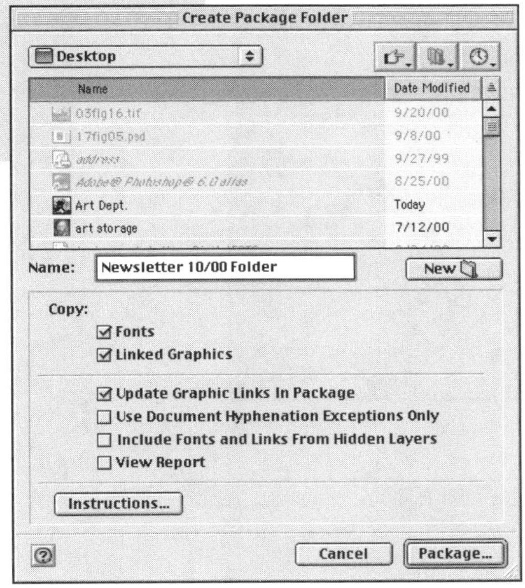

Figure 23.3
Save to a disk that has enough space for all of your files.

TIP

If you don't want an information file, don't click Cancel. That exits the preflight tool. Instead, just click Continue without filling in the form.

Decide where you want to place the folder, give it a name, and check the appropriate boxes. Most of the time, you will want to copy fonts and linked graphics, and you should also click Update Graphic Links in Package to ensure that your links are current. Because the package doesn't normally include spelling or hyphenation information, it's a good idea to check the Use Document Hyphenation Exceptions Only check box so your type doesn't reflow if you have used anything other than the most standard hyphenation.

The next screen you see, after you click Package, won't be the package of files. Instead, it will be the warning screen shown in Figure 23.4. This friendly reminder about copyrights is unfortunately necessary. Fonts, like any other software you buy, aren't meant to be shared. Your agreement with Adobe, or any other vendor of fonts, specifically tells you what you can do and can't do. Your service bureau will generally be licensed to use fonts from many different sources, but that's one more thing to check when you talk to them. Figure 23.5 shows your final package, neat and complete, and ready to send out.

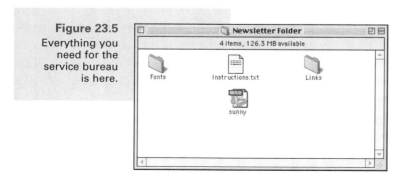

Figure 23.4
Be aware of copyrights.

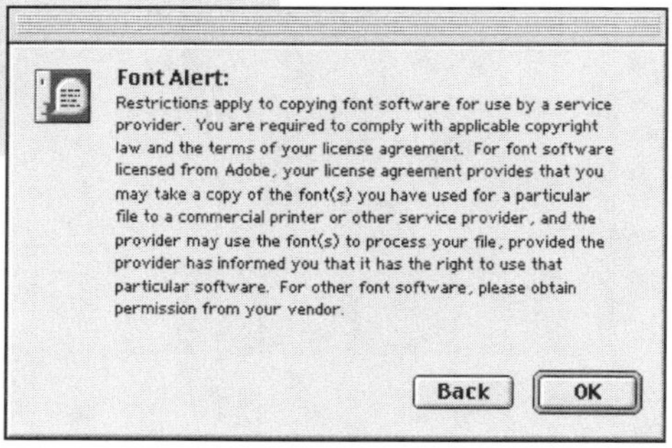

Figure 23.5
Everything you need for the service bureau is here.

Outputting to PDF Format

Sending your files as an InDesign package is fine, if the service bureau can handle it. Most can, but many prefer that you send your document as an EPS or PDF. PDF is a document format based on the Adobe PostScript language, and is used to provide total portability between computer platforms and different types of printers. PDF files are compressed files that can hold all the fonts, graphics, and high-resolution print information needed to view and print the document. PDFs are a good way to proof your pages. As long as fonts and graphics appear correctly onscreen, they will print correctly.

Using Adobe Acrobat (the full program, not the free viewer) publishers can review, do simple text and graphics editing, and print any PDF file on the Windows, Macintosh, or UNIX platform, even to non-PostScript printers. Because PDF files are page-independent, you can rearrange, remove, and insert pages without returning to InDesign. When you convert a document to a PDF file, you can then use plug-ins or prepress tools from other vendors to perform tasks such as color separations, trapping, and imposition. There's more information on this at Adobe's Web site, http://www.adobe.com.

To export your document as a PDF, choose Export from the File menu or type Command+E to open the Export dialog box, shown in Figure 23.6. Choose PDF from the Formats pop-up menu, and give your file a name and a place to live. Click OK to open another series of dialog boxes. The first is shown in Figure 23.7. Here you can determine what images are not imported, how color is handled, and whether to crop large photos down to their frame size to save space. You should definitely check the Optimize PDF and View PDF after Exporting options.

The next window deals with compression, and determining how graphics files are optimized for storage. Because PDF files can be rather large, compression of graphics and text is important. Even though this dialog box, as you can see in Figure 23.8, is primarily for graphics, there's a very important check box down at the bottom of the frame. Be sure that you check Compress Text and Line Art.

Click Next to move on to Pages and Page Marks, shown in Figure 23.9. You learned about these in the previous chapter. You can select the entire

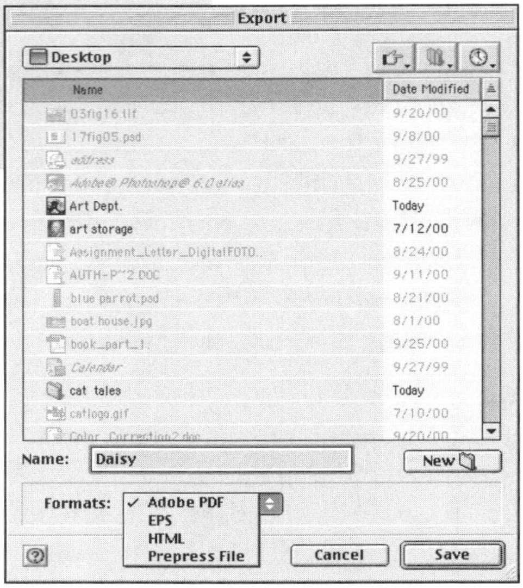

Figure 23.6
You don't need to add the .pdf extension, but I usually do.

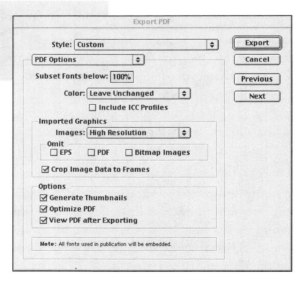

Figure 23.7
When you're done here, click Next.

document, specific pages, or ranges of pages to convert. If your PDF document is going to a print shop or service bureau, ask them which page marks you should include. If there are color photos or colored art involved, they'll want registration marks and color bars, and they might also want crop marks.

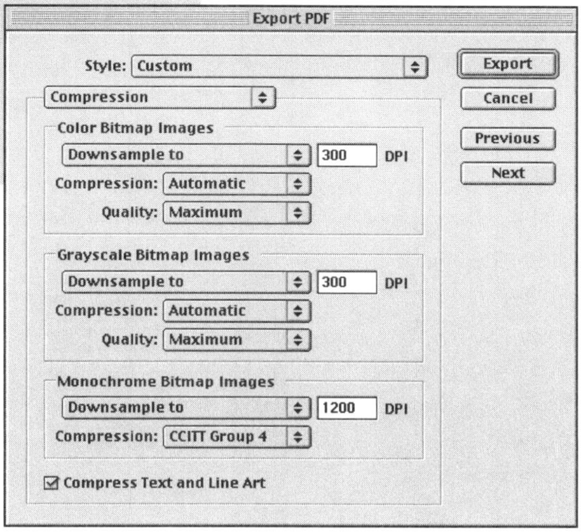

Figure 23.8
Compression makes your PDF files smaller, with no loss of quality.

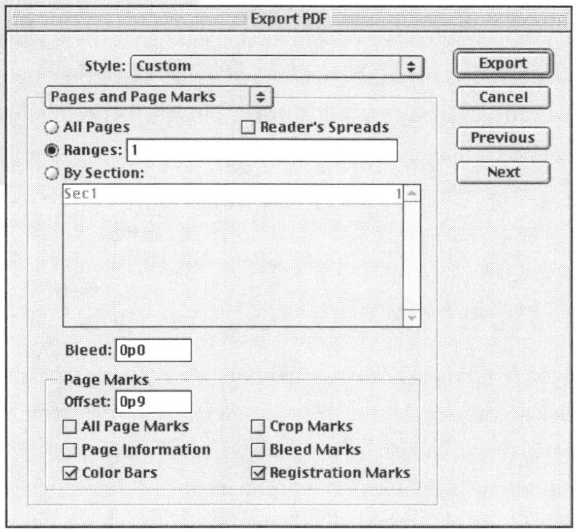

Figure 23.9
If your document is being sent as a PDF to other readers, skip the page marks.

Click Next again to move on to the final window, called Security (see Figure 23.10). Normally, you won't need to use this window. You want the document to be manageable by the service bureau in case there are things that need to be added or changed. However, if you are sending your PDF to co-workers for

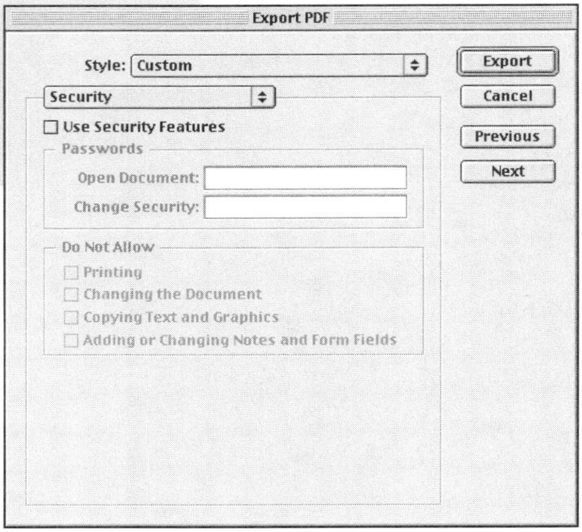

Figure 23.10
Passwords can be any combination of letters and numbers.

comments, you might decide to password-protect it for security reasons, or to disable copying or printing. Click the Use Security Features check box to enable the options. To make your document tamper-proof, set different passwords for opening the document and changing the level of security.

When you click Export, the document will be saved as a PDF and opened with the Acrobat Reader so that you can see it.

Sharing Documents over a Server

Using PDF files is one good way to share your documents after they're finished, but sometimes you need to share the creation. Workgroups are a relatively new phenomenon, made possible by networking computers to a server. It's now common for something like an annual report or company newsletter to be the work of a team, rather than a single person. Therein lies a problem—when several people are working on the same document and passing it back and forth, it's easy for changes to get lost, or for one of the team to add words to the dictionary that the others don't have, so hyphenation and text flow get lost as the pages are passed along. Default settings can differ from one Macintosh to the next, as well as from Mac to PC, which can change parts of the publication based on the default settings. And those are just a couple of the many things that can go wrong.

How can you avoid these pitfalls? First, by keeping the master document on a central server. If you have one location for all the related files, each member of the workgroup can access them without moving them, and everyone will know where to find what they need.

> **TIP**
> Computers crash—that's no surprise to anyone. Be sure you keep a backup of the project, and update it when changes are made.

If you are sharing a document the old-fashioned way, by sneakernet, one person should be responsible for keeping a set of master disks for the project and uploading the files to each person's computer. The same person will need to download and share the changes each time someone revises the document.

Working with Cross-Platform Issues

Macs and PCs can co-exist peacefully when using InDesign. Most of what you do when working on your Mac will transfer smoothly over to your co-workers using Windows. However, there are a few things you need to do to guarantee the successful transfer. The first is to use file extensions. The Windows operating system doesn't recognize file types in the same way that the Mac OS does; it needs those extra letters. The file extensions for InDesign are .INDD for documents and .INDT for stationery (which Windows calls templates). The second thing you need to do is remember that when you import an InDesign file from Windows, you need to select the All Files option in the Open dialog box (Command+O) and open PC files from the dialog box, rather than trying to double-click them.

Most elements transfer seamlessly within the program. Color, tint, and gradient swatches stay with the document. Swatch libraries can be exported if you add the file extension .AI to those going to Windows, and you open any exported from Windows within InDesign to add a Mac resource fork. Styles are retained and exported with the document. Hyphenation and spelling exceptions are retained. If you have added words to the spelling or hyphenation dictionaries, you'll need to export those files, too. Hyphenation and spelling files use the same file extensions on both Mac and Windows. For spelling additions, the file extension is .UDC, for hyphenation, it's .NOT. If you haven't added words to the dictionaries, you don't need to export them.

Document preferences are transferred across platforms, but default settings are not. If you're working with Windows users, make a list of defaults and set them to be the same on all machines. You can set defaults by changing them in InDesign with no document open.

Document naming is accomplished differently on Macs and Windows. Windows files need an extension. Mac files are limited to names of 31 characters or less, and can use any character except the colon. Windows names can be as many as 250 characters long, but most punctuation, other than periods, is illegal. For both, case doesn't matter. For example, REPORT is the same as report and Report. To avoid file name problems, keep file names down to 26 characters or less, plus the extension. Avoid punctuation other than the period setting off the extension.

As for fonts, most have counterparts on both platforms. However, they might not have the same attributes. For example, the Mac uses ligatures; Windows does not. Tracking and kerning might be different, possibly altering text flow. Symbols often change across platforms, because Mac and Windows systems map them differently. The best thing to do is to proofread your documents carefully on the platform from which they will be printed or converted to EPS or PDF. Catching mistakes at this point, rather than after the job is printed, will save you time, money, and frustration.

This chapter has taken your document from the screen to the printed page. You learned about service bureaus and how to work efficiently with them, and about how to make PDF files. You also learned about sharing documents, and going cross-platform. In the next (and final!) chapter, you'll learn about the new frontier in publishing—putting your pages on the Web!

24
Adobe InDesign

Going from Print to the Web

I must admit, InDesign is not my first choice as a Web design program. It doesn't have all the tools I'm used to in GoLive or Dreamweaver, but nevertheless, I do use it when I have a print document that I also want to put on a Web page. InDesign can convert your publication into HTML (Hypertext Markup Language), which is the universal standard for Web publishing. However, there are many factors to consider when you move a document from the printed page to the Web.

Understanding the Differences between Web and Print

When you are accustomed to using a desktop publishing program like InDesign, you're already aware of how things look on the monitor because that's where you first see them. You understand that colors can be displayed differently on different machines, and that there are fewer Web-safe colors than printable colors.

> *Web-safe colors are the 216 system colors that Macintosh and Windows computers have in common.*

One of the main differences between Web and print is page size. Printers use a certain page size, because that's the size of the paper. Page size is irrelevant on the Web; the page can be long or short. While your printed document might have 600 words to a page, the Web version can have 6,000, if you desire. There's really no limit, but when you look at a Web page, you might have to scroll down to see it all.

Another difference is in the way pages are used. We tend to read printed material a page at a time, rather than skipping around the document. In HTML, it's easy to put clickable links in the middle of a sentence to jump the reader to a different page. These hyperlinks are a Web feature that printed material can never duplicate. Alas, InDesign doesn't duplicate them either. To use hyperlinks on your page, you'll have to go into the source code after the page is built and add the links yourself. BBEdit, from BareBones Software, is a good application to use for this. It cleans up your source code and lets you do the things InDesign can't, with relatively little knowledge of HTML coding. If you'd rather not get involved in coding at all, Microsoft Word can handle HTML pages and add links easily, using a dialog box.

A third major difference is that you, as the creator, have only limited control over what your readers will see. Web browsers and computer platforms differ—if the reader doesn't have the same fonts installed that you do, the browser will apply a default font, which might not be what you had in mind.

Browsers don't understand the concept of columns. You're accustomed to seeing type on a page in two or three columns, but the browser can't deal with it. It will, instead, accept the margin you set for one column, and extend that column down as many screens as necessary to hold all the text. If the page is put up on a small monitor, wide-set text can be truncated, or cut off at the side.

Colors, surprisingly, might be *more* accurate on the Web than they are in print. You create and view the colors you use in the same medium—onscreen. Printed colors can never quite match the colors on your monitor, even though they can come close. That's because of the differences between RGB computer displays and CMYK process inks. Still, when you're putting your pages out to be seen by the world, the chances are good that no one will see the colors quite the way you do. Monitors differ, and the way they are set up also affects the colors they display. Brightness and contrast make a big difference in displayed color, as does the ambient lighting in the room where the monitor is located. Also, Macintosh and Windows monitors use a different gamma point, so what looks like a cool white on the Mac is a warm white on the PC. Subtle color differences will get lost, because your monitor is probably set to display thousands, if not millions, of colors. When the document is translated by a Web browser, it gets reduced to the 216 colors that both Mac and Windows browsers have in common.

Desktop publishing people are used to fine-tuning the appearance of the page. Every little detail and hairline has to be just right before the page goes to print. Web publishers, however, already know that what the readers will see is at best an approximation of what they've sent out. Therefore, they don't worry too much about the "look" of the pages. Instead, they concentrate on making the content easy to access with hyperlinks to other pages, sometimes placing multiple frames per page. A frame, in Web terms, is a sort of master page that remains on the screen while other pages are displayed inside it. Figure 24.1 shows one of my Web pages that uses two frames. The one on the left holds thumbnails of some of my art. If you click on one, it opens a linked picture—much larger—in the frame on the right.

Figure 24.1
You can find this page online at http://www.graphicalcat.com.

Preparing Files for the Web

When you think about turning your printed pages into Web pages, consider the content. Long documents full of text, with few or no pictures, are much better converted to a PDF document that can be downloaded from the Web site, rather than read onscreen. Many people still pay by the minute for Web access, and it's considered bad "netiquette" to make them wade through long pages.

Planning a Site

Before you start converting pages to HTML, stop and think about the Web site. Who's the audience for it? What should and shouldn't be included? What can you do to make it simple to navigate and appealing to read? If these questions seem a little bit familiar, they're the same questions you should have asked yourself before you started working on the publication you're now converting.

You also need to think about how the page you're working on relates to other pages on the Web site. The structure of the site can be drawn as a map. First, you have a home page, which might have a lot of information on it, or possibly just the company logo and some buttons to click. Clicking these buttons might

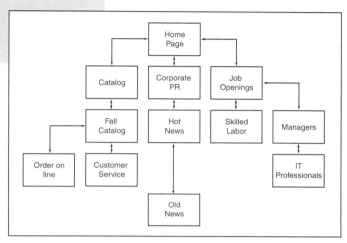

Figure 24.2
Planning a site is critical.

take you to a catalog of products, corporate press releases, or job openings. Figure 24.2 shows a fairly typical but simple site map.

Pages link to other pages in a logical order. Readers can use the Back button when navigating the site, or you can place a link back to "home" at the bottom of each additional page. Each of these pages would be set up as a separate InDesign document. When you upload the pages to your Web site, you'll use the page titles as links to the pages when a button is clicked. For example, from the home page, clicking on Job Openings takes you to the job page, where you can choose Skilled Labor or Managers. From the Managers page, you click a link to open IT Professionals. (I don't know what this mythical company *does*, but it does have a nice Web site.)

Constructing Documents for Web Publishing

There's actually not much point in starting a Web page from scratch in InDesign if you have another page creation program available to you. Netscape's browser includes Netscape Composer, a simple but effective Web page creator. It's included with the Netscape Communicator package, which is a free download from http://www.netscape.com. There are many more complex page creation programs that can handle animation, sounds, and movies that are not supported by InDesign. If, like me, you find these programs a bit intimidating and far more complicated than necessary, you can stick with InDesign and know that your page will work, even if it's not the jazziest site on the Web. If you are converting pages to HTML and you still have the original text and graphics files (of course you do, you *always* keep backups), it will probably be a lot easier to duplicate the page in another program instead of working through it in InDesign.

Assuming that you are going to create a Web page from scratch, here are some things you'll need to know. InDesign, as you've already learned, works with pages. Print pages and Web pages, however, are two different objects. Print pages within a document are all the same size, whether it's 4×6 inches, 8½×11 inches, or 17×22 inches. InDesign can support pages up to 216 inches long and wide, but those really have no practical use. Web pages have no preset length or width. The width of the page as you see it on your browser depends on how the browser is configured and what size monitor you have. The page the reader sees depends on his or her monitor and browser. However, a small monitor cuts off the edge of a wide page. It's always a good idea to plan for the minimum size rather than the maximum. Figure 24.3 shows a fairly typical Web site. Notice that the actual text frame is only about six inches wide. There's a wide border on the right, which is a design element and also fills in the gap between the text and the edge of the frame.

Figure 24.3
This page should be visible on any monitor.

When you set up your pages for the Web, keep these few things in mind:

- **Start with a page width no greater than six-and-a-half inches.** This allows plenty of room at the side to accommodate wide-screen viewers as well as those working on laptops.
- **If you use a gradient or color block as a border, be sure to use the same one on each page on the site.** Otherwise, your readers will get disoriented and wonder whether they've inadvertently jumped to some other part of cyberspace. Also, try to keep your typefaces consistent from page to page. Saving them as styles is an excellent way to do so.
- **Allow empty space at the top of the page for banner ads.** Banner ads are a nuisance, but they're a fact of life, particularly if you're using a free Web host like Geocities or Yahoo!. Leave some empty space at the top of the page and you won't lose your headline.
- **Keep the layout simple.** One column of text and an index up the side of the page is fine. Sure, you've seen a million pages like that, but it's because it works.
- **Use the Web-safe palette for adding color.** That way, you'll know more or less what your readers will see. The palette is found under Window, Swatch Libraries, and it shows the RGB amounts for each colors. Unlike Photoshop, though, it doesn't give you the six-digit binary code for HTML use. You can find the codes, after you have created and saved the document in HTML form, by opening the page in your browser and viewing the source code. A piece of source code looks like this:

```
<body bgcolor="#FFFFFF" text="#000000">

<table bgcolor=#EEEEEE cellpadding=0cellspacing=0
width=100%  border=0>
```

`#FFFFFF` stands for white and `#000000` is black. `#EEEEEE` is a very pale gray, and `#336699` is an interesting sort of country blue.

When you're placing graphics on a Web page, remember that there are only three formats that work for the Web: JPEG, GIF, and PNG. Not all browsers support PNG graphics, so you're better off with either GIF or JPEG. Which one should you use? As a general rule, use GIF for any art that has limited color, and use JPEG for photos and continuous tone art. The reason for using either one is that graphics files are very large, and both GIF and JPEG use compression to save file space, making the pictures load faster on the page. JPEG saves colors more subtly, while GIF immediately translates them into Web-safe colors. JPEG, however uses a pixel-averaging system called "lossy" compression. Every time you resave a file as a JPEG, your image quality degrades a little. It's like making a photocopy of a photocopy.

Still on the subject of graphics, InDesign can handle text wrap for Web page use. It has trouble with wrapping tightly around irregular shapes, but heck, so do bluejeans. Leave a little extra space and you'll be fine.

Exporting a Page as HTML

After all your hard work in creating this HTML page, it should come as a relief that saving it will be relatively easy. First, save your work as an InDesign document. Then, press Command+E or use File, Export to open the Export dialog box. Select HTML from the pop-up menu, as shown in Figure 24.4.

One good thing leads to another, and this dialog box leads you to a series of four more dialog boxes that control the HTML conversion. The first of these is shown in Figure 24.5. Use this box to give your HTML file a name, and to decide which pages of a long document will be converted. If you want to

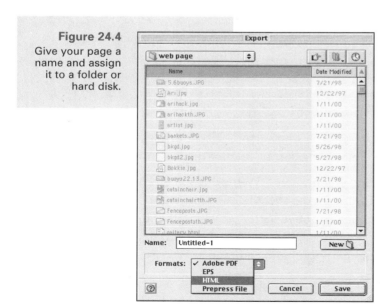

Figure 24.4
Give your page a name and assign it to a folder or hard disk.

CHAPTER 24 • GOING FROM PRINT TO THE WEB

Figure 24.5
Choose a browser in which to view your page from the bottom pop-up menu.

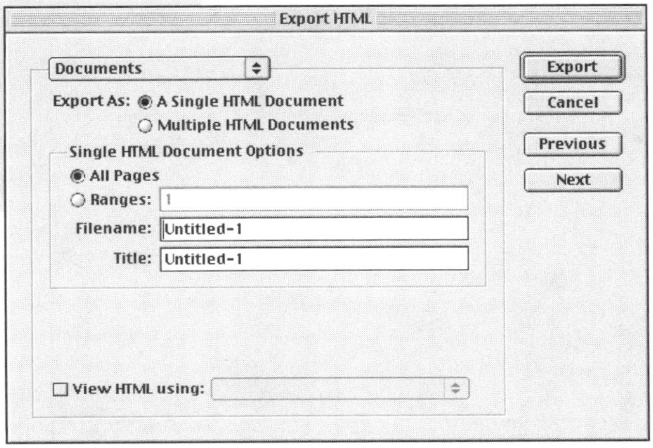

change the name you just gave the document, or if you goofed like I did and saved it as Untitled, you can correct that in this box, too.

Click OK to move on to the Formatting dialog box, shown in Figure 24.6. This box is fun! You can assign colors for your text and background, or import a picture to use as a tiled background for your page. The background tile I'm using is shown in the window on the dialog box.

By comparison, the Layout dialog box is very drab (see Figure 24.7). Stick with the defaults, unless you know for sure that you don't want margins or a navigation bar on your page.

Figure 24.6
Background tiles can be quite small, as long as they blend well at the seams.

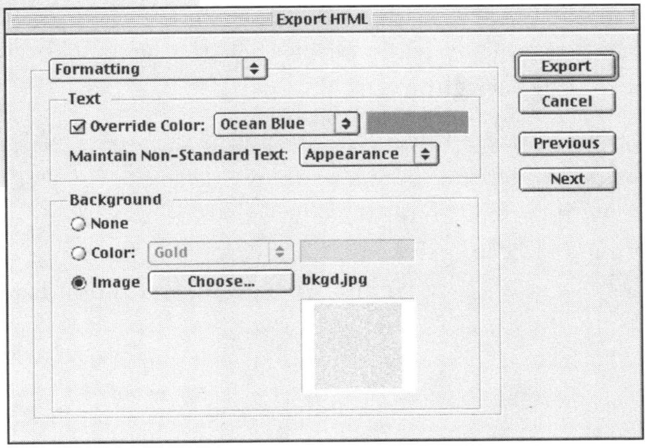

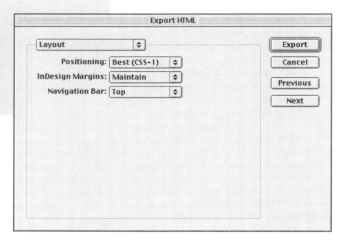

Figure 24.7
You can place the Navigation bar, if you are using one, at the top or bottom of your page.

And finally, there's the Graphics box. This box controls how graphics are exported with your HTML page. Use the Automatic setting (the default) in the Save Images As pop-up menu. InDesign is good at sorting out which pictures should be GIF and which should be JPEG. Checking the Use Images Sub-Folder option places your images in a folder inside the folder that contains the HTML file. It's really optional—either way works fine. You also get to make some decisions about the quality of your GIFs and JPEGs and how they'll load. Loading interlaced GIFs and progressive JPEGs isn't really any faster than loading them one line at a time. It just feels that way, because you can watch them take shape.

So, that's that. Click Export, and in a few seconds your browser will open and, as Chef Emeril says, "Bada boom, bada bang." There's your page. If it's not just as perfect as you'd hoped, open it in a dedicated Web creation program and tweak it until it's right.

So that brings us to the end of our journey through InDesign. Now you know the basics—which are about a tenth of what it can do. You've got the tools; what you do with them is up to you. The only limit to your creativity is you! Keep on exploring and keep on learning. Above all else, have fun! As one of my favorite people once said, "If you're not having fun, you're not doing it right."

Appendix

Keyboard Shortcuts for the Toolbox

Many of the tools and menu commands in InDesign have keyboard shortcuts. If you're like me, and you tend to type with one hand while moving the mouse with the other, you might never need to know these. You can click or pull down a menu to find the tool or action you need. On the other hand, if you regularly do most of your work from the keyboard, these shortcuts can be extremely helpful.

Action	Shortcut
Selection tool	V
Direct-Selection tool	A
Type Tool	Shift+T will cycle through the type tools
Pen tool	Shift+P will cycle through the pen tools
Add Anchor Point	+ (Plus sign)
Delete Anchor Point	- (Minus sign)
Shape tools	Shift+M will cycle through the shape tools
Frame tools	Shift+F will cycle through the frame tools
Rotate tool	R
Scale tool	S
Shear tool	O

Action	Shortcut
Scissors tool	C
Hand tool	H
Temporary Hand tool	Shift+Spacebar
Zoom tool	Z
Temporary Zoom-in tool	Command+Spacebar
Temporary Zoom-out tool	Option+Command+Spacebar
Gradient tool	G
Apply Color box	< (Less than)
Apply Gradient box	> (Greater than)
Apply None box	/ (Slash)
Fill Box	X
Stroke Box	X
Swap Fill and Stroke	Shift+X

Glossary

8-bit. An image that has 256 colors. This was the standard color display for computer monitors until S(uper)VGA graphics came along, using a 16-bit image and thousands of colors.

Anti-aliasing. Refers to any method that smoothes or removes jagged pixels from 2D images or 3D renderings. For example, a diagonal line running across your screen will probably reveal rough edges. To smooth the line, the edge pixels can be made gray to reduce the stair-step jagged lines. Low-resolution graphics look jagged; anti-aliasing can fool the eye into thinking that screen lines are smooth.

Ascender. The part of some lowercase letters, such as h or b, that rises above the letter's x height. (See *x height*)

Backup copy. A duplicate of an original, made in case of loss or damage of the original. Always back up your work!

Banding. A defect in halftone screens, or screen tints output by laser printers or imagesetters, in which parallel lines or streaks appear in the dot pattern.

Banner. A large headline, usually across the full width of a page.

Baseline. An imaginary line under a line of type, used to align characters.

Basis weight. In the United States and Canada, the weight, in pounds, of a ream (five hundred sheets) of paper cut to the basic size.

Bindery. A place where printed products are collated, trimmed, folded, and/or bound.

Bleed. Printing that extends to the edge of a page after trimming.

Blurb. A brief note about the author, appearing as part of an article by that person.

BMP. The PC file extension for *bitmap*, the type of file you get when a computer saves a graphics image by mapping the image pixel by pixel, color by color.

Body copy. Copy set in text type, as compared to display type.

Bold type. Type that appears darker than the normal type of the same typeface.

Bond paper. A category of paper commonly used for writing, printing, and photocopying.

Book paper. A category of paper suitable for newsletters and general printing needs. Book paper is divided into uncoated paper (also called offset paper), coated paper (also called art paper, enamel paper, gloss paper, or slick paper), and text paper.

Brightness. A characteristic of paper or ink referring to how much light it reflects.

Bulk mail. A type of mailing used to save postage. Using bulk mail requires a mailing permit, and presorting of mail by ZIP code.

Bullet. A bold dot or other symbol used for emphasis or to identify elements in a list.

Business reply card. A pre-addressed card that meets postal regulations for size, bar coding, and prepayment.

By-line. The name of the author. The by-line can appear at the beginning or end of an article. Be sure articles are attributed to their authors.

Callout. A word that identifies part of an illustration.

Camera-ready copy. Pages prepared for reproduction according to the technical requirements of the printing process used. Imagesetter output is camera-ready.

Cap height. Height of capital letters in one type size of a font.

Caption. Identifying or descriptive text accompanying a photograph, illustration, map, chart, or other visual element.

CD-RW and **CD-ROM**. Two types of compact disks used for storage of data. ROM stands for Read Only Memory; once written, the disk can only be read. RW represents a disk that can be read and written to repeatedly.

Change order. Written instructions about changes to a job already in progress.

Character. Any letter, numeral, punctuation mark, or other alphanumeric symbol.

Clip art. Copyright-free drawings available for purchase for unlimited reproduction. Clip art was formerly printed on glossy paper, but now is distributed on CD or via the Web.

CMYK. An acronym for Cyan, Magenta, Yellow, and Keyline (black), which are colors used in process printing.

Coated paper. Paper with a coating of clay and other substances that improve reflectivity and ink holdout.

Column rule. A thin, vertical line that separates columns.

Commercial printer. A printer that produces a wide range of products such as stationery, newsletters, flyers, and posters.

Composition. In photography and art, the way the subject is placed and framed against its background. In graphic design, the arrangement of type, graphics, and other elements on a page.

Comprehensive dummy. A simulation of a newsletter, complete with type, graphics, and colors. Often just called a *comp*. *Comping* is making up a dummy.

Condensed type. Characters that are narrow in proportion to their height, in order to seem tall and tightly spaced.

Continuous-tone art. All photographs and those illustrations having a range of shades not made up of dots, as compared to line art or halftones.

Copy. To an editor or typesetter, any and all written material, from headlines to footnotes.

Copy editor. A person who checks and corrects a manuscript for spelling, grammar, punctuation, inconsistencies, inaccuracies, and conformity to style requirements. Copy editors frequently save authors from embarrassment.

Copyfit. To calculate the space needed by a given amount of text in a specific typeface and point size. Also, to edit writing and adjust typography to make the text fit the space available.

GLOSSARY

Copyright. Ownership of creative work by the writer, photographer, or artist who created it or, if the creator was work-for-hire, the organization that paid for it.

Copyright notice. A statement of copyright ownership that has the word "copyright" or the symbol ©, the year of publication, and the name of the copyright owner. For example, ©2000, Carla Rose. Copyright certificates can be obtained from the Library of Congress.

Corner marks. Lines on a mechanical, negative, plate, or press sheet showing locations of the corners of a page or finished piece.

Credit line. A line of relatively small type next to a photo or illustration, giving its source and/or the name of the photographer or artist. The credit line is of great importance to the photographer or artist.

Crop. To eliminate unneeded portions of an image so the remainder is better composed or fits the layout.

Crop marks. Lines near the edge of an image, indicating portions to be removed.

Cropping frame. Pieces of paper or cardboard cut into L shapes that, when overlapped, can be adjusted to frame a photograph.

Crossover. Type or art that continues from one page across the gutter to the opposite page.

Dash. Typographic mark that indicates a break between thoughts. Also called em dash because in text, the dash should be one em wide (width of the letter M in same font). En dashes are used with numbers and are one en wide (width of the letter N).

Descender. The portion of a lowercase letter falling below its baseline. Lowercase g,p,q, and y have descenders.

Dingbat. A typographic symbol, such as a bullet (*), used for emphasis or decoration.

Display type. Type used for headlines, advertising, and signs.

Drop cap. A large capital letter that extends down into the first two or more lines of text.

Drop shadow. A screen tint or rule placed behind an illustration, box, or type to give a three-dimensional shadow effect.

Dual-purpose bond paper. Bond paper suitable for printing by either lithography (offset) or xerography (photocopy).

Dull finish. Flat finish paper, which is slightly smoother than matte.

Dummy. A mock-up simulating the final product. Dummies range from very rough (showing the approximate layout) to very complicated (showing the position and color of type and art).

Edition. One version of a newsletter or other publication, such as a regional edition.

Electronic mechanical. Pages assembled on the computer and submitted for printing as files, rather than as physical pages.

Element. One part of an image or page. Elements of a page can include headlines, body copy, charts, tables, and illustrations.

EPS. An acronym for Encapsulated PostScript File. An EPS file is a special kind of file for PostScript printers. Some graphics, computer-aided design (CAD), and word processing programs can read and/or convert these files, too.

Extended type. Characters that are wide in proportion to their height, thus seeming fat.

Feature. An article that provides general knowledge, entertainment, or background. May be the lead article in a newsletter.

Fillers. Short items, such as proverbs or announcements, kept on hand to fill small blank spaces in a layout.

GLOSSARY

Finish. The surface characteristics of paper.

Finished size. The size of the product after production is complete, as compared to flat size. Many newsletters are printed on 11" × 17" paper, and folded to 8½" × 11", then to 8½" × 5½" for mailing.

Fixed costs. Costs that don't depend on the number of pieces printed, as compared to variable costs. The costs of copy writing, photography, and design are examples of fixed costs, as are printer's charges for plate making, ink color change, and so on.

Flat size. The size of the product after printing and trimming but before folding, as compared to finished size.

Floating rule. A rule, usually between columns, whose ends don't touch other rules.

Flop. To reverse an image so it is a mirror image of itself.

Flush left. Type aligned vertically along the left side of the column.

Flush right. Type aligned vertically along the right side of the column.

Font family. A complete assortment of uppercase and lowercase characters, numerals, punctuation, and other symbols of one typeface. Font families come in different point sizes.

Footer. Information, such as page number or chapter title, that appears at the bottom of every page.

Freelancer. A professional, such as a writer or photographer, who is self-employed and accepts work from many clients.

GIF. An acronym for Graphics Interchange Format (developed by CompuServe). A method of compressing a bitmapped image to make the file size smaller and therefore easily viewable by different types of computers. The file extension .gif indicates these files.

Gloss finish. Paper with a shiny coating, as opposed to dull- or matte-coated paper.

Graphic arts. The crafts, industries, and professions related to designing and printing on paper and other substances.

Graphic design. The arrangement of type and visual elements along with specifications for paper, ink colors, and printing processes that together create a printed or on-screen page.

Graphics. Visual elements that supplement type to make printed messages clearer or more interesting.

Grid. A pattern of lines representing the layout of a newsletter. Grids help align and organize copy.

Gutter. A line or fold at which facing pages meet. Also, space between adjacent columns.

Hairline. The thinnest visible space or rule.

Halftone. A photograph or illustration that has been converted into dots for reproduction.

Hard copy. A copy on paper, as opposed to a *soft copy*.

Hard mechanical. A mechanical consisting of paper and/or acetate, as opposed to an electronic mechanical.

Hard proof. Proof on paper, as opposed to a soft proof, which is viewed on the computer screen.

Header. Information, such as page number or chapter title, that appears at the top of every page of a newsletter or other publication.

Hickey. A spot or imperfection in printing ink coverage, caused by dirt on the printing plate or offset blanket. Also called a bull's eye.

High/Low Resolution. The number of pixels per inch (or centimeter) or, more recently, the depth of color measurement. The higher the resolution of an image, the closer to photo-quality and the larger the file.

Highlights. The lightest portions of a photograph or halftone, as compared to midtones and shadows.

House organ. A newsletter published for employees or members of an organization.

House sheet. Paper kept in stock by a printer and suitable for a variety of printing jobs. It's usually cheaper than other papers because printers buy in bulk.

House style. Guidelines for grammar, typography, color, and other graphic features, as adopted by a specific organization.

Image. A complete page, reproduced on the computer screen, film, printing plate, or paper.

Imagesetter. A laser output device that puts a high-resolution image on paper or film.

Imposition. The arrangement of pages on mechanicals or flats so they will appear in proper sequence after press sheets are folded and bound.

Imprint. To print new copy on a previously printed sheet, such as imprinting an employee's name on business cards.

Indicia. Postal permit information printed on objects to be mailed.

Ink holdout. A characteristic of paper that prevents it from absorbing ink, thus allowing ink to dry on the surface of the paper. With poor ink holdout, print appears fuzzy.

ISSN. An acronym for International Standard Serial Number. An ISSN is created for each edition of a commercial publication such as a magazine.

Issue. All copies of a newsletter having content related to one theme, such as the Tenth Anniversary issue, or one location, such as the Western issue.

Issue date. The year, month, or date on which a newsletter was mailed or released.

Italic type. Type slanted to the right to resemble handwriting, as compared to Roman type.

JPEG or JPG. Pronounced "jay-peg," a graphics file format that compresses large files into small files with a minimal loss of visual clarity. The extension .jpg (sometimes .jpeg) indicates these files.

Jump. The point at which text moves from one page to another. Unless the reader is jumping to an adjacent page, the jump is usually designated by "Continued on page. . . ."

Jumper. Type that continues from above a photo or illustration to below it, so the reader's eyes jump over the visual to continue reading the text.

Justified type. Type set flush right and left.

Kern. To reduce the space between pairs of characters so they fit together better.

Laddering. Three or more hyphenated words in a series at the edge of a justified column. Laddering is to be avoided, if possible.

Laser printer. A device using a laser beam and xerography to reproduce type, graphics, and halftone dots.

Layout. A sketch or plan of how a page or sheet will look when printed.

Lead. (Pronounced *leed*.) The main story in a newsletter or newspaper, or the first paragraph of a story.

Leaders. Dots, dashes, or other symbols that lead the eye from one item to another, as in a table of contents.

Leading. (Pronounced *ledding*.) The space between lines of type expressed as the distance between baselines. The word comes from the early days of typesetting, when spacing was done with strips of lead.

Legible. Referring to type that has sufficient contrast with its background so readers can easily perceive the characters, as compared to *readable*.

Letter fold. Two folds creating three panels, which allows a sheet of letterhead to fit into a business envelope.

Letter spacing. The amount of space between characters. This is adjusted by tracking.

Line art. Any high-contrast image, as compared to continuous-tone photographs.

Lines per inch. A linear measure of screen ruling, describing how many lines of dots there are per inch in a screen tint, halftone, or separation.

Logo. An abbreviation for logotype, a combination of type and art forming a distinctive symbol unique to a business, product, or group.

Masthead. A block of information in a newsletter that indicates its publisher and editor, and might include information about advertising and subscribing. May also include a copyright notice.

Matte finish. A flat (not glossy) finish on photographic paper or coated printing paper.

Measure. The width of a column of type.

Moiré. An undesirable pattern resulting when halftones and screen tints are made with improperly aligned screens, or when a pattern in a photo, such as a plaid, interferes with a halftone dot pattern.

Multicolor printing. Printing in more than one ink color (but not four-color process).

Nameplate. Often confused with a *banner*, the portion of the front page of a newsletter that graphically presents its name, subtitle, and date line.

Newsletter. A short, usually informal periodical presenting specialized information to a limited audience.

Offset printing. A printing technique that transfers ink from a plate to a blanket to paper instead of directly from a plate to paper.

Opacity. A characteristic of paper that prevents print on one side from showing through the other.

Original art. An initial photo or illustration prepared for reproduction.

Overprint. To print one image over a previously printed image, such as printing type over a screen tint.

Overrun. The number of pieces printed or paper made in excess of the quantity ordered. Printers often expect clients to pay for overruns.

Page. One side of a leaf in a newsletter.

Page count. The total number of pages in a publication.

Page proof. A proof of type and graphics as they will look on the finished page, complete with elements such as headings and rules.

Pantone colors. The brand name of colors in the Pantone Matching System.

Pica. An Anglo-American unit of typographic measure equal to .166 inch (4.128mm). There are six picas to an inch. Picas are subdivided into points; one pica has twelve points.

Pixel. Thousands of individual dots that make up the image on your computer screen.

PNG. A new kind of compressed image file used on the World Wide Web. PNG files have not yet gained the popularity of GIF or JPEG files.

Point. Regarding type, a unit of measure used to express size (height) of type, distance between lines (leading), and thickness of rules. 12 points equal a pica.

GLOSSARY

PostScript. The brand name for Adobe's page description language used in laser printers and imagesetters.

Prepress. Camera work, color separating, stripping, platemaking, and other functions performed by the printer, separator, or service bureau before printing.

Process color. A printing process that uses cyan, magenta, yellow, and black inks to reproduce all colors.

Proof. A test sheet made before printing to catch mistakes before a printing job is finished.

Proofread. To examine a manuscript or proof for errors in writing or typesetting.

Proofreader marks. Standard symbols and abbreviations used to mark up manuscripts and proofs.

Pull quote. Words from an article printed in large type and inserted in the page in the same manner as an illustration.

Quick printing. Printing using small sheetfed presses, called duplicators, and precut sizes of bond and offset paper. Also called *instant printing*.

Quotation. The price offered by a printer to produce a specific job. Also called an *estimate*.

Quoted price. The printer's price for a job based on specifications from the customer. It acts as a contract in most circumstances.

Ragged-left or **ragged-right type**. Type whose line beginnings or endings are not aligned vertically.

Readable. A characteristic of printed text that is both easy to read and to understand.

Register. To place printing properly with regard to the edges of paper and other printing on the same sheet. Done so that colors will print properly.

Register marks. Crosshair lines on mechanicals and film that help keep printing plates in register. They are lined up to ensure that full color or spot color plates are aligned.

Resolution. The sharpness of an image on film, paper, a computer screen, or other medium.

Reverse. Type, graphic, or an illustration reproduced by printing ink around its outline, thus allowing the underlying color or paper to show through and form the image. Type printed this way is said to be "reversed out."

Roman type. Upright type with serifs, as compared to italic. Roman is the basic typeface in any type family.

Rough layout. A sketch giving a general idea of size and placement of text and graphics in the final product. Also called a *rough*.

Rule. A line used as a graphics element to separate or organize copy.

Runaround. Type set to conform to part or all of the shape of a photograph or illustration.

Saddle stitch. To bind by stapling sheets together where they fold at the spine, as compared to *side stitch*.

Sans-serif type. Type without *serifs*.

Satin finish. An alternative term for dull finish on coated paper.

Scale. To identify the percentage by which photographs or art should be enlarged or reduced to achieve the correct size for printing.

Scanner. An electronic device used to copy an image from paper into the computer. Scanners with Optical Character Recognition software can also scan and translate text from a page into an editable computer file.

Screen. To convert a continuous-tone image into a halftone or a solid into a screen tint.

Screen density. The amount of ink that a screen tint allows to print. Expressed as percentage of ink coverage.

Screen ruling. The number of rows or lines of dots per inch or centimeter in a screen used for making a screen tint or halftone.

Self-mailer. Printed piece designed to mail without an envelope. Newsletters are frequently done as self-mailers, with half of the back page reserved for the indicia, mailing label, and return address.

Semibold type. Type darker than normal but lighter than bold. Also called *demibold*.

Serif. A short line that crosses the ending strokes of most characters in Roman typefaces.

Service bureau. A business that uses imagesetters to make high-resolution printouts of files prepared on microcomputers. Many also do job printing.

Shadows. The darkest areas of a photograph or illustration, as compared to midtones and highlights.

Show through. Printing on one side of a sheet that is visible from the other side. Caused by paper that's too transparent.

Side stitch. Compiling pages by stapling the stack from front to back.

Small caps. Capital letters approximately the x height of lowercase letters in the same font. Small caps are often used for headlines.

Smooth finish. The most even finish available on offset paper.

Soft copy. Copy viewed on a computer screen, as opposed to printed *hard copy*.

Solid. Any area of the page receiving 100 percent ink coverage, as compared to a screen tint. An area of an image on film or a plate that will print as 100 percent coverage is also called a solid.

Soy-based inks. Inks using soybean oils as pigment vehicles. These inks are easier on the environment.

Spot color. Color printed on a page with a single-colored ink, as opposed to process color which uses cyan, magenta, yellow, and black inks to reproduce all colors.

Spread. 1. Two pages that face each other and are designed as one visual or production unit. **2.** The arrangement of two or more photos across facing pages.

Standing headline. A headline whose words and position stay the same with every issue, such as "Today's Weather."

Style. 1. In typography, the set of type attributes that define a headline, text, and so on. **2.** Copyediting rules for handling modes of address, titles, and numerals, usually decided by the editor.

Style sheet. A document containing rules for copyediting and typography to be used for a newsletter or other publication.

Subhead. A small heading within a story or chapter.

Substance weight. An alternative term for basis weight, usually referring to bond papers.

Subtitle. A phrase in a nameplate that supplements information in the newsletter name. May be a motto or descriptor.

Summary deck. Two or three sentences that condense the highlights of an article and appear between the headline and the lead paragraph.

Tabloid. A newsletter with trim size 11" × 17" or A3.

Tag line. An alternative term for subtitle.

Template. 1. A pattern used to draw illustrations or make page formats. **2.** A selection of text styles to be applied in a word processor and then translated by InDesign.

Terms and conditions. The specifics of an order for printing that a printer and a customer include as part of their contract.

Text. The main portion of type on a page, as opposed to such elements as headlines and captions. Also known as body type, body text, or body copy.

Text paper. A designation for printing papers with textured surfaces, such as laid or linen.

Text type. A small font size used for text and captions, as compared to *display type*.

Thumbnail sketch. A small, rough sketch of a design, layout, or art.

TIFF. An acronym for Tagged-Image File Format. TIFFs are commonly used for high-resolution graphics, layout, and desktop publishing needs.

Tight register. A subjective term referring to almost, but not quite, perfect register.

Tint. A color created by dots instead of solid ink coverage.

Tombstone. Two headlines next to each other so that, at first glance, they appear to be one headline. Can result in some very funny headlines.

Toner. 1. The powder that forms the images in photocopying and laser printing. 2. The powder or liquid that forms the images in some color proofing systems.

Trim size. When nonstandard-sized documents are printed on standard-sized paper and must be trimmed to size, the resulting page size is called the trim size.

Type. Letters, numerals, punctuation marks, and other symbols produced by a machine and reproduced by printing.

Typeface. A set of characters with similar design features and weight.

Type family. A group of typefaces with similar letter forms and a unique name. For example, all the styles and weights of a particular font, such as Helvetica, including light, semibold, and bold italic.

Type size. The height of a typeface measured from the top of its ascenders to the bottom of its descenders, expressed in points.

Type style. A characteristic of a typeface, such as bold, italic, or light.

Typography. 1. The art and science of composing type to make it legible and readable. 2. The arrangement of type on a page.

Ultrabold type. Type that is heavier than bold.

Uncoated paper. Paper that has not been coated with clay.

Underrun. When the printed pieces delivered are less than the number ordered.

Unit cost. The cost of one item in a print run. Unit cost is computed by dividing the total cost of the printing job—variable costs plus fixed costs—by the quantity of pieces delivered.

Uppercase letters. An alternative term for capital letters.

Variable costs. The costs of a printing job that change depending on how many pieces are produced, as compared to *fixed costs*. An example would be paper stock.

Vellum finish. A somewhat rough, leatherlike finish.

Viewer. Types of programs that allow the user to look at BMP, JPEG, and GIF files. Graphic Converter is a good viewer.

Wallpaper. A graphics image designed for decorating your computer's desktop. If it's on your Web page, it's called a background.

Washed out. A characteristic of printing or a photograph whose images appear faded.

Waste. Unusable paper, or paper damaged during normal printing or bindery operations, as compared to spoilage.

White space. The area of a printed piece that does not contain images or type.

Wide-angle lens. A camera lens whose field of view is wider than the eye can normally see, as compared to a telephoto lens.

WYSIWYG. (Pronounced *wiz-ee-wig*.) An acronym for What You See Is What You Get. It's a desktop publishing term meaning what's on your screen is (theoretically) what comes out of the printer.

X height. The vertical height of a lowercase x in a typeface. X height varies from one typeface to another.

ZIP code. A five-number code that identifies every post office and substation in the United States.

ZIP+4. A five-digit ZIP code plus four additional numerals giving more precise information about the address, carrier route, or city block.

Index

A

accessing
    Character palette, 182
    Preferences dialog box, 33
activating layers, 131
Add/Strip, downloading, 146
adding
    borders to images, 263-264
    bullets, 214–216
    fills to frames, 92–94
    gradients to frames, 96–99
    items to Object Library, 138
    objects to layers, 132
    page numbers to master pages, 115–116
    pages
        to documents, 61–62
        to spreads, 63
    tab leaders, 165
    text to frames
        by drag-and-drop placement, 170
        by pasting from Clipboard, 169–170
        by typing, 168–169
        using Place command, 171
adjusting
    column guides, 24
    document preferences, 34–35

    kerning, 190
Adobe Online Preferences dialog box, 35
Adobe Type Reunion utility, 185
Adobe Web site, 349
AI file formats, 244
Align palette, 51
aligning text frames to grids, 79–81
anchor points, 101
    moving, 288
Application Color Settings dialog box, 304
applying
    color to objects, 55
    fill to shapes, 293–294
    kerning, 189–190
    leading, 188
    stroke to shapes, 293–294
    styles, 203–204
Arrange command (Object menu), 223
Attributes palette, 52

B

backgrounds, 262
baseline grids, 66
    aligning to, 195
bitmaps, 242
BMP file formats, 243

borders, adding to images, 262–264
bulleted lists, 213–214
bullets, inserting, 214–216
Bullets and Numbering dialog box, 214

C

changing. *See also* editing
    font families, 183–184
    frame size, 41
    lines
        color of, 106
        weight of, 105
    margins
        default settings, 61
        in master pages, 112
    master pages, 121
    text, 156
        formatted, 160
    text frames to graphic frames, 76
    tints, percentage of, 317
    tracking, 191
Character palette, accessing, 182
character styles
    creating, 206
    defined, 9, 205
characters, foreign, 219
Check Spelling dialog box, 161–162
Chooser dialog box, 329
Clipboard, pasting text from, 169–170
Clipping Path dialog box, 278
clipping paths
    creating automatic, 278–281
    defined, 254, 276
    saving paths as, 277–278
closed shapes, drawing, 284
closing dialog boxes, 36
CMS (color management)
    color calibrations, 304

    profiles, obtaining, 307–308
    turning on, 303
CMYK model, 298–301
color management. *See* CMS
color models
    CMYK, 300–301
    LAB, 301–302
    RGB, 299
    types of, 298
color modes
    defined, 302
    switching, 303
Color palette, 53
color profiles, 305–306
Color Settings dialog box, 36
Color Settings command (Edit menu), 304
colors
    applying to objects, 55
    consistency in, 306–307
    copying with Eyedropper tool, 46
    defining, 313–315
    indirect lighting of, 308
    of lines, changing, 106
    setting default, 53
    spot, 312–313
        defining, 315–317
    tints, 319–320
        changing percentage of, 54, 317
        creating, 317
    trapping, 345
column guides, adjusting, 24
command key combinations, 33
commands
    Edit menu
        Color Settings, 304
        Edit Dictionary, 162
        Find/Change, 23
        Paste In Place, 22

Step and Repeat, 22
Undo, 21
File menu
   Document Setup, 20, 61
   Export, 349
   New, 18, 58
   Open, 18, 59, 247
   Place, 19–20, 171, 234
   Preflight, 346
   Save, 19
   Save As, 19, 64, 68
Layout menu
   Create Guides, 24–25
   First Page, 25
   Insert Page Number, 25, 115
   Last Page, 25
   Layout Adjustment, 25
   Margins and Columns, 24, 60, 112
   Next Page, 25
   Previous Page, 25
   Ruler Guides, 24
Object menu
   Arrange, 223
   Compound Paths, 291
   Transform, 233
Revert, 19
Type menu
   Fill with Placeholder Text, 27
   Insert Character, 26–27
   Show Hidden Characters, 153
   Story, 26
View menu
   Display Master Items, 119
   Entire Pasteboard, 16
   Fit Spread in Window, 112
   Hide Guides, 131
   Show Document Grid, 112
   Show Rulers, 65

compound paths, 292
   closing, 102
   defined, 290
   grouping paths for, 291
   releasing, 293
copying
   color with Eyedropper tool, 46
   text attributes, 46
Corner Effects dialog box, 88
corner points, 286
corners
   Bevel, 89
   Rounded, 89
   treatments, 88
Create Guides command (Layout menu), 24–25
Create Guides dialog box, 24
Create Package Folder dialog box, 347
creating
   character styles, 206
   clipping paths, automatic, 278–281
   curves, 286–287
   documents, new, 58–59
   graphics frames, 84–85
   hanging indents, 213
   layers, 130
   master pages, 110–111
      multiple, 118
   stationery, 67–69
   styles, 199–203
      character, 206
   tagged text, 148–150
   templates, 67–69
   tints, 317
cropping pictures, 252–254
curves
   creating, 286–287
   sharp, 102
cutting paths, 289–290

D

decorative fonts, 229
defining
    colors, 313–315
    spot colors, 315–317
deleting
    frames, 86
    layers, 135–136
    pages, 63
    styles, 204–207
    text, 159
dialog boxes
    Adobe Online Preferences, 35
    Application Color Settings, 304
    Bullets and Numbering, 214
    Check Spelling, 161–162
    Chooser, 329
    Clipping Path, 278
    closing, 36
    Color Settings, 36
    Corner Effects, 88
    Create Guides, 24
    Create Package Folder, 347
    Dictionary, 163
    Document Color Settings, 304
    Document Setup, 20, 61, 121
    Export, 350, 362
    Export HTML, 363
    Eyedropper Options, 203
    Find/Change, 155
    Find Format Settings, 161
    Formatting, 363
    General Preferences, 116
    Grids Preferences, 114
    Image Import Options, 248
    Insert Character, 26, 215, 220
    Insert Pages, 62, 121
    Layout, 364
    Margins and Columns, 24, 60, 113
    Modify Paragraph Style Options, 201
    New, 18
    New Document, 16, 58
    New Gradient Swatch, 97
    New Layer, 130
    New Tint Swatch, 95, 318
    Paragraph Rules, 224
    Place, 144, 171, 248
    Preferences, 33–34
    Preflight, 334
    Print
        Advanced Page Control window, 338
        Color Window, 338–339
        Edit Trapping Inks window, 341
        Graphics window, 339
        Page Marks window, 340
        Printer Specific Options, 342
        Scale and Fit window, 339
    Printing Instructions, 347
    Rotate, 233
    Ruler Guides, 24
    Save As, 68
    Scale, 258
    Section Options, 117
    Shear, 261
    Stationery, 68
    Step and Repeat, 22
    Style, 149
    Subset, 137
    Swatch Options, 55
    Text Frame Options, 77
    Text Import Options, 171
    TIFF Options, 245
dictionary, adding words to, 162
Dictionary dialog box, 163
dingbats, 218
    defined, 212
    uses for, 217

Direct-Selection tool
   example of, 40
   uses for, 39
Display Master Items (View menu), 119
Document Color Settings dialog box, 304
Document grids, 66
document pages, 7
Document Setup command (File menu), 20, 61
Document Setup dialog box, 20, 61, 121
documents
   adding pages to, 61–62
   creating new, 58–59
   exporting as PDF, 349–352
   margins, resizing, 60
   moving pages in, 122–123
   opening, 59
   removing pages from, 122
   saving, 64
      as stationery, 68
   sharing over servers, 352–353
   switching between, 120
downloading Add/Strip, 146
drag-and-drop, 170
drawing
   lines, 104, 286
   shapes, 86
      closed, 284
      filled, 87
      open, 285
      sharp curves, 102
drop caps, 195–196

E

Edit Dictionary command (Edit menu), 162
Edit menu commands
   Color Settings, 304
   Edit Dictionary, 162
   Find/Change, 23
   Paste In Place, 22
   Step and Repeat, 22
   Undo, 21
editing. *See also* changing
   styles, 204
   tints, 318
Ellipse tools, 42
ellipsis, 19
EMF file formats, 244
endpoints, 288
Entire Pasteboard command (View menu), 16
EPS file formats
   defined, 243
   problems with, 245–246
Export command (File menu), 349
Export dialog box, 350, 362
Export HTML dialog box, 363
exporting pages as HTML, 362–364
Extensis Suitcase 9 utility, 185
Eyedropper Options dialog box, 203
Eyedropper tool, 46

F

F-keys (keyboard shortcuts), 32
file formats
   choosing best, 244–245
   cross-platform issues, 353–354
   list of, 243–244
File menu commands
   Document Setup, 20, 61
   Export, 349
   New, 18, 58
   Open, 18, 59, 247
   Place, 19–20, 171, 234
   Preflight, 346
   Save, 19
   Save As, 19, 64, 68

Fill tool, uses for, 47–48
Fill with Placeholder Text command (Type menu), 27
filled shapes, drawing, 87
filling
   shapes, 285
   text with graphics, 323–324
fills
   adding to frames, 92–94
   applying to shapes, 293–294
Find/Change command (Edit menu), 23
Find/Change dialog box, 155
Find Format Settings dialog box, 161
finding. *See* searching
First Page command (Layout menu), 25
Fit Spread in Window command (View menu), 112
flattening, 133–134
flowing text
   automatically, 173
   manually, 172
font families
   changing, 183–184
   defined, 183
fonts. *See also* type
   Adobe Type Reunion utility, 185
   choosing, 185
   decorative, 229
   defined, 183
   Extensis Suitcase 9 utility, 185, 231
   FontReserve utility, 231
   graphics, 230
   monotype, 229
   sans serif, 228–229
   script, 229
   serif, 228
   styles options, 186–187
   typewriter, 229
foreign characters, 219
formatting. *See also* setting paragraphs
   alignment of, 193–194
   indents, 194–195
   spacing of, 195
   tables, 221–223
Formatting dialog box, 363
frames. *See also* text frames
   adding
      fills to, 92–95
      gradients to, 96–99
   centering images within, 254–256
   changing size of, 41
   deleting, 86
   graphic
      creating, 84–85
      versus text, 8–9
   moving, 41, 81–83
   overview, 7
   reshaping, 256
   resizing, 81–84
   rotating, 44
   stroking, 84–85
   text
      changing to graphics, 76
      versus graphic, 8–9
      versus type, 74
Free Transform tools, 43–45

G

gamma, 305
General Preferences dialog box, 116
GIF file formats, 243
Gradient palette, 52
Gradient tool, 47

gradients, adding to frames, 96–99
graphics frames
    changing to text frames, 76
    creating, 84–85
    versus text frames, 8–9
graphics
    file formats for, 243–244
    filling text with, 323–324
    fonts, 230
    importing, 247–249
    inline, 249–250
    moving behind text, 273
    rotating, 258–260
    vector, 242
grids
    aligning text frames to, 79–81
    applying to master pages, 112–113
    baseline, aligning to, 195
    defined, 66
    Document, 66
    setting, 66
Grids Preferences dialog box, 114
guidelines, horizontal, placing, 64
gutters, 78

H

Hand tool, 47
hanging indents
    creating, 213
    defined, 212
headings, importing from Illustrator or Photoshop, 234
Help menu, 30–31
Hide Guides command (View menu), 131
horizontal guidelines, placing, 64
horizontal scaling, 192–193

HTML (Hypertext Markup Language)
    exporting pages as, 362–364
    style sheets, 207–208
Hypertext Markup Language. *See* HTML
hyphenating words, 163

I

icons
    New Layer, 130
    Place Graphics, 20
    Place Text, 20
    Thread, 175
    Trash can, 63
Image Import Options dialog box, 248
images. *See also* pictures
    adding borders to, 263
    centering within frames, 254–256
    resizing, 257–258
    skewing, 261–262
importing
    graphics, 247–249
    headlines from Illustrator or Photoshop, 234
    text
        choosing formats for, 147
        using Add/Strip, 146
        using import filters, 143–145
indents
    hanging, 212–213
    setting, 194–195
InDesign
    installing, 10–12
    registration screen, 12
    system requirements for, 10–11
inline graphics, 249–250
Insert Character command (Type menu), 26
Insert Character dialog box, 26, 215, 220

Insert Page Number command (Layout menu), 25, 115
Insert Pages dialog box, 62, 121
inserting. *See* adding
insets, 76
installing InDesign, 10–12
island spreads. *See* spreads

J

JPEG file formats, 243

K

kerning
    adjusting, 190
    applying, 189–190
    defined, 188
    optical, 189
    turning off, 190
keyboard shortcuts
    command key combinations, 33
    F-keys, 32
    for styles, 201
    for symbols, 220

L

LAB model, 298–302
Last Page command (Layout menu), 25
layers
    activating, 131
    creating, 130
    defined, 126–128
    deleting, 135–136
    merging, 133–134
    moving objects on, 133
    naming, 130
    objects, adding to Object Library, 136–137
    placing objects on, 132
    selecting objects on, 132
Layers palette, 50
    overview of, 128–129
    reducing icon size, 136
Layout Adjustment command (Layout menu), 25
Layout dialog box, 364
Layout menu commands
    Create Guides, 24–25
    First Page, 25
    Insert Page Number, 25, 115
    Last Page, 25
    Layout Adjustment, 25
    Margins and Columns, 24, 60, 112
    Next Page, 25
    Previous Page, 25
    Ruler Guides, 24
lead-ins, 219
leading, applying, 188
line art, 243
Line tool, uses for, 42
lines
    changing
        color of, 106
        weight of, 105
    drawing, 104, 286
    ending, 105
    moving, 106, 288
    resizing, 106
    starting, 105
    stroking, 104
links, managing, 176–179
Links palette, 176–179
loading styles, 199

M

margins
  changing
    default settings, 61
    in master pages, 112
  resizing, 60
Margins and Columns command (Layout menu), 24, 60
Margins and Columns dialog box, 24, 60, 113
master pages. *See also* pages
  applying grids to, 112–113
  changing
    margins, 112
    number of, 121
    size of, 112
  creating, 110–111
    multiple, 118
  defined, 7
  moving in documents, 122–123
  overriding, 119–120
  page number markers, 114–116
  removing, 122
menus
  Edit commands
    Find/Change, 23
    Paste In Place, 22
    Step and Repeat, 22
    Undo, 21
  ellipsis, 19
  File commands
    Document Setup, 20
    New, 18
    Open, 18
    Place, 19–20
    Save, 19
    Save As, 19
  Help, 30–31
  Layout commands, 23
    Create Guides, 24–25
    First Page, 25
    Last Page, 25
    Layout Adjustment, 25
    Margins and Columns, 24
    Next Page, 25
    Previous Page, 25
    Ruler Guides, 24
  Object, 27–28
  Type commands
    Fill with Placeholder Text, 27
    Insert Character, 26
    Story, 26
  View, 29
  Window, 30
merging layers, 133–134
metacharacters
  codes for, 158
  defined, 153
  searching text by, 156–159
misregistration, trapping, 345
models. *See* color models
modes. *See* color modes
Modify Paragraph Style Options dialog box, 201
monotype fonts, 229
moving
  anchor points, 288
  frames, 41, 81–83
  graphics behind text, 273
  layers, objects on, 133
  lines, 106, 288
  pages in documents, 122–123
  text frames, 75

N

naming layers, 130
Navigator palette, 50
Netscape Web site, 359
New command (File menu), 18, 58
New dialog box, 18
New Document dialog box, 16, 58
New Gradient Swatch dialog box, 97
New Layer dialog box, 130
New Tint Swatch dialog box, 95, 318
Next Page command (Layout menu), 25
numbered lists, 213–217
numbering pages, 114–117

O

Object Library
    adding items to, 136–138
    defined, 136
    removing items from, 138
Object menu commands, 27–28
    Arrange, 223
    Compound Paths, 291
    Transform, 233
objects, adding
    color to, 55
    to layers, 132
    to Object Library, 138
Open command (File menu), 18, 59, 247
opening
    documents, 59
    Place dialog box, 20
optical kerning, 189
overriding master pages, 119
overset text, 82, 172

P

packaging for service bureaus, 346–348
pages. *See also* master pages
    adding
        to documents, 61–62
        to spreads, 63
    changing number of, 121
    deleting, 63
    exporting as HTML, 362–364
    moving in documents, 122–123
    opening new, 59
    removing from documents, 122
    saving, 64
    switching between, 120
    types of, 7
Pages palette, 50
palettes, 48
    Align, 51
    Attributes, 52
    Character, 182
    Color, 53
    docking, 49
    Gradient, 52
    Layers, 50
        overview of, 128–129
        reducing icon size, 136
    Links, 176–179
    menus for, 49
    Navigator, 50
    options, accessing, 49
    Pages, 50
    Stroke, 51
    Swatches, 53
    Tabs, 164
    Transform, 51

INDEX

Paragraph Rules dialog box, 224
paragraph styles, 9
paragraphs
    aligning to baseline grid, 195
    drop caps, 195–196
    setting
        alignment of, 193–194
        indents for, 194–195
        spacing of, 195
Paste In Paste command (Edit menu), 22
Pasteboard, 17
    overview, 6–7
    viewing contents on, 16
pasting text from Clipboard, 169–170
paths
    clipping. *See* clipping paths
    compound
        closing, 102
        defined, 290
        releasing, 293
    cutting, 289–290
    grouping for compound paths, 291
    removing sections of, 103
    saving as clipping paths, 277–278
PCX file format, 244
PDF file format, 244, 246–247
    exporting documents as, 349–352
Pen tool, 100–102, 285–287
    uses for, 40
PICT file format, 244, 247
pictures, cropping. *See also* images, 252–254
Place command (File menu), 19–20, 171, 234
Place dialog box, 144, 171, 248
Place Graphic icon, 20
Place Text icon, 20
plug-ins, 10

PNG file format, 244
points
    anchor, 288
    corner, 286
    endpoints, 288
    smooth, 101, 286
Polygon tool, 42
polygons, changing number of sides, 42
PostScript, history of, 4
preferences
    adjusting document, 34–35
    setting, 33
Preferences dialog box, 34
Preflight command (File menu), 346
Preflight dialog box, 334
Preflight summary
    fonts, 333–334
    links, 335
    print settings, 336
Previous Page command (Layout menu), 25
Print dialog box
    Advanced Page Control window, 338
    Color Window, 338
    Edit Trapping Inks window, 341
    Graphics window, 339
    Page Marks window, 340
    Printer Specific Options, 342
    Scale and Fit window, 339
printers
    inkjet, printing to, 330–331
    setup of, checking, 328–329
printing
    to inkjet printers, 330–331
    setting pages for, 331–332
Printing Instructions dialog box, 347
PSD file format, 244

publications
    attracting readers to, 237–238
    dividing into sections, 116–117

R

ramp, 298
Rectangle tool, 42
registration marks, 54
removing
    overrides, 119–120
    pages from documents, 122
    tabs, 165
Rendering Intent, 309
resizing
    frames, 81–84
    images, 257–258
    lines, 106
Revert command, 19
RGB model, 298–299
Rich Text Format. *See* RTF
Rotate dialog box, 233
Rotate tools, 43–45
rotating
    frames, 44
    graphics, 258–260
    text, 232–233
RTF (Rich Text Format), 143
Ruler Guides command (Layout menu), 24
Ruler Guides dialog box, 24
rulers, 65
run-in heads, 219

S

sans serif fonts, 228–229
Save As command (File menu), 19, 64, 68
Save As dialog box, 68

Save command (File menu), 19
saving
    documents, 64
        as stationery, 68
    paths as clipping paths, 277–278
Scale dialog box, 258
Scale tools, 43–45
scaling, 192–193
Scissors tool, 103
Scitex CT file formats, 244
script fonts, 229
searching text, 155–156
    formatted, 160
    by metacharacters, 156–159
Section Options dialog box, 117
sections, dividing publications into, 116–117
selecting tools, 38–39
serif fonts, 228
service bureaus
    defined, 331
    file preparation for, 344–345
    packaging for, 346–348
    questions to ask, 344
setting. *See also* formatting
    gridlines, 66
    pages for printing, 331–332
    preferences, 33
    tabs, 164
shapes
    applying
        fill to, 293–294
        stroke to, 293–294
    drawing, 86
        closed, 284
        filled, 87
        open, 285
    filling, 285

sharing documents over servers, 352–353
sharp curves, 102
Shear dialog box, 261
Shear tool, 261–262
shortcut keys
    command key combinations, 33
    F-keys, 32
    for styles, 201
    for symbols, 220
Show Document Grid (View menu), 112
Show Hidden Characters command (Type menu), 153
Show Rulers command (View menu), 65
skewing, 192–193
    images, 261–262
smooth points, 101, 286
spelling checker, 161
spot colors, 54, 95–96, 312–313
    defined, 94
    defining, 315–317
spreads
    adding pages to, 63
    defined, 58
    island, 63
stationery
    creating, 67–69
    saving documents as, 68
Stationery Option dialog box, 68
Step and Repeat command (Edit menu), 22
Step and Repeat dialog box, 22
Story command (Type menu), 26
stroke, applying to shapes, 293–294
Stroke palette, 51
Stroke tool, uses for, 47–48
stroking lines, 104
Style dialog box, 149

style sheets, 148
    HTML (Hypertext Markup Language), 207–208
styles
    applying, 203–204
    character, 205
    creating, 199–203
    defined, 198
    deleting, 204–207
    editing, 204
    keystroke shortcuts of, 201
    loading, 199
    overview, 9
    types of, 9
Subset dialog box, 137
swatch libraries, 313
Swatch Options dialog box, 55
Swatches palette, 53
Switch Libraries menu, 30
switching color modes, 303
symbols, shortcuts for, 220

T

tables
    formatting, 221–223
    placing rules into, 223–226
tabs
    adding leaders to, 165
    clearing, 165
    removing single, 165
    repeating, 165
    setting, 164
Tabs palette, 164
tagged text, creating, 148–150
templates, creating, 67–69

text
- adding to frames
  - by drag-and-drop placement, 170
  - by pasting from Clipboard, 169–170
  - by typing, 168–169
  - using Place command, 171
- changing, 156
  - formatted, 160
- deleting, 159
- filling, 235–236
  - with graphics, 323–324
- flowing
  - manually, 172
  - semi-automatically, 173
- importing, 147
  - choosing formats for, 147
  - using Add/Strip, 146
  - using import filters, 143–145
- jumping, 272
- leftover, 176
- moving graphics behind, 273
- overset, 82, 172
- pasting from Clipboard, 169–170
- rotating, 232–233
- searching, 155–156
  - formatted, 160
  - by metacharacters, 156–159
- Show Hidden Characters command, 152–154
- spelling checker, 161–162
- tagged, creating, 148–150
- viewing, 152
- wrapping. *See* wrapping text

Text Frame Options dialog box, 77

text frames. *See also* frames
- adding to existing threads, 175–176
- aligning to grids, 79–81
- changing to graphics frames, 76
- drawing with Text tool, 75
- versus graphic frames, 8–9
- sizing, 75
- threading, 174–175
- versus type frames, 74
- unthreading, 176

Text Import Options dialog box, 171

Thread icon, 175

threading, 174–176

TIFF file formats
- defined, 244
- Options dialog box, 245

tints, 319–320
- creating, 317
- editing, 318
- percentages, 54
  - changing, 317

toolbox
- diagram of, 38
- layout, changing from two columns to one, 39
- tools. *See* tools

tools
- Direct-Selection, 39–40
- Ellipse, 42
- Eyedropper, 46
- Fill, 47–48
- Free Transform, 43–45
- Gradient, 47
- Hand, 47
- Line, 42
- Pen, 40, 100–102, 285–287
- Polygon, 42
- Rectangle, 42
- Rotate, 43–45
- Scale, 43–45
- Scissors, 103
- selecting, 38–39
- Shear, 261–262
- Stroke, 47–48

Type, 41
Zoom, 47
tracking
    changing, 191
    default for, 191
    defined, 188
Transform command (Object menu), 233
Transform palette, 51
transformation, 44–45
trapping, 345
Trash Can icon, 63
troubleshooting wrapping text, 274–276
turning off kerning, 190
turning on
    CMS (color management), 303
    Rulers, 65
type. *See also* fonts
    sans serif, 228–229
    serif, 228
Type menu commands
    Fill with Placeholder Text, 27
    Insert Character, 26–27
    Show Hidden Characters, 153
    Story, 26
Type tools, 41
typewriter fonts, 229
typography, 182

U

Undo command (Edit menu), 21
unthreading frames, 176

V

vector graphics, 242
vertical scaling, 192–193

View menu commands, 29
    Display Master Items, 119
    Entire Pasteboard, 16
    Fit Spread in Window, 112
    Hide Guides, 131
    Show Document Grid, 112
    Show Rulers, 65
viewing text, 152

W

Web
    preparing files for, 358–359
    publishing, constructing documents for, 359–362
Web sites
    Adobe, 349
    Netscape, 359
Webdings, 217
white space, 236–237
Wind, Jon, 146
word processor formats, 143
words
    adding to spell checker dictionary, 162
    changing hyphenation of, 163
wrapping text
    around bounding boxes, 270–271
    around frames, 268–269
    options for, 268
    troubleshooting, 274–276

Z

zero point, resetting, 65
Zoom tool, 152